KILL
OR GET
KILLED

RIOT CONTROL TECHNIQUES,
MANHANDLING, AND CLOSE COMBAT
FOR POLICE AND THE MILITARY

Also by Rex Applegate:

Bullseyes Don't Shoot Back (with Michael D. Janich)
Close-Combat Files of Colonel Rex Applegate (with Maj. Chuck Melson)
Combat Use of the Double-Edged Fighting Knife
Kill or Get Killed (1943 Edition)
Point Shooting (video)
Scouting and Patrolling
Shooting for Keeps (video)

Kill or Get Killed:
Riot Control Techniques, Manhandling, and Close Combat,
for Police and the Military
by Col. Rex Applegate

Copyright © 1976 by Col. Rex Applegate

ISBN 13: 978-1-58160-558-7
Printed in the United States of America

Published by Paladin Press, a division of
Paladin Enterprises, Inc.
Gunbarrel Tech Center
7077 Winchester Circle
Boulder, Colorado 80301 USA
+1.303.443.7250

Direct inquiries and/or orders to the above address.

PALADIN, PALADIN PRESS, and the "horse head" design
are trademarks belonging to Paladin Enterprises and
registered in United States Patent and Trademark Office.

Visit our Web site at www.paladin-press.com

To

GUS PERET

and those officers and men of the Combat Section, Military Intelligence Training Center, Camp Ritchie, Maryland, whose accumulated experience and training helped make this text possible.

INTRODUCTION

KILL OR GET KILLED

With the bombing of Pearl Harbor, war burst upon an unprepared America. Our young men, wrenched from a world where "fair play" was the code by which all games were conducted, were faced with a foe trained to ruthless killing. They had to be taught to be tougher, meaner, more efficient and more merciless than the enemy if this country was to survive.

It was of this necessity that the book, "Kill or Get Killed" was born. Techniques of hand to hand fighting worked out by then Captain Rex Applegate and his staff were taught to thousands of men going into combat. Many of these returned to verify the rightness of these techniques or to give information by which they were corrected or refined. In 1943, Applegate published this volume which became, and has remained, the basic classic text on close combat. Now long out of print, the few copies still in existence have been treasured by fighting men the world over.

As a nation, we are not now formally at war. As a society, menaced by ever escalating crime, the need for this book was never greater. Study and practice of the principles explained and illustrated will help you and those dependent on you to survive. It's reprinting was long overdue.

Bill Jordan
Asst. Chief, U.S. Border Patrol (Ret.)
Major, USMCR (Ret.)
Shooting Editor, Guns Magazine
Author, "No Second Place Winner"

Publisher's Foreword

Human life is precious. To guard it and to permit the individual to enjoy various rights and privileges, society has established rules of human behavior and has organized itself against unlawful violence. Police provide protection against individual criminals or gangster groups and mob violence; military forces guard against organized armed aggression. The presence of peace enforcement officers is a deterrent to the criminally inclined individual. Similarly, peace loving nations, such as our own, find it necessary to maintain armed forces to deter aggressor nations. Both our communities and our nation seek to preserve the domestic tranquility and international peace. Sometimes, in spite of these efforts, the peace is broken and a war must be fought—to defend our homes, our way of life, or our peace loving neighbors, and to restore peace. In our communities we must always maintain law and order.

War is a brutal business, whether it be war against an enemy or war against the criminal who strikes from within. And personal combat, at close quarters, is its most brutal aspect.

Personal combat conforms to no set rules of conduct, as the fighting in Korea so plainly proved. Were we, the United States, the choosers, it would not be thus; the decencies of human conduct would be observed. But we must be ready to fight against an utterly ruthless Communist enemy, one who feels he must win at any cost, even at the cost of human decency.

The American soldier who meets such an enemy is forced to adapt himself to a pattern of behavior that is foreign to his education and his religious beliefs. If he would win the fight— indeed, if he himself would survive—he must know all the dirty tricks of close combat, even as the enemy knows them. He must match them trick for trick. Further, he must be able to take the initiative and attack an enemy soldier as ruthlessly as he, in turn, would be attacked if he waited. It is a split

vii

second business. There is no time allowed for moral debate. In close combat, it is now or never.

The same principles hold when the enemy is domestic—when he is a brutal criminal running at large; or when he, with other subversives, in a critical hour strikes at our communities. In any case—enemy soldier, dangerous criminal, or fifth columnist—the opponent is playing for keeps. Whether we like it or not, we can defeat him and defend our decent standards only by beating him at his own game.

This book is designed to meet this situation. It is an intensely practical and forthright description of the techniques of hand-to-hand combat and of mob control. It is written primarily for members of our Armed Forces and those of our Allies (in the performance of their military duties); for the police officer; and for those members of civil defense organizations who may some day be forced to deal with the criminal subversives in our midst, including professional fifth columnists who would stir up dissension and incite disorders and riots.

The first edition of the book was written during World War II and was used by the various military branches of the United States and our Allies, as a textbook and reference, in training for individual combat and survival. Subsequent editions have been broadened to cover the civilian law enforcement field as well as the military. Over thirty thousand copies are now in circulation. We believe this text is alone and unique in its field. The completeness of the coverage of the subject has resulted in a steady demand for its material. It is felt that publication of this text is a public service, both to enable those who have to fight in close combat to survive, and to make more effective those who serve in the field of law enforcement

This edition is being published at a time when the world is in a state of unrest. Race riots, intolerance, Communist-inspired mob violence, and nationalism emphasize the importance of mob control by the established forces of law and order. Three new chapters have been added on the techniques involved in riot control. The timely incorporation of these new chapters has again added greatly to the value of this text to law enforcement agencies.

There is probably nobody better qualified than Colonel Applegate to describe the techniques of close combat. During World War II, as an infantry officer, he served with military police units, the Office of Strategic Services (OSS), the Counter Intelligence Corps, and the Military Intelligence

Division of the War Department. During the latter part of the war, he was in charge of special training in close combat at the Military Intelligence Training Center at Camp Ritchie, Maryland, where high priority intelligence personnel were given the training described in this book.

Colonel Applegate has attended many of the principal police schools in the United States, has studied in foreign police and special combat schools, and has undergone British commando training. He has worked and studied with famous experts, including W. E. Fairbairn and E. A. Sykes of Shanghai police and British commando fame; with Gus Peret of the Remington Arms Company, J. H. Fitzgerald of the Colt Firearms Company, and Colonel Biddle of the U. S. Marine Corps. At one time, he was assigned to special duty with President Roosevelt's bodyguard.

During recent years Colonel Applegate has been actively engaged in the field of riot control. He has had an opportunity to observe at first hand several violent mob actions. He has also had the satisfaction of seeing riot control units which he has trained, successfully dominate a mob and restore order.

Like the publishers, Colonel Applegate believes that the techniques he describes should be taught under careful supervision and used only for legitimate purposes and in appropriate combat or law enforcement situations.

Author's Preface

This book was first conceived and published early in World War II. If it had not been for the type of conflict experienced, combined with the circumstances and opportunities of my own personal assignments, it would never have been written.

Frequent armed conflict and mob violence since the end of World War II has brought about an increasing demand for a text on these very difficult subjects.

This fifth edition represents a further effort to broaden the scope of the text to cover adequately the combat and mob control problems of the civilian law enforcement officer as well as the military.

Weapons, tactics and strategy of modern warfare may be changing, but the age-old aspects of military and police individual combat and of mob control are still the same.

Since the time of the caveman, techniques of personal combat have been in the process of evolution. There are many methods and systems of personal combat. The methods of teaching them are equally varied. Some are good, some bad, some practical, others nonpractical. This book does not, and could not, cover all methods. It is a compilation of the most practical methods known to the writer, methods that have been developed and used during and after World War II by our own police and military, those of our Allies and even our enemies.

The soldier must be trained and indoctrinated in the offensive. Combat between armies is only won by offensive tactics.

The law enforcement officer has a different problem. He must first master restraint and manhandling tactics. He must also be able, under extreme or necessary circumstances, to take strong defensive or offensive action.

The "Cold" War has placed increased emphasis on guerrilla, mob control, and fifth column tactics. This furnishes an additional reason why members of the Military and of law enforcement and civil defense agencies must be trained in some or all of the offensive tactics covered in this book.

The tactics, training, and strategy of the enemy are in process of improvement and change. This is especially true of the direction and manipulation of a mob as an instrument of gaining or destroying political power.

I do not expect that all the answers as to how best to combat the professional mob will be found here, but they are the best known to the author at this time. It is sincerely hoped that the new material I have added on this subject will be of interest and help to all legitimate forces of law and order. The counter mob tactics outlined here may not make pleasant reading for Communists. But their willingness to use mob violence as a weapon in their drive to attain world domination is well known. The field of mob control and its tactics is not a new one, but the interjection into the picture of the professional Communist agitator, trained in all aspects of mob psychology and incitation, is relatively recent. New counter measures and tactics must now be employed by police elements to meet the situation. The Communists have taken over forty years to perfect their techniques of mob persuasion and direction. Police and military units will find difficulty in trying to meet such a threat with hurriedly improvised counter measures.

Other than mentioning general training aids, I have purposely avoided laying out specific, detailed training programs. Each organization—military or civilian—has its own problems, some phases of training demanding more emphasis than others.

Although this text has been pointed toward the training of large groups of men, I hope that those individuals who have sufficient interest to study it will, as a result, find themselves better prepared should they suddenly find themselves opposed by a killer.

REX APPLEGATE

Contents

Chapter 1

INTRODUCTION TO UNARMED COMBAT

A NY subject with as many variations in theory, training, and application as there are in hand-to-hand combat should be presented to the trainee in a simple manner, so as to be easily understood. The history and background of close combat without weapons is a desirable beginning for such a training program.

Unarmed combat is just what the name implies—a system of fighting intended for use when weapons are not available or when their use is not advisable. A soldier or police officer carries weapons in addition to those given him by nature; but he must not depend solely on his firearm, baton, or other issue equipment. These are only mechanical aids and will not always sustain him. Long before the existence of the stone knife and the bow and arrow, primitive man fought with his hands, teeth, legs, feet, and body. But through the centuries, unarmed combat tactics became more refined and skillful, until they reached their peak in the commando-type training given in certain of our military units during World War II.

Tibetan monks of the 12th century are reputed to have been among the first to develop a definite system of fighting without weapons. These monks, prohibited by the rules of their order from bearing arms, developed a system of unarmed combat to protect themselves from the brigands and robber bands of that era. Their system of combat involved many of the basic principles from which our body-contact sports and jiu jitsu have been developed. Some time after the 12th century, the Japanese learned of this method of combat and, characteristically, copied it and claimed its origin. They gave it the name of jiu jitsu, and claimed that it was developed during their mythological age. For centuries jiu jitsu was practiced, with many variations and interpretations, by the Samurai warrior clans. About 1885, a Japanese professor by the name of Kano established a school in which a unified version of the best of the many jiu jitsu techniques was taught. He called his improved version "judo." Today the terms jiu jitsu and judo are synonymous, judo being in reality the modern version of jiu jitsu.

Judo as a sport, and, with certain restrictions, as a method of combat, was practiced universally in Japan until recently. It was advocated by the military as a means of body-building and of developing individual competitive spirit. Jiu jitsu, or judo, employs a group of basic principles that are common to body-contact sports, such as wrestling, boxing, and football. Basically it is a system of holds and throws based on the use of the mechanical principle of the lever and fulcrum. Properly employed, jiu jitsu enables a small man to overcome a larger opponent by using his opponent's greater weight and strength to the latter's disadvantage.

For years prior to World War II, this Japanese method of combat was cloaked in mystery. It was regarded by the public as a somewhat miraculous power that enabled the user to conquer a hapless opponent by a mere flick of the wrist. As long as there was lack of knowledge on the subject and an element of mystery surrounded its use, this was to some degree true. Taking advantage of the element of surprise, the jiu jitsu expert did not fight as his opponent expected and could thereby gain the initial advantage, which he never relinquished. This was evident, but not understood, when certain jiu jitsu experts publicly overcame unskilled opponents in scheduled exhibitions.

The most optimistic experts estimate that it takes several years of consistent, intelligent practice before an individual can use judo as a dependable method of unarmed combat. As a sport, it is practiced in this country by a small group of devotees, but there are relatively few experts who can use their skill effectively against determined opponents. Based on the application of holds, throws, and on the destruction of the opponent's balance, the jiu jitsu user has to be really expert if he is to overcome a determined assault by an individual skilled in the use of blows of the hands or feet.

Soldiers and police can expect to encounter few individuals who will use judo against them successfully. They will, however, probably encounter certain judo tricks which have been combined with the type of rough and ready fighting tactics advocated in the commando style of personal combat.

The danger of overrating judo as an effective means of

combat lies not only in the aura of mystery that has been allowed to surround it, but also in the overemphasis placed on it as an effective means of hand-to-hand combat training in World War II. As a result of that war and a demand by the public for books and techniques on methods of fighting, bookstores were flooded with books and pamphlets on the subject of unarmed combat. Many of these, purporting to be genuine jiu jitsu, bore titles and slogans intended to appeal to the gullible. Courses which would take a sincere judo student months to master were offered in "ten easy, self-taught lessons."

Extravagant claims of success of the unarmed judo exponent against an armed enemy are frequently made. Students of many judo courses, given recently, are "quickly" taught a specific number of jiu jitsu tricks. When the course is completed and students are called upon to use what they have learned against a determined opponent, they usually find themselves helpless, unless the attacker performs in the specified manner taught in the course. Such courses obviously do not give the student the training necessary to adapt him to the uncertainties of combat. Many tricks advocated in jiu jitsu, and certain combat books, are not practical because they cannot be applied quickly enough. They are based on the assumption that the opponent will stand still, allowing the hold or throw to be applied.

The illusion of ease in subduing an opponent and the implication that this can be accomplished without personal risk or injury to the user, are also fallacies evident in many instruction courses in close combat offered the public. An individual can test the efficacy of such combat methods and holds by asking himself a simple question: "*Will this work so that I can use it instinctively in vital combat against an opponent who is determined to prevent me from doing so, and who is striving to eliminate me by fair means or foul?*" Considering the small amount of time devoted to instruction in fundamentals and the scanty practice demanded of the student in these courses, it is evident that many highly advertised techniques cannot measure up to this simple standard.

To sum up, the average American lacks the time, patience and usually the interest to become a genuine expert at judo. He does not really need a complete course in jiu jitsu, as is often claimed, to be able to take care of his opponent in unarmed combat. His athletic background, physique and temperament are usually adaptable to a style of fighting which is based more on the use of blows than on finesse. Military experience, in combat and training centers throughout the world, has shown that the average man can be quickly turned into a dangerous, offensive fighter by concentrating on a few basic principles of combat and by advocating principally the use of blows executed by the hands, feet and other parts of the body.

All types of combat can be divided into two phases, offensive and defensive. Knowledge of both is necessary to any fighting man. In training for warfare, the emphasis is usually on the offensive. In the case of the military police or civil law enforcement officers, the emphasis should be at least equal. Only the local situation, as it affects himself personally and his mission, can determine which type of combat a police officer should use. At times, he will have to resort to extreme offensive methods, because they may be his only means of defense. In other situations, only simple defense and restraint methods may be necessary. The judgment of the officer will determine what tactics he must use. He usually carries a loaded gun and is expected to exercise proper judgment in firing it. Also, he must decide for himself whether a given situation calls for personal unarmed combat tactics, and which of those tactics he will use.

The unarmed combat methods presented in the initial chapters represent a selection and combination of techniques taken from judo, wrestling and other body-contact sports, from combat methods used in other lands, and from self-defense tactics, and those used in rough and tumble fighting. The techniques presented have been used successfully in training and in recent combat. They can be learned easily and applied quickly and instinctively—but only after adequate, but not excessive, practice.

No text, no matter how well-illustrated or clearly explained can, alone, teach a man to fight. It can only serve as an instructional guide. Closely supervised intensive practice is the only path to practical knowledge. There are no easy methods or short cuts. Practice must be intensive enough to render the mechanics of each technique automatic. There is seldom time to stop and think when the pressure of combat is on. *Being able* to throw a man is much different from *knowing how.*

Expert boxers and wrestlers will already be far along the road to proficiency in personal combat. The use of boxing, wrestling and other body-contact sports in training and conditioning programs will add materially to the student's progress and will speed up his development as an aggressive fighter. An athletic background develops the necessary coordination and muscular ability, and enables the student to learn combat techniques more easily. However, experience has shown that such techniques can also be developed in the trainee who has had no previous athletic experience. His progress may be slower, but practice and a desire to learn can develop the average trainee, who possesses normal courage, physique and the will to fight, into a dangerous antagonist at close quarters.

Chapter 2

OFFENSIVE
UNARMED COMBAT

NEITHER war nor individual combat is won solely by defensive, Maginot Line psychology or tactics. In personal combat, it is often difficult to determine where defense ends and offense begins. Often the only defense is a good offense. However, in all cases, a knowledge of possible methods of attack enables a defense to be better planned.

The methods advocated in this chapter are simple and are based on a style of fighting that knows no rules, that depends on speed and ruthlessness for results. Boxing and wrestling are sports. They can be used only to a limited extent in vital combat. The fighting tactics discussed here, however, are designed to knock out, maim, or kill, as the situation may demand.

Types of hand-to-hand combat that demand set positions and complicated maneuvers—for the attacker and his opponent—are practically useless when the ordinary man finds himself projected into physical combat at an unexpected time. To be able to rely upon and use instinctively a specific hold or throw for each set or different position of an opponent is a difficult task. To be able to do so swiftly and instinctively demands months and sometimes years of practice. It takes time to train the mind and body to react to each set of conditions instinctively and in the prescribed method. This is one of the weaknesses of the jiu jitsu technique. By certain maneuvers and movements, a jiu jitsu expert can place an antagonist in the proper position for a specific throw; but for the layman it is much too complicated and, according to American standards, takes too long to learn.

The combat tactics advocated here do not depend on any set stance or position to achieve results. They are based on what the smallest man can do to the largest, using the element of surprise when possible, with ruthless disregard for the opponent. In the homespun philosophy of David Harum "Do unto others as they would do unto you, *but do it first.*"

VULNERABLE PARTS OF THE BODY

The human body is made up of many vulnerable spots. Some are nerve centers, some are organs unprotected by a bony or muscular structure, and some are areas only lightly protected by bone or muscle tissue. About a dozen such spots can be attacked with marked results in combat. A well-timed blow or pressure brought to bear on one of these vital areas will disable an opponent or force him to cease offensive action. Man has many natural weapons—his head, teeth, elbows, feet, knees, hands and fingers—which he may use in attacking vulnerable spots. These spots are listed below in the order of their vulnerability and accessibility.

Testicles. These organs are the most sensitive and vulnerable of man's body. A hand, knee, or foot blow to the crotch

GROIN BLOW
The best way to finish quickly any close-quarter fight is to use a strong hand, knee or foot blow to the groin—the testicle area.

will disable the strongest opponent. The best and strongest of holds can be broken if the testicles can be grasped or hit. Because of their extremely vulnerable location in the body, they are the most likely spot at which to expect an attack from an unscrupulous opponent. It should always be remembered, when closing in vital combat, that a good knee blow delivered to the testicle area will not only finish the fight, but also, while in the process of being delivered, will protect the user's groin area by blocking with the thigh a similar attempt by an opponent. These vulnerable organs are the principal reason why we have referees in such sports as boxing and wrestling. Not only the testicles, but the entire groin area, is susceptible to attack. They are the Achilles heel of man's anatomy.

Eyes. The eyes are delicate, easy to reach, and like the testicles, are parts which any man instinctively strives to protect. A gouge with thumb or finger to the eye will be effec-

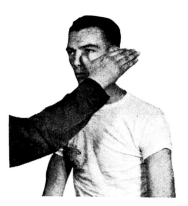

FINGER OR EYE GOUGE

The eyes, like the testicles, are extremely vulnerable. A finger or eye gouge will stop the most determined attack.

tive in breaking up the most determined hold or attack. A blow aimed or feinted at the eyes, or "family jewels" (testicles), will cause a man to move instinctively to cover them. Many times this will leave him wide open for other types of attack.

Neck Area. An edge-of-the-hand blow across the windpipe, in the Adam's apple area, will have fatal results. It has the same effect as the crushing of a piece of copper tubing with a blow from a sharp-edged instrument.

Blows delivered by the edge of the hand to the sides of the throat and to the back of the neck, at the base of the skull, have a knockout effect. Few physiques can stand up to these blows, the only exceptions being wrestlers and such, who have exceptionally well-muscled necks.

The effect of a blow to the windpipe can be demonstrated by placing the thumb in the hollow at the base of the throat, below the Adam's apple, and pressing gently. Light, edge-of-the-hand blows, delivered to the sides and back of the neck, will demonstrate their effectiveness to the most skeptical person.

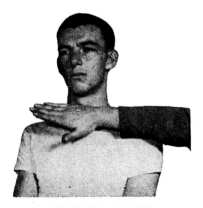

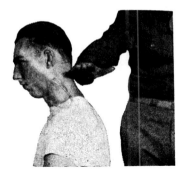

WINDPIPE BLOW

The windpipe is unprotected. A sharp blow here will have fatal results. The area just below the Adam's apple is the most vulnerable.

NAPE OF NECK BLOW

An edge-of-hand blow here will cause a knock-out. A light blow will demonstrate the stunning effect.

Back and Kidney Area. A physiology book will show that the main muscle cords and nerves of the body branch out from the base of the spine at a point very near the surface. This region is commonly known as the small of the back. In it the kidneys are located, just above the hips on each side of the spine. A horizontal blow with the fist or edge of the hand, or a kick delivered there, will have a disabling, if not a knockout, effect. Care must be taken to hit the area above the hip bones and below the heavy back muscles. Not for nothing are kidney pads worn by football players.

A low blow delivered by the edge of the hand to the end of the spine is often effective. It is easiest to deliver when the opponent is stooping over, as he would be when grappling some one about the waist. A kick delivered by the point of the toe to this area often produces a disabling effect.

Stomach Area. It is a big one and easy to hit. A hard blow here by the fist, knee, or head is very effective, particularly if the opponent's muscles are relaxed. The solar plexus can be hit by driving the fist up and under the rib structure at a point about one inch above the navel. At a point about one inch below the navel is another vulnerable spot, which can be reached by a knuckle jab.

Chin. A blow by a *skilled* boxer to the point of the chin will put a man down for the count. The same result can be obtained by a blow using the heel of the hand. An edge-of-the-hand blow, directed downward at the point of the chin, will cause a break or dislocation of the lower jaw bone.

Nose. A horizontal blow, by the edge of the hand, at that part of the nose which is ordinarily covered by the bridge of a pair of glasses will result in a knockout, and possibly death. The most fragile bones of the facial structure are crushed when this blow is used. It usually results in a hemorrhage, from which a fatal infection can develop.

By placing the index fingers on both sides of the base of the nose, where it joins the face, and pressing inward and upward, another vulnerable spot is reached. An edge-of-the-hand blow directed upward at the base of the nose also is most effective.

Temples. Blows delivered by the knuckles, or edge-of-the-hand, to the temple area will often put an opponent down for the count. This area is small, but it is one of the most sensitive on the head. By placing the thumbs on the temple and exerting a firm, steady, inward pressure, then moving them about, this most vulnerable area can be located.

Jaw Hinge Area. Where the lower jaw hinges to the upper, near the base of the ears, is a sensitive point that is vulnerable to a knuckle blow. By placing the finger tips just under the ear lobe and pressing in and *up*, another sensitive area is located. Pressure applied here is particularly effective in forcing an opponent to release a hold or stop offensive action.

Joints. Nature made the joints of the knee, wrist, arm, elbow, finger, and other members to bend only in certain directions. Enough pressure or strong blows applied to these joints in the *opposite* direction will cause a break or dislocation, or will at least force the opponent to yield temporarily.

Sensitive Bones. Many bones of the body are sensitive to blows or pressure because they have not been furnished with protective coverings of flesh or tissue. Kicks to the shins, edge-of-the-hand blows to the collar bones, forearm, or wrist will often cause a break or effect a release. Many grips may be broken by forcing the point of a thumb or knuckle between the small bones of the back of the hand, or by placing the point of the thumb in the hollow spot where the opponent's thumb joins his wrist. Pressure applied on such points is not disabling in itself, but is very good in effecting releases.

Other Sensitive Areas. Nature has given man numerous other unprotected spots which can be hurt locally, to effect releases and create openings. The following actions are effective: Pulling hair, tearing a lip, grasping and twisting (or tearing) the nose. A grip with the point of thumb and forefinger, or bite, on the thick muscles that extend from the neck to the shoulder; a thumb and forefinger grip, or bite, across the breast muscles to the arm; kicking or biting the Achilles tendon back of the heel—all are effective.

FUNDAMENTAL PRINCIPLES

There are a number of fundamental principles in hand-to-hand combat. Some must be observed at all times, others are used in special situations. Where the use of one begins and the other leaves off is difficult to define and can only be determined by the user. Often their application is separated only by a split second.

Balance. The most basic fundamental of all is that of balance. Mental balance, or stability, is a state of mind that is necessary before physical balance can be achieved. In exciting circumstances, such as vital combat, the mental balance of the opponent can often be upset by the surprise of the attack. The use of yells, feints or deception; throwing dirt or other objects in the opponent's face; or the use of any strategy that he does not expect forces him to take time to condition his mind to a new set of circumstances. The time necessary for the mind to adjust itself varies with the individual, but it is during this period of adjustment that the attacker can destroy his opponent's physical balance and undertake offensive action. Surprise is as effective in man-to-man combat as it is in the strategy of armies. That is why the successful fighter conceals his true intentions, so that he never "telegraphs" his intention. He always strives to do the unexpected.

Physical balance must be retained by the attacker and destroyed in the opponent. The fighter who retains his body balance can utilize his entire strength. Conversely, he can have his lack of balance used against him by a skilled antagonist. The destruction of the opponent's body balance, after he has been led by finesse and movements into an off-balance position, is a fundamental of jiu jitsu technique. A sudden push or pull applied to the shoulders, or other part of the body, will weaken or break body balance. Once this is accomplished, an opponent's offensive power and strength, no matter how great, cannot be fully utilized. The man who attacks first and destroys his opponent's balance has a decided

DESTROYING BALANCE   CHIN PUSH

Greater physique and strength mean nothing if you do not have balance. In the illustration at the left, the larger and stronger man easily lifts the smaller man. The illustration at the right shows how, by pushing back on the opponent's chin, the smaller man destroys the big man's physical balance, thus preventing the use of his superior strength. The larger man is unable to lift the smaller man when this occurs.

advantage, regardless of a difference in size, weight, or physique. Once the opponent is knocked off-balance, he should be kept struggling to regain it and should never be allowed to get set. The destruction of body balance should be followed immediately by offensive tactics.

To get into a good balance position which offers a fighting stance, place the feet apart, about the distance of the width of the shoulders, with the body crouched and bent slightly forward and with the knees slightly bent. In this position the individual can change stance readily and can move about, facing his opponent, so that he is always in a state of physical balance.

Momentum. Do not work directly against, or try to stop, the momentum of an opponent in motion. Utilize his impetus

BODY BALANCE IN ATTACK

A good, balanced position with which to meet an attack or from which to launch one—body crouched and bent slightly forward, feet apart and knees flexed. The hands are out in front, to be used as a defense, or to strike a blow.

DESTROYING WALKING BALANCE

Another simple demonstration of the value of balance. Let the victim start to walk past you. Then reach out and, by placing the forefinger under his nose and by forcing his head back, prevent him from walking past you. His body is no longer in a state of physical balance.

by directing its force, once he comes in contact. For example, if a man rushes you and you side-step and apply a trip, you are utilizing his momentum and his resultant lack of balance to throw him. If, on the other hand, you remain in his path and try to stop him and throw him in the opposite direction, it becomes much more difficult; it takes a great deal more strength and energy to accomplish the same result. The same principle applies if an opponent takes a wild swing at you. Duck, and let the momentum of the swing take him off balance; then attack.

Another useful element is potential momentum. Assume that an opponent has grasped you by the wrist and is endeavoring to pull you off balance, and that you are pulling in the opposite direction to keep him from doing so. If you suddenly change your tactics and effect a wrist release, or cease to resist the force of his pull by stepping toward him, he will fall backwards in the direction in which he was trying to pull you. When this happens, he loses balance and becomes vulnerable to attack. The same principle would apply if you were resisting a push, and suddenly gave way instead of opposing.

Maximum Force. The principle of maximum force means the concentration of the greatest proportion of your strength against some weak spot or area on your opponent's body. In other words, attack parts of your opponent's body that are easily hurt, or concentrate on an area that will cause him intense pain if he does not move away. Instead of putting your entire strength against him in an area where he is equally strong, or perhaps stronger, try to pit his weakest point against your strongest. A good example is the use of the wrist throw, or a finger twist, where you concentrate great pressure against a weak part of the body which is easily broken.

The principle of maximum force is not a magic formula, to bring an individual through all types of combat unscathed; but it will help by inflicting as much damage as quickly as possible, while receiving as little damage as possible.

One school of thought, in unarmed combat circles, advocates first closing with the enemy, throwing him to the ground, then dispatching him. The other, and most successful, insists that blows used to down the opponent are preferable to throws, and that they can be taught to and used by the average man much more speedily. Naturally, throws will have to be used in many instances; but actual combat has shown that well-placed blows by the hands or feet, in many instances, can accomplish the desired result more quickly and more easily. Two good general rules in unarmed combat are: *(1) Keep your opponent at arm's length by the use of hand and foot blows.* Many times, when you are in a position to start to close with an opponent so as to throw or trip him, you will be able to use blows instead. *(2) Avoid, if at all possible, going to the ground with your adversary.* Try to avoid getting close to him. Being close, you will not have room to see what he is up to or be able to work with the best effect. If you are smaller than your opponent and go to the ground with him, his superior weight and strength will always give him an advantage, whether he utilizes it or not. The danger of being stunned upon impact with the ground surface also presents a good reason for not closing with the opponent if it can be avoided.

Falls. A knowledge of the art of falling is very useful, because, in the varied conditions of combat, there will be times when the cardinal rule of never going to the ground will be violated. Many practice and training hours could be devoted to training the student in how to fall correctly, without harm to himself. Knowledge of this subject can be obtained from any good book on tumbling or jiu jitsu. In a training program, such sports as wrestling, football, and gymnastics will teach a great deal about proper methods of falling. However, there is a vast difference between falling on gymnasium mats and falling on a hard, uneven surface—as is likely to happen in combat. It is obvious that you should stay on your feet.

One injunction you should heed: Once going to the ground, never stop moving. Start rolling and try to get back on your feet as quickly as possible. If you can't get up and can't roll, pivot on your hips and shoulders so you can face your opponent and block with your feet any attempt to close with you.

Remember, it is not necessary to go to the ground once you have placed your opponent there. You can finish him off with your feet. Your enemy can do likewise if you remain immobile on the ground and stay within range.

MAN'S NATURAL WEAPONS AND THEIR USES

Offensive Tactics Using the Feet. The proper use of the feet as weapons of combat is not generally appreciated. Properly used, feet can be the most potent of all natural weapons. The Chinese and the French long ago developed methods of using the feet in fighting; and loggers of the Pacific Northwest and Canada have long used their heavy boots as offensive weapons. However the average person usually considers the feet only as a means of locomotion.

USE OF FOOT IN KICKING

The best kick utilizes the whole length of the foot, the striking surface being large enough to insure accuracy.

TOE KICK

A kick delivered toe first at a standing or moving opponent is likely to miss, causing the kicker to lose his balance.

Many fights can be stopped before they have a chance to start by a well-placed kick to the opponent's knee. When the opponent is standing, kicks should generally be delivered by using only the outside edge, sole, or inside edge of the foot. A kick delivered toe foremost, aimed at a narrow target, is not accurate; the slightest movement by the opponent will cause a miss and leave the kicker in an off-balance position where he is wide open for retaliation. When he is left off balance, the opponent may grab his foot and twist it for a throw.

Feet often can be used offensively, before body contact is made, after contact is made, and as weapons to stun or kill, once the opponent is down. They can be used defensively against attack with bladed weapons or striking implements. When on the ground, subjected to attack from a standing opponent, the individual can use his feet to prevent the adversary from closing in or administering a *coup de grace.*

A proper kick makes use of the length of the foot (heel to toe) and utilizes footwear, the heavier the better. The kick delivered toe foremost makes use of a striking area of only the width of the toe of the shoe, whereas the kick delivered correctly, with the full length of the foot as the striking area, uses a weapon almost four times larger. This is especially important in view of the fact that the opponent

THE BEST WAY TO USE THE FEET

Face sideways to the target, raise the leg, and lash out. Body balance is retained by bending the body in the direction opposite to the kick.

KNEE KICK

A determined attack can be stopped quickly by using the knee kick. This blow, directed at the knee cap, will break or dislodge the knee hinge. It is very effective against any type of frontal attack, even though the opponent is armed with a club or bladed weapon. Notice how the kicker's body trunk is bent back, out of arm's reach, as the kick is delivered.

KNEE JOINT KICK

Kicks to the side of the knee joint will either destroy balance or cause a break or dislocation.

may not be standing absolutely still when the kick is launched.

The knee is particularly susceptible to a kick, since it is built to bend in only one direction. Forceful kicks delivered on the knee cap area from the right or left side will cause a break or a dislocation. A kick delivered to the back of the knee and accompanied by a shoulder pull to the rear will destroy balance and take any opponent to the ground.

The knee kick, properly used, almost always will be effective. It should be one of the first basic attack methods learned. The knee kick is correctly delivered by raising the leg first and then lashing straight out with the foot, withdrawing after contact. Balance is retained by bending the body from the hips in a direction opposite to the force of the kick. When a kick is made from this position, body balance is always retained even though the target is missed. Thus the danger of falling into the opponent if he should evade the blow is avoided.

Ordinarily it is difficult to kick a standing opponent at

BACK OF KNEE KICK

A kick against the back of the knee will cause an opponent to topple backward, especially if it is accompanied by a shoulder pull.

any spot above his knee height and still retain body balance. There may be instances, particularly when the opponent is crouching, when a kick can be delivered by the toe or side of the foot to the groin area, but the particular situation must determine whether or not this attempt should be made. A kick that is too high can be dangerous, and a miss causes a very precarious balance position.

Too much cannot be said about the desirability of using this type of attack. It can be learned without an excessive amount of practice and can be executed simply and effectively, particularly when accompanied by the element of surprise.

Other types of kicks are also effective, at close quarters, in creating openings or effecting releases. A kick delivered directly to the shins will cause an opponent to release a hold, or, if not in contact, will usually cause him to lurch forward, leaving him wide open for an uppercut or chin jab. A kick delivered to the shins in a downward direction, by the inside or outside edge of the shoe, can be directed a little below the knee, scraping all the way down the shin bone and ending by crushing the small bones on the top of the opponent's foot. If grasped around the body from the rear by an opponent, a stamp by the heel on the top of his foot, or a backward kick to the shin, will usually effect a release.

If thrown to the ground and unable to regain a standing position, kicks are most effective in preventing the enemy from closing. Turn on the back and spin, so that the feet are always toward the enemy. By pivoting on the hips and shoulders, and by using the hands to help propel the body, the feet can be kept in such a position that a kick can be

SHIN BONE KICK

A kick, with the outside edge of the shoe scraping down the shin bone and ending with full force on the small bones at the top of the opponent's foot, is extremely effective.

executed before the opponent can close in. The flutter type kick should not be used. Rather, one leg should be bent back, with the knee in a bent position, and the other extended with knee slightly bent, to be used as a parry. If the opponent attempts to close, a short kick can be made with the extended leg. This can be followed by a more powerful blow from the leg in the more fully bent position. When this last kick is made, it should be done in a piston-like movement with all the force of the big leg muscles behind it. Naturally an individual cannot maintain this tiring, defensive position indefinitely. At the first opportunity he should try to regain his feet.

Kicks to Stun or Kill. Once an opponent has been downed, the rest of the job should be done with the feet. This can be accomplished by a toe kick to the temple, throat or arm pit area, or by driving the back edge of the heel into the ribs, face, heart, stomach, throat, kidney or groin areas. The back edge of the heel is much more effective than the whole flat of the

KICK TO TEMPLE

A toe kick to the temple area will cause a concussion or a kill, if forceful enough.

foot inasmuch as all the force is concentrated in a small sharp area, thus getting more penetration. When using the feet for the *coup de grace*, it is best to stand at one side and use one leg only as the striking weapon, retaining balance on the other leg. If you jump on the opponent with both feet, as some methods advocate, there is always danger of losing balance in case of a miss caused by movement of the opponent.

KICK TO RIBS

The flat, or back edge, of the heel will crush the rib cage and cause a fatal injury.

BLOWS USING THE HANDS

Hand blows can be delivered by using the fists, edge of the hand, palm, or knuckle. To use the fists effectively, a knowledge of boxing is a prerequisite. Experts state that it takes up to six months to learn to deliver a knockout blow with either fist. The ability to box is very desirable and the other principles boxing teaches, such as the use of body balance, should not be underestimated. However, there are other means of using the hands which the layman can learn and use more swiftly, and at times more effectively.

The Chin Jab. Knockout blows delivered to the chin by the fist may not only be ineffective, they also present the danger of a dislocated finger or knuckle, or a cut from the opponent's bony facial structure. The use of the fist has another shortcoming; that it does not concentrate the force of the blow sufficiently. Any part of the anatomy will collapse if it is struck many times in one place; but the average individual cannot use the fist effectively enough to do great damage in a single blow. The novice should limit the use of his fists to such soft, vulnerable areas as the stomach, groin and kidneys, and rely on other types of blows for other parts of the body.

The extremely effective chin jab is so called because it is used principally in the chin area. It must be delivered *up and under* the chin with the heel of the palm, fingers extended and spread for palm rigidity. The more directly underneath the chin the blow falls, the more power it will pack. It is executed with a stiff, locked wrist and a bent elbow; and a great deal of upward body force can be utilized at the time of impact. The further forward the chin is extended at the time of the blow, the more devastating the result. If a knee thrust to the testicles or groin is used in connection with the chin jab, the body will be automatically bent forward, leaving a perfect setup for this particular blow. It results in unconsciousness and possible neck fracture, if delivered with sufficient force.

CHIN JAB

Correct hand and arm position for chin jab. Note how the fingers are spread apart, giving the palm rigidity.

CHIN JAB WITH GROIN BLOW

A knee to the groin, causing the opponent to lurch forward, followed by a chin jab, will result in a knockout.

The arm, or hand, does not have to be drawn back in beginning execution of the blow. It can be hanging at the side, fingers hooked in belt, hand resting on a lapel, or in any other nonchalant position. An average man can cause a knockout with only six inches of traveling distance from the start of the blow to the point of impact. The element of surprise is most useful in close quarters, where time, space, or circumstances do not allow the hand and arm to be withdrawn for a long haymaker. A neck fracture can be caused by gripping an opponent's belt with the left hand and jerking him forward, at the moment of impact with the right. It is also desirable to use the fingers of the striking hand on the eyes following the blow. The heel of the hand also can be used to strike a stunning blow at the base of the skull.

Edge of the Hand. The most effective of all hand blows is that using the edge of the hand. It is valuable because it can be utilized against, and will penetrate to, vulnerable spots of the body which would not be susceptible to blows from the fist or heel of the hand. It can be delivered with varying degrees of effectiveness, from almost any position of the body and arms. The edge-of-the-hand blow is properly delivered with the fingers extended, close together, *thumb upright* and wrist locked. The striking surface is the cushioned part of the hand between the base of the little finger and the edge of the palm, where it joins the wrist. It is very important that the thumb be raised to an upright position. Doing so prevents the hand from remaining in a relaxed, clenched position, and it insures that the fingers automatically extend. The striking surface is well padded, and its length, varying with the sizes of hands, is usually about two inches. Contrast the striking surface of this area, in square inches, with that of a clenched fist. The fist provides roughly eight square inches of striking surface, but with the edge of the hand the striking surface is only two or three square inches. Therefore, a blow delivered by the

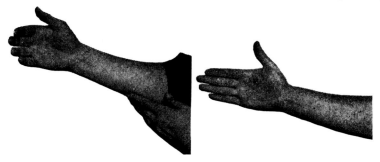

INCORRECT USE OF HAND   CORRECT USE OF THE HAND

The illustration at the left shows the hand in a relaxed, bent position, thus preventing its use as a weapon. At the right, above, the fingers are extended and the thumb is in the *up* position. This turns the edge of the hand into a sharp, hard weapon.

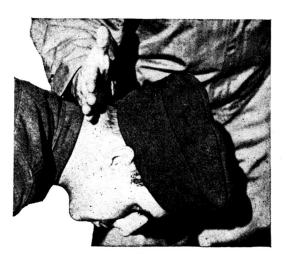

RABBIT PUNCH

This blow, delivered at the point where the skull joins the spine, will cause a knockout. In sporting circles it is called "the rabbit punch."

BASE OF NOSE BLOW

This edge-of-hand blow, directed upward and landing on the point where the base of the nose joins the face, will cause unconsciousness and possible hemorrhage.

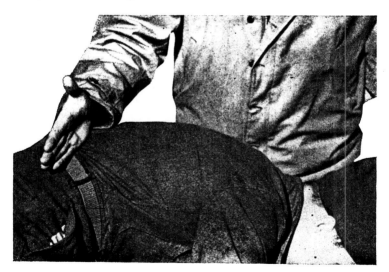

KIDNEY BLOW

A kidney blow will have a temporary stunning effect. It is most effective when the opponent is stooping over.

TAIL BONE BLOW

A blow to the tail bone area, like the kick with the point of the toe, is dangerous.

hand gives a sharp-edged effect, causing a break, fracture or concussion. The force is expended on a relatively small area.

When applied to the area around the neck, the cords on either side of the back of the neck, the base of the skull, the sides of the neck, the windpipe area just below the Adam's apple, the bridge of the nose, the kidneys, and the

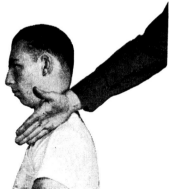

SIDE OF NECK BLOW

A blow to the side of the neck will hit vital nerves and the carotid artery, causing a knock-out.

COLLAR BONE BLOW

A downward blow, like the blow of a police baton, will fracture the collar bone and incapacitate the opponent.

end of the spine—this type of blow has a devastating effect. The bones of the forearm, the collar bone, the end of the chin, and the wrist area will fracture when subjected to such a blow. It should be delivered with the elbow bent, utilizing body force by a chopping motion. Chopping is important because it tends to localize the force of the blow even more

WRIST OR BICEPS BLOW

A sharp chopping blow to the wrist or forearm will often cause a fracture. Delivered to the muscles of the biceps, it will cause them to cramp.

BRIDGE OF NOSE BLOW

This blow will crush the most delicate bones of the facial structure. Delivered at the bridge of the nose, where the brow and nose join, it will cause concussion. Cerebral hemorrhage is a possibility.

in a small area. If the edge-of-the-hand blow is delivered without the chopping motion, it will still be effective, but a great deal of the striking force will be expended over a larger area than when it is delivered properly.

Edge-of-the-hand blows can be delivered with either hand in a downward direction, or can be directed horizontally, palm down, as in a backhand saber stroke. The best position from which to use the horizontal edge-of-the-hand blow is with the right foot forward, using the favorite hand (usually the right). From this position, body weight can be utilized more fully. The reverse foot position applies for the left hand. With a somewhat lessened effect, the blow can be delivered with either hand and from any free position where the arm can be swung.

The Knuckles. Many sensitive spots have been well protected by nature and can only be reached by a striking weapon that is small and pointed. This particularly applies to the head and face area, where the knuckle is the best weapon to use. By "knuckle" is meant the second joint of the second or third finger, protruding from the front of the clenched fist. It is best used at close quarters where accuracy

USE OF KNUCKLE

The knuckle is very effective against the temple or hinge of the jaw.

is more certain. Properly employed, the knuckle can be used against the temple or hinge of the jaw area. It can cause a knockout or inflict enough pain to effect a release from an opponent's hold; or it can create another, more vulnerable opening. Of course, the thumb and all the fingers can be used as weapons, principally for exerting pressure on vulnerable points, for gouging, and for pinching large muscles.

The Bent Elbow. The point of the bent elbow is long and sharp and can often be used against tender parts of the anatomy, such as the stomach, groin, and throat. The elbow is generally best used when it is impossible to swing the fist or hand, or to use the feet because the opponent is too close. It is very effective when used against the jaw, as a follow through from a wrist release, or as a jabbing instrument to the opponent's groin or mid-section.

USE OF ELBOW

Use of the point of the elbow in a horizontal blow against the jaw or temple. Jab it into the groin, stomach, kidneys, or rib section when the opportunity arises.

Other Body Members. The head will make a good battering ram against soft areas, such as the small of the back or the stomach. If covered by a protective helmet, it can be used against the bony facial area.

The knees are capable of delivering extremely powerful blows to the groin or testicles, or to the small of the back and kidney areas. If the opponent is bent forward, they are very damaging against the chin and face.

The teeth, in spite of any mental qualms as to their use, are very effective weapons. The jaw muscles can exert terrific pressure and a deep bite to almost any tender or exposed area will effect a release or cause an opponent to cease offensive action.

THROWS

Blows should always be used in preference to throws; but a well-rounded fighting man must understand, and will at times use, the principles of throwing. In executing a throw he will utilize some or all of the fundamental principles discussed at the beginning of this chapter. When an opponent is falling, he is off balance, unable to fight back, and therefore susceptible to blows. If a throw is correctly applied, the adversary is usually momentarily stunned on impact with the ground, making a good target for hand and foot blows.

The average man simply cannot pick up a determined adversary and throw him to the ground by use of strength alone. A person of great size and strength might be able to accomplish such a feat, but the average individual must apply the scientific principles of throwing.

After an opponent has been placed in an *unbalanced position*, he is thrown by the use of leverage, or by stopping or sweeping aside some part of his body. His body balance may be destroyed by lifting him, stopping him from advancing, pulling or pushing him. When any of these things happen, he is momentarily off balance, and it is then that a throw is applied. Leverage is applied by forcing the extremities of the opponent's body in opposite directions. For example, kick your opponent's legs out from under him and at the same time shove his head in the opposite direction.

Sweeping away part of the body is exemplified, in throwing an opponent, by tripping him. When an individual is walking forward and his forefoot is caught and jerked just as he is about to put it down, he topples to the ground.

There are many ways to throw any opponent, but most of them are variations of the few fundamental throws described below. Although every situation in combat cannot be foreseen, the adoption and use of these simple tactics will suffice in most instances. Some may be more adaptable by individual fighters than others, but they may serve as a foundation around which to build variations that will apply in most situations.

The Hip Throw. The principle of the see-saw is here applied. The hip, acting as a fulcrum, is placed under the center of the adversary's body and his head is pulled toward the ground. One specific type of hip throw can be executed as follows: Facing your opponent, grasp his right wrist with your left hand; place your right arm under his left arm pit and around his back. Using the left foot as a pivot, step across in front of him with your right foot, so that your right side and hip are against his stomach area. Use your right arm to force the upper part of his body down and your left hand to pull down on his right arm while he is being forced over the hip by your right arm. If successfully executed, he will hit the ground head first. Simple variations of this throw can be used from the same initial position. This throw may be initiated from a locked embrace or by stepping be-

THE HIP THROW

The hip throw can be initiated in any situation where the upper part of the opponent's trunk can be grasped and the hip placed in a position to act as a fulcrum. At the left, above, enough clearance has been obtained by a testicle blow (or similar blow) to allow the left leg to cross in front, thus placing the hip where it acts as a fulcrum (right above). The upper part of the body is then pulled down across this pivot point to complete the throw.

hind the opponent and pulling him backward over your right or left hip. The important thing is to get your hip in the center of the opponent's body before downward leverage is applied.

Shoulder Throw. Another simple, effective throw is the "flying mare." It can be applied swiftly by grasping your opponent's right wrist with both hands, stepping in with your right foot and bringing his arm over your right shoulder with the hinge joint of his elbow up. In this position, you will have a firm grasp of his arm. Pressure on the arm will be exerted against the hinge resting on your shoulder, so that any sudden downward movement of your body, combined with a quick back thrust of your hips, will send him sailing through the air. If he doesn't go, his arm will break from

THE FLYING MARE

This is the more vicious version of the popular wrestling throw. Grasp the opponent's right arm (left above). Step across in front of him, turning your back; then pull his arm over the right shoulder, inside of elbow up. Pull downward and thrust back with the hips, as at the right above. The opponent will be thrown over your shoulder and will suffer a possible fracture of the elbow, in addition to a neck fracture or concussion on impact with the ground.

the leverage exerted. He can then be finished off in some other way. The flying mare, used with the elbow hinge reversed, has been used in wrestling circles for years as a spectacular type of throw. If you are working on a hard surface, instead of letting go of your opponent, after you flip him over your shoulder, maintain your hold on his arm and bring him down at your feet on his head and shoulders. A concussion or neck fracture will result when he strikes the ground.

The shoulder throw is effective against an opponent who has grasped you around the neck, or around the shoulders from behind. Reaching up, grasp your opponent's right arm above the elbow with both hands. Pull his arm forward, so that his armpit is over the point of your right shoulder. As you do so, step forward, bend down and bring your elbows sharply down to a point level with the knees. The step forward or the use of a backward thrust of the hips will lift him off the ground; the downward pull on his arm will finish the throw.

In any of these throws, the body must always be bent slightly forward when the throw is initiated. If it is bent backward, the use of powerful stomach muscles, as well as balance, can be lost. This is why the victim should always be pulled backward into an off-balance position in a skillful attack from the rear.

Sometimes a fall back may be used if an opponent has grasped your body from the rear and bent it backward so that a shoulder throw cannot be applied. To execute this, step to the outside and back of one of his legs, slam backward with the upper part of the body and sit down. The opponent will land between you and the ground and the possibilities are good of stunning him, knocking him out, or breaking his hold.

The Leg Hook. This is a surprise tactic that will usually catch an adversary off guard, particularly if he is coming in swinging. Drop your whole body to a crouch position under his swing as he closes in. From this crouch, drive upward so that the shoulder meets the pit of his stomach. At the same time hook the arms around his legs and lift upward. He will hit the ground hard.

These tactics can often be preceded by a feinted blow to his head before the drop. Flying tackles, or dives, at an on-rushing opponent are dangerous because the arms swinging wide and the crouching body telegraph your intentions. Be

careful to use a trick, such as a leg hook, just before contact is established, not when the opponent is some distance
away. If you are unable to grasp both legs from the crouch,
when contact is made, grasp the ankle or lower part of one
leg and use the shoulder against the knee.

Throws From the Rear. Many throws can be applied against
a man who is approached from the rear, but the use of blows
to the neck or a kick to the hinge of the knee is very simple
and effective. If body contact is desired, a variation of the
hip throw can be used; or the opponent can be smashed to
the ground by driving against his buttocks with the shoulder,
as the hands pull his ankles backward.

STRANGLES

A properly applied strangle should eliminate all resistance
within five seconds or less. Great pressure must be applied,
either to the windpipe or to the large arteries on both sides
of the neck. A strangle which affects both these areas is most
effective. Strangling can be accomplished by use of mechanical aids (which will be discussed in a later chapter), by use
of pressure against the hard bones of the wrist or forearm
(against a standing opponent), or by the use of thumbs and
fingers, if the opponent is down. The pressure applied by a
strangle must be great, and must be applied in such a way
that the victim's neck muscles do not have a chance to resist.
In many cases a neck fracture will accompany strangulation.

Whenever the edge-of-the-hand blow can be delivered
across the windpipe or Adam's apple area, it should be used
in preference to more complicated methods. It is advisable
to use it even after a strangle has been completed.

The Judo Choke. This is best performed on the ground.
The pressure is applied against the large carotid arteries on
both sides of the neck. These vessels supply blood to the
brain. Unconsciousness results within a few seconds when
they are closed by pinching. This choke is performed by utilizing the shirt, or coat, collar of the victim as a base for the
application of leverage.

There are two principal methods. The cross-arm choke is
performed by crossing the forearms, grasping the inside of
the collar with each hand (palm up) in a high up position,
so that the thumbs are under the ears. By taking a firm hold
and pulling the victim toward you while you force your
elbows out, strangulation is accomplished.

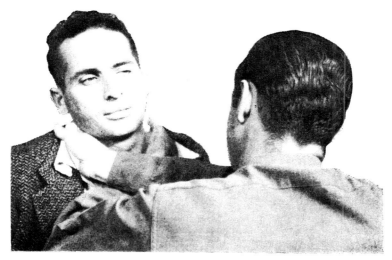

CROSS-ARM CHOKE

The cross-arm choke utilizes the garment of the victim. Note that the grasp on the collar is well back.

OUTSIDE CHOKE

The outside choke will cut off the blood supply to the brain. It, too, uses the garment of the victim.

The outside choke, best applied on the ground, is accomplished in the following manner. Astride your opponent, who is on his back, grip the inside of his collar high up on both sides, so that the little fingers are next to the ground and the thumbs toward you. The elbows should be close to the ground when gripping the collar. Keep the wrists rigid, straighten out the elbows and bring them together. The leverage that results will force the knuckles and thumb into the arteries at the sides of the neck, causing the blood supply to the brain to be shut off. Intense pain is caused by pressure against nerves in the neck.

Finger Strangle. The muscles of the throat are strong and often are developed to the point where they can resist pressure brought to bear by the fingers across the front of the throat. To execute a strangle using the fingers, therefore, an area not so well protected must be attacked. The best point is the windpipe, in an area as near the lower jaw as possible. Drive the fingers and thumb of the hand in a tongs-like action around and behind the windpipe. Close them together, and pull out to cause strangulation.

Japanese Strangle. This attack should be launched from the rear against a standing opponent. The fist should be driven into the victim's right kidney section with such force that he will be caused to bend backward and thus lose balance. At the same time, your left forearm should be swung around his neck in such manner as to strike him across the Adam's apple. These two blows are enough, initially, to stun him—for the fraction of a second necessary to complete the strangle.

From this position, with your left forearm across his neck, place your right hand on the back of his head and hook your left hand inside the bend in the elbow of your right arm. With your hand in this position, you are able to exert enormous leverage by pushing forward with your right hand and pulling him back with your left at the same time. In a matter of seconds, you have strangled him completely or broken his neck. One of the most important things to remember is that you must continually pull your victim backward, so that he is off balance at all times. This is even more important if you are shorter than your victim. In that case, the use of the knee, instead of the fist, in the kidney section is best for the first blow. Another satisfactory way to get your victim off balance is to thrust your foot into the back of his knee. This will cause him to topple backward and enable you to apply the hold more easily.

JAPANESE STRANGLE

The victim is approached silently and is put off balance by a fist blow to the kidney or by a kick to the back of the knee, as at the left above. Simultaneously, the arm is put around the neck, so that a blow is struck across the Adam's apple area by the forearm; as in the center above. The right hand is placed against the back of the head. The left hand **grasps your right arm.** The victim is then pulled back, while forward pressure is exerted by the right hand. **Swift strangulation, and a possible neck fracture, will result.**

FRONT STRANGLE

If the victim is standing, initiate the attack by cupping the hand and striking, against the back of his neck, a guiding blow that stuns him and brings his head down; as at the left above. Place his head under your left arm pit, with your forearm across his throat. By putting pressure against the throat, slow strangulation will result (see right above.) A neck fracture can be made by pushing forward with the hips and jerking upward with the left arm simultaneously.

Front Strangle. A strangle hold may also be applied from the front. In this application, it is easier when a man's head happens to be lowered, as it would be if he were attempting to make a grab for your legs or waist. If he is standing upright, it can be initiated as follows: Swing your right arm forward and around, bringing the palm of the hand against the back of his neck. By giving your body weight to the swing, you will cause him to bring his head forward and downward, to a position where your left forearm can be brought across, up and under his throat and locked around his neck, with your right hand taking a grip on your left hand as a reinforcement. When you have him in this position, all you need to do to cause strangulation, or a neck break, is to push your hips forward and your shoulders well back, lifting upward as you do so. (See preceding page.)

Rear Straight Choke. This choke can be executed from a standing or kneeling position in any situation where the attacker is in back of the opponent. Place the bony part of your right forearm across the front or side of the opponent's neck. Grasp the wrist of the right hand with the left and exert backward pressure so that the forearm comes hard against the throat. Place the point of the right shoulder against the back of the victim's head, forcing it forward while the forearm is being pulled back.

Criminals often attack their robbery victims from the rear with either the rear straight choke or the Japanese strangle.

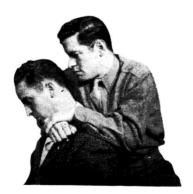

STRANGLE HOLD

By placing the bony part of the left forearm across the neck, grasping the left wrist, and pulling back, a strangle can be made at the time of back pressure against the neck. The point of the right shoulder is pressed against the back of the head, pushing it forward.

CHIN JAB AND TRIP

When opposite your opponent, time your steps so that your right leg can be placed in rear of his right heel. Execute a chin jab at the same time, as in left above. The blow to the chin can be as hard as desired; even a light push will send him down. A hard blow, coupled with the trip, will result in a knockout and possible concussion, as is shown at the right above.

Although the intent in most cases is only robbery, many victims have lost their lives when they attempted to struggle. The attacker has often lost his head and applied too much pressure to subdue the victim, with fatal results. This form of attack is called "mugging" in some police circles.

SPECIFIC METHODS OF ATTACK

The following are additional tried and proved methods of attack in given situations, when the element of surprise may be applied.

Chin Jab and Trip. If, as you pass by an opponent, you wish to down him by utilizing your advantage of surprise, this is a very simple and effective method. It can be used without any suspicious warning movements. As you pass your opponent, on his right side, and are directly opposite him, place your right leg in the rear of his right leg and execute a chin jab from a starting position of hands at side. He will go down and out. The leg in the rear has a tripping effect. It causes the body to go up, then down with more force.

SITTING NECK-BREAK

This surprise attack from the rear is deadly and simple. It will result in an instant neck fracture,

Sitting Neck-Break. If your opponent is sitting in a low-backed chair, approach him from the rear. As you pass by, on the right or left side, and are opposite him, with the arm nearest the victim reach across and under his chin, with the hand coming around to the back of the neck. From this position, a contraction of the arm muscles plus an upward and backward jerk, will cause his neck to break instantaneously. It can be done almost without breaking your stride.

Wrist Throw. The wrist throw has several practical applications. The most practical would be in a situation in which a man has reached out and grabbed your shirt, coat lapel, or belt strap, with his right hand. With your left hand reach over to the inside of the grasping hand and place your left thumb in the back of his hand across the small knuckle bones. Your fingers will pass underneath the palm of his hand. With your hand in this position, twist his hand back sharply toward him and to his right and force it toward a point on the ground three or four feet from his right foot. He will immediately be forced to drop to the ground. From there, you can either release your hold on his hand as he goes down or retain it, pulling his arm out straight above his head as he goes down, and kicking him in the temple with your foot. In many cases, particularly when there is a great difference in size of opponents, it is advisable, after making the initial hold with your left hand, to use your right to give additional pressure and leverage in completing the throw. The same technique can be applied by doing just the opposite in the case of left-handed procedure. After practice, the individual

WRIST THROW

Grasp the opponent's hand so that your thumb is across his knuckles, as in the upper picture. Twist the opponent's hand to his right, and out. Use your other hand to add strength, once the initial grip and twist is made with the left, (See lower picture).

Continue the downward shove and step in as he starts to fall; as at

left. The grip can be released at any point, once balance is destroyed. If desired, the grip on the wrist can be retained and a follow-up kick to the head can be made, as at right.

can initiate the same wrist throws against the opponent who has his hands hanging at his sides.

Pushing Counter. Many times the soldier or police officer has been in a position where a belligerent drunk has attempted to antagonize him by placing a hand on his chest and shoving him backward. The counter is simple and effective. As your opponent's hand is placed on your chest, take your own two hands and, laying one flat on top of the other, raise them above your opponent's pushing hand, then come down sharply with the edge of your hands at the angular bend where his wrist joins his hand. Press his hand against your chest. As you do this, bend forward and step back. Your opponent will go down, for a very simple reason. When he is pushing you, his wrist is already at a right angle bend. Any additional bend will cause a break. When you strike his wrist with the edge of your hands and bend the body forward, he can do nothing but go to the ground to protect himself from a broken wrist. As he goes down, you can use your knee against his chin, or you can hit him on the shoulder so as to destroy his balance. It is important that you bend forward in applying the hold, at the time of the blow on the wrist angle. By so doing, you force him to the ground and also pin his hand against your chest so he cannot pull away.

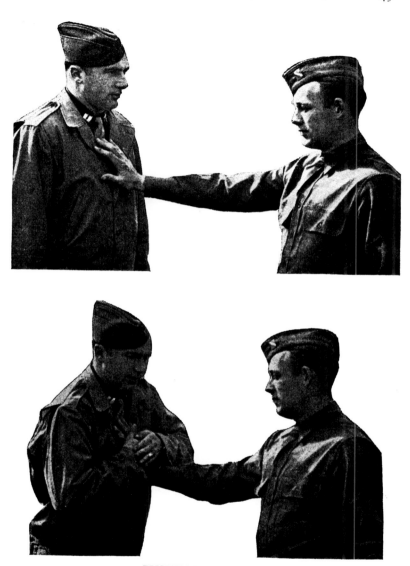

PUSHING COUNTER

In the position shown in upper picture, the opponent's wrist is bent back, and he lays himself open to attack. Place both hands on his pushing hand and press back against your chest. Be sure the edges of your hands are directly on the wrist joint. Bend swiftly forward and step back with one foot, as in the lower illustration.

PUSHING COUNTER (Continued)

If a knockout is desired, a follow with the knee to the chin can be made, as in lower left above. If it is desired merely to spill the opponent, reach around in back of him, as he goes down, and pull him by grasping his shirt or the point of his shoulder, as in lower right above.

Ear Concussion Blow. Approaching your opponent from the rear, you can rupture his eardrums by cupping both hands and simultaneously striking them against his ears. A type of concussion results which causes the victim to become "slap happy" and makes him an easy subject to do with as you will.

Elbow Break. This is a particularly effective hold from a hand-shake position. At the moment when your right hand grasps the outstretched right hand of the victim, jerk him forward and step forward with the left foot. Retaining your grip on the hand, strike the outside of his right elbow with the palm of your left hand, or with your left forearm. A break will result.

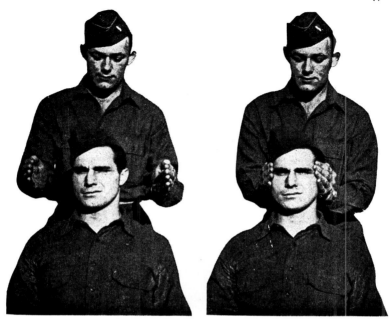

EAR CONCUSSION

Surprise approach from the rear, as shown left above, and the simultaneous boxing of the opponent's ears, will rupture both ear drums and cause a blackout.

Testicle Blow. If you are standing beside an opponent and, for some reason, such as a difference in size, a direct blow to his neck or head is not advisable, try the following. Clench the fist of the hand next to him and swing it into his groin, or testicle, area. When he bends forward from the blow, use the edge of either hand on the back of his neck.

These specific attacks are only a few of many possible ones, once the use of foot and hand blows is mastered and other fundamentals of offensive combat are achieved. The individual can work out those best suited to his need.

OFFENSIVE GROUND FIGHTING

Once an opponent has been thrown, blows should be used to finish him off. Most of the throws and trips described can be used so that after practice they are all completed with the attacker still retaining a controlling grip on the opponent's wrist or arm. If the impact of the throw has not stunned him enough to permit the use of the feet, he may attempt to roll away. If so, a jerk, spin, or a pull on the arm that you have retained in your grasp (or grasped again if it has been dropped), will usually slow him up to the point where you can use a kick. Always try to keep the opponent from regaining his feet or from getting his feet or his arms solidly under him. If he falls free and tries to get up by scrambling forward on his hands and knees, a well-placed kick to the kidney or tail bone area will stop him. If he evades a kick, jump astraddle his back, as you would that of a horse, then drive your feet backward under his body and between the legs. Straighten the hips and lean forward. At the same time, reach under his chin and pull up hard. He will flatten out, and a strangle can be applied that should remain unbroken, even if he rolls over with you underneath him. Naturally, an edge-of-the-hand blow should be used if possible at any time during this maneuver. If a general melee ensues, when both of you are on the ground striving for position and holds, the first to resort to blows, bites and gouges will come out on top. Always attack parts of your opponent's body that are easily hurt. If the enemy can be kept in pain, he will be unable to do much offensive fighting.

CONCLUSION

Again, unarmed combat tactics should be used when weapons are not available. It is not intended that the soldier or policeman lay aside his rifle and other weapons to engage in such combat. However, he must not be dependent on his weapons to the point where he is helpless without them—for psychological as well as practical reasons. Training and skill in this type of fighting creates all-around self-confidence and enables the soldier or policeman to handle all situations in which he must depend only on those weapons given him by nature.

Chapter 3

DEFENSIVE
UNARMED COMBAT

MUCH of the reader's combat experience will begin with the defensive phase. Circumstances will often be such that he is attacked first, or at least must wait for an initial offensive gesture from the enemy. When he meets such an attack, his first movements may have to be defensive. From this defense he will either undertake some degree of offensive action or apply restraint methods, as the situation dictates. In the case of the law enforcement officer, as guardian of the law he is primarily concerned with defense rather than offense.

An attack by an opponent will usually be launched in one of three ways. He may try to strike the defender by using blows of fists, hands, or feet—if he is skillful enough. He may attempt to throw the defender to the ground by securing a hold on his body; or third, he may simply rush him, trying to upset him by the momentum and impact. When they can be foreseen, all these attempts should be met by having the body in the balanced, crouched position, with the hands poised, forearms in almost a vertical position, palms of the hands about six inches apart and facing each other, in position to protect the face and throat. The hands in this position are used to ward off and parry blows. They are also in a position from which fist or edge-of-the-hand blows can best be launched. In the balanced position, the body is slightly crouched, so that the upper middle part of the body, which is the natural target for blows, is at a maximum distance from the opponent. To reach vulnerable parts, the attacker must not only break through the protective screen of the hands, he must also lunge and possibly overreach in order to make contact.

TYPES OF ATTACK

The Striking Attack. Most individuals who use blows to attack will probably be unskilled in boxing and will attempt

49

to hit by using wide, frequently wild, swinging blows with the fists. Such blows may be parried outward with the edges of the hands and forearms, while closing *inside* the opponent's arms—where his arm and shoulders can be grasped preparatory to a throw, fist or edge-of-the-hand blows, a chin jab, or a knee to the testicles.

If you are a skilled boxer, the attack can be met with well-delivered blows of your own. Usually the knee kick will be the simplest defensive (or offensive) measure. Frequently an upright swinging attack of this type will be delivered with little thought given to balance. One knee or the other of the attacker will be well-advanced, so that it presents a vulnerable target for a well-placed kick.

A successful alternative to meeting an attack by blows is to use the hands and arms to parry the striking arm *out*, so that you are on the *inside* of the striking arms. The parry should be forceful and the body should be moved sidewise in the opposite direction to the opponent's swinging arm. In this manner the force of the opponent's swing, coupled with your parry, will leave him in an unbalanced position and will permit you to move in to his side, where a blow, throw, trip, or spin will put him on the ground.

A man who is trained in boxing usually leads with his left, following up with his right. If confronted by such an antagonist, duck quickly to his left as he jabs with his left fist. At the same time, slap the outer side of his left elbow with your right hand. He will spin into an off-balance position. Place your foot behind him and shove or hit him backwards so that he trips over your foot.

The leg hook, described in chapter 2, is another good method of meeting a skilled striking attack. It must be executed when the opponent is very near and the element of surprise is present.

Defense against an opponent who attempts a kick usually will also be against an unskillful individual, one who tries to kick, toe first, to the crotch or knee. By pivoting aside and grasping the heel and toe of his foot and twisting it, you can easily throw him. Defense against a man who uses his feet properly is more difficult. The best tactic is to kick him first.

The Rushing Attack. The attacker who charges like the proverbial mad bull, at a well-balanced and trained opponent, can be easily handled in a number of ways. His momentum can be used to his disadvantage and downfall. In such an attack, he usually strives to grab the upper or middle part of the body or drive into the legs. He must not be met head on, as the force of his drive will carry a standing defender backward, and often to the ground. The simplest counter to this type attack is to step aside and apply a leg trip, particularly when attacked with great speed and momentum. A drop and leg hook can be used if he is coming in upright; but your own weight and body strength must be enough to counteract any advantage he gains by momentum.

When the opponent drives in with his head lowered and strives for a grip about the waist, he can best be met by a blow into his face with the knee. It is also often possible to deliver a trip and a blow by using the hands against this attack. At other times, his drive can be met squarely and a front strangle applied. Whenever any type of rush attack is met head on, contact should be made with the defender's legs stretched out to the rear and his body leaning forward.

EYE GOUGE AS A RELEASE

The eye gouge will almost always be an effective release. It is best to use the thumb against the inside of the eye socket, with force exerted toward the outside of the head.

MOUTH OR NOSTRIL HOLD AS A RELEASE

Hooking the thumb in the corner of the mouth, or in the nostril, is an effective release.

BREAKING REAR BEAR HUG

From a rear bear hug that pins the arms, the point of the elbow can be used against the attacker's mid-section.

EFFECTIVE RELEASE—BLOW TO GROIN

The simplest and most effective of all releases is a knee to the groin or testicles.

No attempt should be made to stop the opponent's drive completely. Rather, the legs should be kept extended, and the force of the impact and momentum should be absorbed by "riding it out," letting the attack carry you to the rear. The opponent who tries to drive to the legs in a football-type tackle can be handled as he is by the ball carrier—by simply sidestepping and pushing down on his head. He will drive himself into the ground.

BREAKING ENCUMBERING BODY HOLDS

The following breaks are intended for use in situations in which the bodies of the attacker and defender are in close contact. They will result from a surprise attack, or from faulty execution of a blow or throw. Obviously, no defender in possession of his normal faculties would permit any such blows to be used if he could see them coming. Many of them are of a type which would be applied only by an inexperienced individual. Generally, in such situations, there is not

BREAKING REAR ATTACK

A rear attack in which the arms are not pinned can be broken by grasping a finger and bending it back, or by stamping on the instep with the heel.

BREAKING FRONTAL HOLD

This type of encumbering hold can be broken by a kick to the shins with the inside edge of the foot, or by grasping the opponent's testicles.

much motion and the encumbering or offensive action of the attacker must be broken by some sort of a blow, or release, before counter action can begin.

When a hold such as a bear hug, arm hug, or strangle is applied and the trunk of the attacker's body is pressed against that of the defender, the following general rules should be observed: (1) Strive to keep balance; try to prevent your body from being pulled, pushed, or bent off balance. (2) The instant contact is made, drop the body into a slight crouch and force the opponent to support part of your weight. (3) Attack sensitive points. The opponent's testicles, eyes, toes, and shins are either collectively or singly vulnerable—almost invariably when he is applying encumbering holds. Blows and kicks to these areas will loosen his grip, or break it so that other blows and types of releases can be used, or a counter attack launched.

BREAKING FRONTAL HOLD ABOUT THE WAIST

A frontal hold about the waist can be broken simply by pushing back on the chin and destroying the aggressor's balance.

The Wrist Release. The principles of the wrist release should be familiar to every soldier and police officer. The wrist release has long been known in wrestling and jiu jitsu circles and has a practical application in lifesaving techniques. A knowledge of the wrist release enables any person to break any grip, no matter now strong, that is applied to his wrists or arms by the opponent's thumb and fingers. This is important, since defenses and many attacks, or throws, are started when an opponent grasps one or both wrists with his hands.

When an opponent grabs your wrist or forearm with his hand, he will have four fingers on one side of the arm and his thumb on the other. Regardless of the strength of the grip, it will never be stronger on the thumb side than the strength of your entire arm. The thumb side of the grip is weak. The necessary force to effect a release is concentrated against the thumb by always rolling the wrist outward against it, and by jerking as the roll is started. The opponent's grip will be broken, no matter whether the grip is left- or right-handed, as long as the roll is outward against the thumb.

If a two-handed grip is applied to the wrist, a sharp pull against the thumbs will break it. It is advisable in this case

BREAKING WRIST GRIP

A grip that pinions the wrist, (illustrated at top), is weakest on the thumb side. To break it, forcefully turn the wrist *outward*, in the direction of the thumb (see bottom photo) and jerk the arm away. Follow up with the point of the elbow to the opponent's chin, as the arm is jerked away.

to use your free hand to grasp the pinioned hand and help in the outward jerk against the thumbs. If the opponent's thumbs are on the underneath side of the arm, reach under with the free hand and pull down. Another reason why this grip is so effective is that at the time the release is made a follow-through blow, with the elbow of the previously pinioned arm against the body or face, can be made without any extra motion. Practice of the wrist release should be so thorough that it can be done instinctively, and at the instant a grip is made. The principle of the wrist release can also be applied to break a grip made on the coat sleeve. Make a circular, backward and upward motion with the pinioned arm. As the down swing is completed, the grip will be broken.

Arm Jerk. An arm jerk, prior to the application of a come-along or an attack, will help soften up the opponent. It will help destroy his physical balance and will result in a slight concussion when forcefully applied. Grasp the opponent's arm at the wrist with both hands. Lift his arm about six inches and jerk it sharply downward. This often destroys his body balance and causes a jolt to the brain. If the right arm is jerked, the force of the jolt will be felt on the left side of the head. This tactic must be practiced gently. Although it sounds mild, it does have a very marked effect on the opponent. Some judo experts use it instinctively whenever they can grasp an opponent's arm. A policeman may well use it, before applying many of the come-along holds, to destroy, momentarily, the opponent's mental and physical balance.

COMBAT WITH TWO OPPONENTS

The defender may be confronted by two assailants at the same time. In cases where offensive action by his opponents is imminent, he should always take advantage of the element of surprise by launching his attack first. A quick kick to the knee, or an edge-of-the-hand blow, delivered without warning at one of the assailants, will incapacitate him long enough to permit special attention to the remaining opponent. The attack should be launched before the two opponents can maneuver. Prior to any action, the defender should try to keep the opponents in front of him. He should never allow them to close in simultaneously from the sides or to attack from the rear. If a surprise attack is launched against a defender by two or more assailants, there is every justification for using the quickest and most effective tactics to put them out of action. Restraint methods are ineffective and foolish in such a situation.

ARM RELEASE

If the arm is grasped with two hands, as shown at the top, the thumb side is still the weakest. Force must be exerted against it. With the free hand, reach over and grasp the pinioned fist, as in the lower picture, and jerk out against the thumbs. Follow with the point of the elbow to the opponent's chin.

Crowd Escape. A defender cannot always choose the time and place to fight. Frequently escape should be his only object, especially when he is unarmed and is faced by several opponents. He may be caught in the midst of a riot or may be the victim of a surprise gang attack.

The only hope of escape from an overwhelming number of opponents is continual movement. Each time the defender takes a new position a few seconds are required for his antagonist to balance himself for a forceful attack. This constant movement should be accompanied by indiscriminate blows of the hands, feet, elbows, knees. Movement may be in any direction, but must never cease. The body should be kept low, with the knees bent. A bobbing motion is most successful. Any of these movements, made rapidly, will bewilder the opponent. By the use of blows, and by shoving one opponent against the other, it will often be possible to create more room in which to keep moving. This technique can be practiced by hanging dummies in a small space and letting the trainee work his way through them. It should be remembered that the object is to get away, not to stay and fight it out against hopeless odds.

COME-ALONGS AND RESTRAINT HOLDS

Military and civil police officers have frequent use for come-along type holds. Once the criminal, or law breaker, has been apprehended or subdued, the police must "take him in," in order to complete the arrest. If he is drunk, unruly, or potentially dangerous, he must be kept helpless. By application of the proper come-along, the prisoner is made amenable to movement or to other actions by the officer. A come-along, or other type pressure hold, also is often used before handcuffing.

Usually it is difficult to apply pressure holds when the antagonist is suspicious. Such holds are almost always intended for use after the opponent has been subdued. Certain kinds of come-along can be applied as a type of attack by a skilled man; others can be used after a break from an encumbering hold by the opponent. However, there is always a risk in applying the come-along if the opponent has not been subdued, or if the user does not have a marked superiority of physique, knowledge and experience.

No come-along hold, applied with the bare hands, has been developed that can be maintained successfully over a long period of time against an opponent who is in full possession of his faculties and who is determined to break it. It is true that some escapes from come-alongs may be made—at the expense of broken bones or painful dislocations. If the victim is desperate enough, this will not deter him. If the come-along must be maintained over a considerable distance or for a considerable length of time, it is advisable to keep a dangerous man groggy by edge-of-the-hand blows, short jabs to the chin, or similar blows.

Mechanical come-along devices, such as the iron claw or chain twister—when they are available and if their use is permitted—will often provide better control and allow more freedom of movement by the user. Handcuffs and their correct use is a separate subject, warranting complete training for any law enforcement officer (see chapter 8).

Come-along holds can be divided into two general categories: holds which restrain by inflicting pain or the threat of pain and those which destroy balance or dignity. In the latter category are the holds that cause the victim to lose face and be an object of ridicule and laughter. In some cases, as when evicting a quarrelsome drunk from a room, the policeman should use this type of hold. The come-alongs and restraint holds described below are selected from the best and most practical of many holds.

Where the come-along is used and the victim has a free arm that can be used offensively, he can be made to keep it inside his belt; or his belt can be removed, so that he must hold up his trousers with his free hand. Again, the come-along is not an attack; it is applied as a mastering hold after the victim has been subdued by other means.

The Wrist Come-Along. The following technique is the most effective of all come-alongs, especially when you are forced to walk a man a long distance and keep him under control. You are facing your opponent, who has his arms hanging at his sides. With your right hand outstretched, palm up, hook your thumb inside his left thumb. With your left hand, reach over to the outside of your prisoner's left elbow and pull it toward your right foot to a point where you are directly up against the victim. You will find that the victim's left elbow will be next to your body, with your right elbow between his arm and his body. You have not changed your grip during this process. By keeping his elbow close to your body and locked in place by your right arm, and by

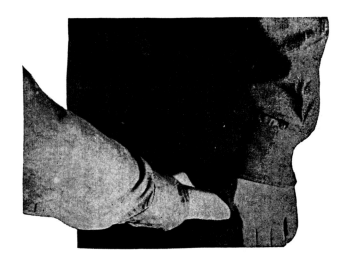

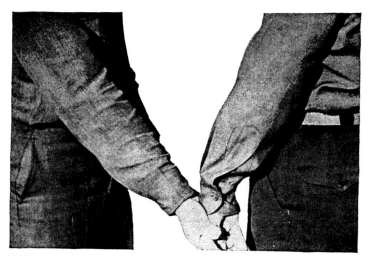

WRIST COME-ALONG

With the palm of the right hand up, hook your thumb with the opponent's left thumb, as shown at top. An alternate initial grip is to grasp the back of the opponent's left hand with your right hand, as in the bottom picture. After applying one of these grips, reach over with your left hand and grasp the outside of your opponent's left elbow, as at left on next page. Pull his elbow toward you and step in to his side. After getting his pinioned . . .

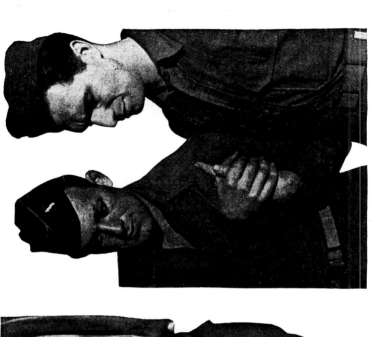

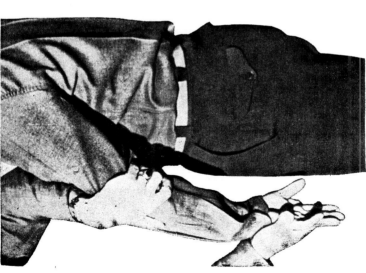

WRIST COME-ALONG (Continued)

. . arm and wrist in this position, twist his wrist toward you and down, as in the picture at right. The victim will rise on his toes when enough pressure is applied; and the come-along is in effect. The victim's free hand can be placed inside his belt, or may be used to hold up his unbuttoned trousers.

raising his forearm to a vertical position, you have a very effective come-along. This position is maintained by twisting his hand and wrist toward you at any sign of rebellion. By applying a few pounds pressure on the wrist, you can raise your victim on his toes, and it is by this means that you will know that he is completely under your control. This come-along has the advantage of allowing you, in most cases, to maintain sufficient pressure with one hand while you walk along with a weapon, or some other implement, in your left hand. This application can be reversed for the purpose of leaving your right hand free.

The Arm Lock Come-Along. Another come-along which has a great deal of merit is the arm lock. Properly applied, it makes a hold strong enough to escort a prisoner a short distance. If pressure is maintained on the forearm, you have complete control of your opponent. This come-along is useful in applying handcuffs or in taking a man to the ground before tying him.

It is applied as follows: Facing your opponent, reach out with your left hand, palm down, and grab the opponent about the right wrist. Shove his arm to the side and rear of his body. As you do this, strike his left arm on the inside of the elbow joint with the flat of your right hand. The hand should be withdrawn immediately after the slap has been given, causing the elbow to bend. Step in and turn his body, so that you are beside him, facing in the same direction. From this position, disengage your left hand, which has been about his wrist, and, grasping his right hand, shove it under and up between the opponent's forearm and his back. Place your left hand on, or just below, the shoulder point on his arm. By bending forward, with his right arm locked in this position, you have him completely under control. Your right hand can then be placed on his left shoulder, to prevent him from pulling sideways out of the hold; or it can be used to exert extra pressure on his pinioned arm by pulling it out from his back. This will force him to do as you wish, because of pain or the possibility of a broken elbow. This come-along can be maintained over a long distance but has a disadvantage in that your own body must be bent forward, alongside and slightly over your opponent's body, in order to keep him under control. However, this liability is offset by the fact that this hold can be used for other purposes than those mentioned above.

ARM LOCK COME-ALONG

Face the opponent; reach out and grasp his right wrist with your left hand, as in left top above. With your right hand strike the inside of his right elbow, so as to bend the arm, as shown in right top above. Step in and turn his body, so that you are beside the opponent, facing in the same direction he is facing. By disengaging your left hand and shoving it up and under, between the opponent's arm and back, the lock is applied (see lower picture). By bending forward and exerting upward pressure on the pinned forearm, the victim is put under control. Your right hand can be used to grasp his shirt collar or left shoulder, to prevent his pulling out sideways.

Forearm Come-Along. Facing your opponent, with your right hand grasp the back of his left hand, at the same time taking a firm hold on his left arm by grasping the outside

FOREARM COME-ALONG

This type of forearm come-along will give you control of the most unruly prisoner. Upward pressure on the arm will cause intense pain.

of it at the elbow with your left hand. Force the opponent's left hand and wrist up behind his back. Use your left hand to hold his elbow tight against the right side of your body. By bending the victim's captured wrist toward his elbow, great pain can be inflicted. Once the hold has been secured, face in the same direction as the opponent. He is forced to walk with you.

Forearm Lock. Face the opponent, reach across and grab his right wrist with your right hand, raising it about waist high. Move over to his right and slip your left arm over his forearm and under his right elbow, at a point just above the elbow. In this position, the sharp bone of your left forearm can be used to lift upward, against the elbow which the right hand can press down. To make the hold more secure, grip your opponent's coat or lapel with your left hand, once the arm is in place.

REAR CLOTHING COME-ALONG

This type of come-along is effective against a troublesome drunk. By grasping the seat of his pants at the rear and lifting, and at the same time shoving forward with the hand that grasps his collar, he can be moved along easily.

CROSS ARM COME-ALONG

This is another come-along that is effective against a small or inebriated person. Grasp both wrists, lift his arms so as to put him off balance, then cross them. Shove him forward. This is a good method to use in putting a man through a narrow hall or door.

HEAD HOLD COME-ALONG

A man sitting in a chair, or in the seat of a car, can easily be pulled out by putting one hand under the point of his chin and the other on the back of his head. By twisting his head and lifting at the same time, he can be forced to come.

NECK PRESSURE POINTS

A man lying on the ground or sitting in a seat can be moved quickly by pushing the forefingers in and up against the nerve centers which are at the hinge of the jaw, under the ears. This is a good way to test faked death or unconsciousness, since the pain is extremely intense. It is also effective as a release.

Two other humorous, but effective, come-alongs against persons who resist getting up from the prone or sitting position, are as follows:

(1) With the thumb and forefinger grasp the short hairs on the back of the head or nape of the neck, and pull forcefully. Although most people can resist the pulling of hairs on top of the head, the short ones on the back of the head and neck are placed where pressure on them causes intense pain. Men are usually more susceptible to this than women.

(2) A drunken man or woman can also usually be handled by using the thumb and forefinger to grab the lower lip. By pinching hard and twisting, as the pull is made, the victim will come along.

Chapter 4

KNIFE ATTACK
AND DEFENSE

IT is probable that the soldier or law enforcement officer sometime will face an enemy, a criminal, or a demented person who is armed with a knife or some other kind of bladed weapon. He may encounter a trained knife fighter, but it is more likely that he will be assigned to duty in areas dominated by racial groups or by underworld elements who rely upon bladed weapons as their principal means of combat.

The average American does not like the idea of encountering a knife in personal combat. He would much rather use his fists, a hand gun or a club as a fighting weapon. He would much rather face such weapons than an opponent armed with a sharp blade. Because of this repugnance, he often shrinks from the possibility of facing an adversary so armed; and this destroys his self-confidence. This condition is especially true if a knife attack is made unexpectedly and the defendant has had no time either to condition himself mentally or to have a defense or weapon ready.

Because of the strong probability of his encountering a bladed weapon, every soldier and law enforcement officer should receive training in knife offense and in the general defensive precautions and techniques to be used in areas where opponents are likely to carry knives.

Before undertaking a successful knife defense—which should be concluded by disarming, subduing, or killing—it is necessary to understand and practice the principal methods of knife attack. Once a person with a defensive mission, such as a policeman, understands how the knife is most likely to be used against him, he will be more confident and proficient.

With respect to technique, knife wielders usually fall into three categories: (1) the trained knife fighter, who uses both a cutting and a slashing type of attack; (2) the unskilled knife user, who usually employs either an upward or downward thrust in attacking; and (3) the slasher, who usually uses a short-bladed knife, or razor, and who takes advantage only of the cutting effect of the blade. There will always be exceptions. Some knife wielders, because of animal courage, past successes or reputation, are, for defense purposes, in the same category as the highly skilled fighting knife wielder, even though they do not use the knife with the approved and best fighting technique. This type of attack can be readily recognized when made from the front, provided there is time to see it coming.

The kinds of bladed weapons encountered may vary from the common pen knife to the World War I fighting knife, complete with brass knuckles. The razor, the popular hunting knife, knives with retracting or snapout blades, the standard pocket knife, the kitchen or butcher knife, or the real fighting knife—may be employed in an assault. All are dangerous and can inflict serious wounds; but some are more to be feared than others.

THE FIGHTING KNIFE

This stiletto type weapon is ideal for close-in fighting. It can be used both for cutting and thrusting, and it is easy to maneuver, because of its design and balance. This last feature is very important. The handle is similar to that of a fencing foil, so the knife can be used for cutting and thrusting in any direction without a change in the grip. The weight is toward the hilt. The blade is about six inches long, is double-edged and tapers to a point. This length blade is ideal for balance, is good for both the cut and the thrust, and is long enough to penetrate heavy clothing without losing its effectiveness. Its width, at its widest part near the guard, usually is not over one inch. It either can be hollow ground or can taper evenly toward both edges, from the strengthening ridge which runs down the center of the blade to the point of the knife.

The handle is round or oval in shape, its largest diameter is toward the center, and it tapers off toward the guard as well as at the butt. The over-all weight is approximately ten ounces. The handle, in addition to being rounded, is checkered.

Such a knife, with balance toward the handle, is adapted more easily to maneuverability, is more easily passed from hand to hand, and, with more weight in the handle, affords a better grip for passing, thrusting and slashing. Its very design

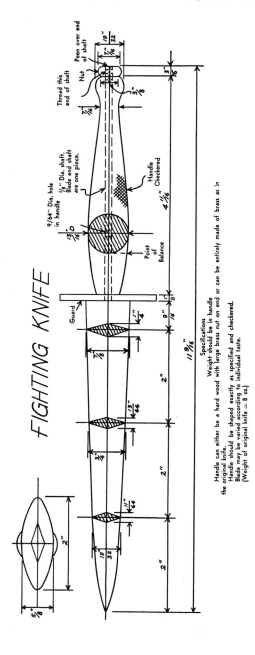

This is the original design of the Fairbairn Fighting Knife, used by Canadian and British commandos, and by some special units of the United States forces, during World War II. It may be purchased from Pasadena Firearms, 1165 E. Colorado Blvd, Pasadena 1, California.

Top: Trench knife, World War I, with case shown above it.
Second: Utility knife, constructed along the lines of a hunting knife.
Third: Fighting knife.

Bottom: Fighting knife, modified from utility knife, issued to United
States troops. The cross guard has been strengthened, the back edge
ground to a cutting edge, and the blade tapered to a point.

makes it a true fighting knife, combining with its double-
edge both cutting and slashing qualities. The double edge is
also useful in preventing an opponent from wresting it from
the hand of the user. The opponent cannot grasp its blade,
in defense, without receiving a severe cut.

The proper grip on the handle of a knife of this type is as
follows: The knife lies diagonally across the outstretched
palm of the hand. The small part of the handle next to the
cross guard is grasped by the thumb and forefinger. The
middle finger lies over the handle at the point where its
largest diameter occurs. With the knife held in this fashion,
it is very easy to maneuver it in all directions. The direction
of the blade can be controllable by a combination movement

CORRECT GRIP OF FIGHTING KNIFE

The proper grip for use on a well-designed fighting knife with handle, as illustrated on page 69.

of the fore and middle fingers, plus a turning of the wrist. When the palm is up it is possible (holding knife in the right hand) to slash to the right. When the palm is turned down, it is possible to slash to the left. The thrust can be executed from either the palm-up or palm-down position. At the time of contact, in the thrust or the slash, the knife is grasped tightly by all fingers. The initial controlling grip of the fore and middle fingers has not changed and the blade becomes a mere continuation of the arm.

Such knife manipulation is fairly simple. Skill can be acquired after a few hours practice, but only if the handle is generally constructed along the lines described above. The handle described here is round. However, a handle of similar size in oval shape works equally well.

The trained man will use this knife, in the attack, from a crouch, with the left hand forward and the knife held (handle diagonally across the palm of the right hand) close to the body. The outstretched left hand will act as a guard, a foil or a parry, and will help to create the opening for a slash or thrust. The left hand also may be used to distract the adversary's attention—by waving it in his face, by throwing something, or by making sudden darting motions toward him. When the knife fighter is in the crouch, with his left

ATTACK WITH KNIFE FROM CROUCH

Beware of the man who holds his knife this way and who attacks from a crouch, with the blade held close to his body and with his free arm out in front to parry or to help create an opening for a slash or thrust.

hand forward to parry, he is in a position of extreme mobility, because his knees are flexed and he is in perfect balance. In the fighting or crouch position, he also is protecting his vital mid-section and throat area from vital thrusts—by an opponent who also may be armed with a knife or a club. In this position, the trained knife fighter can foil the usual knife defenses of the unarmed opponent. Often he can maneuver successfully against such defenses as a chair, a club, or other object used to strike or to throw.

The thrust and slash type of attack is best when used with a knife of correct design. However, any long-bladed, single-edged weapon—such as a jack knife or hunting knife—can be used in the manner described, with a somewhat lessened degree of effectiveness because of poorer basic design. A skilled knife user may employ such tactics as throwing dirt or other objects in his opponent's face when making his attack. This type of strategy is most likely to be used against an opponent who is standing his ground and readying himself for a defense, or when the attacker has not had the advantage of surprise.

THE UNSKILLED ATTACK

If a knife attack is made by an individual gripping his weapon in such a manner that he can deliver only an upward or downward thrust, he probably is unskilled and has received little training in the use of a knife as a weapon. This is the manner in which a demented person will use the weapon, or in which weapons such as the butcher knife are frequently used in crimes of passion. When a knife is so gripped that the handle is directly across the palm, blade protruding from the little finger side, with all fingers wrapped around the hilt (as in using an ice pick), the user is limited to a downward thrust.

The reverse type of grip is equally limiting. If the individual grasps the knife directly around the hilt so that the blade protrudes from the forefinger side of the hand (as in gripping a hammer) the same thing is true. Only an upward thrust can be delivered. To execute either one of these types of attack, the knife wielder must get close to his victim. It is easier to see such an attack coming and to block or parry it. This method of knife attack is the one usually demonstrated by instructors of knife defense, and it is against this type of attack that most common knife defenses have been developed.

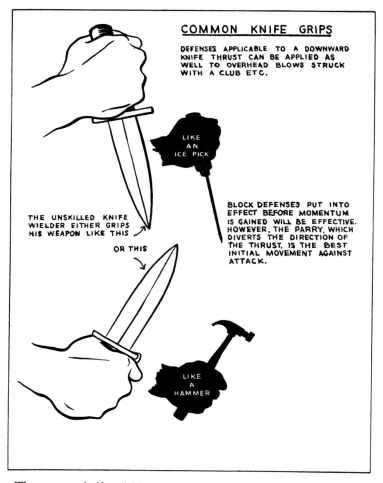

COMMON KNIFE GRIPS

DEFENSES APPLICABLE TO A DOWNWARD KNIFE THRUST CAN BE APPLIED AS WELL TO OVERHEAD BLOWS STRUCK WITH A CLUB ETC.

LIKE AN ICE PICK

THE UNSKILLED KNIFE WIELDER EITHER GRIPS HIS WEAPON LIKE THIS

OR THIS

BLOCK DEFENSES PUT INTO EFFECT BEFORE MOMENTUM IS GAINED WILL BE EFFECTIVE. HOWEVER, THE PARRY, WHICH DIVERTS THE DIRECTION OF THE THRUST, IS THE BEST INITIAL MOVEMENT AGAINST ATTACK.

LIKE A HAMMER

The average knife wielder, who has never had special training, will grip his weapon in one of the two ways shown here.

When depicting a knife attack, even the movies usually resort to this method of use of the knife. From the point of view of the audience, it is much more spectacular for the knife user to be shown charging his victim with a flashing blade upraised above his shoulder, preparatory to making a downward thrust. A knowledge of defense against knife attacks of this kind is necessary, but it is a serious omission by any instructor to place all knife users in this category and to conduct a training program accordingly.

THE SLASH ATTACK

Any type of bladed weapon may be used in this attack. However, those most frequently used are short-bladed pocket knife, pen knives, razors, and similar instruments. Since the blade can be readily concealed, a surprise attack is very easy. A planned defense often is difficult for this reason.

In a slash attack, the knife is commonly held across the palm with fingers wrapped around the handle and with the blade protruding from the little finger side of the palm. The cutting edge is to the outside, or toward the fingers. It is very easy, by this method, to carry a small knife with the handle concealed in the hand and the wrist bent, so that the blade is concealed and lies flat along the inside of the wrist and forearm.

When carried in this manner, the knife is in a ready position, and attack can be made without giving any warning. An unsuspecting person will not have enough warning to

SLASH ATTACK GRIP

Slash attacks with the knife usually are made with the knife held in this manner. Note that the handle lies across the palm, butt on the thumb side and blade facing out. To get the cutting action, a horizontal swing is made. Straight razors, pen knives and such are often used in this manner. Gripped like this, with the palm down, so that the blade points up the arm, the knife is hard to see until the swing actually takes place.

defend himself. By swinging the arm and hand in a horizontal direction across the front of the body (called a "round house"), the sharp edge of the blade will cut anything in its path because of the tremendous force exerted by the swinging arm. By a more skilled user, the blade is sometimes used to execute a thrust on the return of the arm from the cross swing slash. Men who use the knife this way must be classed as skilled, or at least semi-skilled, and should be watched accordingly. The weaknesses of this type of attack, when not accompanied by the element of surprise, is that the wielder must get very close to his victim and that the basic stroke can be blocked.

If the blade of the knife is short, it usually is difficult to deliver an initial disabling wound, such as one to the throat. The penetration is not great enough, and any movement of the opponent's body, or his clothing, will limit the depth of the slash. Knife fighting of this type, common among certain racial minorities, can be and is a very bloody affair. It may result in a protracted fight, due to the inability of the slash type of attack to penetrate deeply enough to reach the vital organs and blood vessels. Naturally, slashes across the throat can be immediately fatal, but usually the cutting is confined to the less vulnerable parts of the arms, face and body.

KNIFE THROWING

Knife throwing can be largely discounted as a practical means of combat. There are few persons who can pick up a knife, throw it at a moving object at an unknown distance, and hit a vital spot. In the main, knife throwing is an art relegated to vaudeville and stage, because, to throw a knife properly, the exact distance from the thrower to the target must be known. Since the knife turns end over end as it travels through the air, the thrower must know the exact distance. He must be able to control the number of turns the knife makes, so that it will hit the target point first.

There are, indeed, methods of knife throwing, at close ranges, without the blade turning end over end in the air; but considering the movement of the target, varying distances, heavy clothing, and the fact that if you miss you are without a weapon, knife throwing is not practical as a means of attack.

Knives with spikes on the end of the hilt or with brass knuckles attached are very fearsome in appearance, but are not commonly used and should not be greatly feared. In reality, these extra features only limit maneuverability and, in a melee, present almost as much threat to the user and his allies as to his opponent. It is very easy to catch such extra attachments as brass knuckles in the clothing. In turn, an attempt to use the brass knuckles for striking a blow makes the blade a hindrance that can cut or catch on the user's own clothing, as well as on that of the victim.

The hacking type of attack with a light, bladed weapon, such as a knife, generally is not effective. Ordinary types of knives do not weigh enough to allow sufficient force to be employed. Machetes, brush knives, axes, and such are sometimes used and are much more effective because of their greater size and weight.

BODY AREAS MOST VULNERABLE TO KNIFE ATTACK

A man attacked from the front by a bladed weapon has two spots he instinctively protects—the throat and the stomach, or abdominal section. Perhaps the reason why he instinctively protects these two areas is that they are easy for an opponent to reach. In any event, the psychological effect of a knife wound in these areas, whether it is serious or not, is so great that the victim is usually momentarily incapacitated.

The throat area is vulnerable to either the thrust or the slash, the thrust being most effective when driven into the hollow at the base of the throat just below the Adam's apple. A thrust there, into the jugular vein, or a slash on either side of the neck, cutting the arteries which furnish the blood to the brain, results in extreme loss of blood and death in a very short time. Thrusts in the abdominal area, which can be combined with the slash as the knife is withdrawn, have a great shocking effect and usually incapacitate the opponent to the point where another blow can be given with the weapon before he has a chance to recover. A deep wound in the abdominal area will cause death if unattended, but it is much slower in taking effect than a good thrust or slash in the throat area. The heart, of course, is a vital spot for the thrust, but the protection of the ribs makes it more difficult to hit. In some cases, knife thrusts directed toward the heart have been stopped by the ribs and the point of the knife broken off by the bony structure, without causing a vital wound. Usually, however, the blade will slide off the rib and go into the vital area. The heart thrust is, of course, fatal.

It is possible to get an effective slash across the sides of the throat from the rear; but one of the most effective knife strokes in the rear of the victim is the thrust delivered into

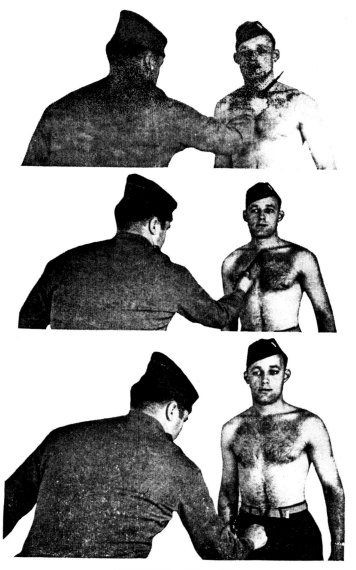

FRONTAL ATTACK

The throat, stomach and abdominal areas are the points most vulnerable to frontal attack. These are the areas that must be defended against any type of attack. A slight wound in any of these will have a serious psychological effect; and a deep wound is potentially fatal.

A slash across the biceps. A slash inside the wrist also is very effective.

the kidney or small-of-the-back area. Penetration here, in the form of a deep thrust, will cause great shock, internal hemorrhage, and often death. This back, or kidney, thrust is best used in the sentry attack, as will be explained later. The vital areas still are the throat, heart and abdominal sections.

The slash attack can be used effectively to sever the tendons on the inside of the wrist of an outstretched hand. This is most effective against a person who is trying to defend himself by striving to grasp the knife hand. A slash renders the hand useless. A slash across the large muscle of the biceps has the same effect. Also, a slash on the inside of the thigh, or arm, will cut arteries and will incapacitate, if delivered deeply enough. Slashes to these areas, in addition to disabling the opponent, cut various veins and arteries. If left unattended, the wounds will cause death from loss of blood.

KILLING ENEMY SENTRY

The following description of the correct attack technique for killing an enemy guard or sentry should be of general interest to any student of knife attack. To the soldier, plant guard, and policeman it will show the need for precautions against a surprise attack from the rear. It is a type of attack for which there is no defense if the victim is taken by surprise. It is not unlikely that it will be used again, since many individuals, in all armies during World War II, received training in it, just as they received training in methods of strangulation.

In killing an enemy sentry, all factors regarding the approach and initial attack, described for use with a rear strangle, apply. The approach from the rear is naturally a noiseless one. At the time of rising, a few feet in the rear of the victim, the knife should be taken either from the sheath where it has been during the crawl, or from the teeth where it may have been carried. The attack is launched from a distance of

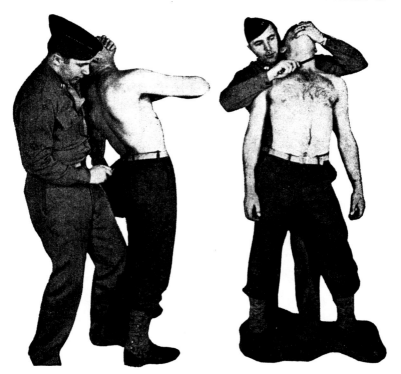

KILLING AN ENEMY SENTRY

This is the best method of surprise knife attack taught in the Armed Forces. Approach from the rear, grasp the nose and mouth with the left hand to prevent outcry, and thrust the knife into the kidney area, as shown at the left. After a short interval, withdraw the knife and cut the throat.

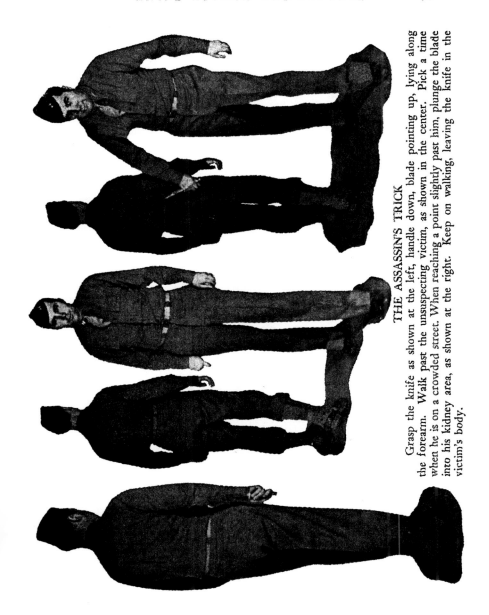

THE ASSASSIN'S TRICK

Grasp the knife as shown at the left, handle down, blade pointing up, lying along the forearm. Walk past the unsuspecting victim, as shown in the center. Pick a time when he is on a crowded street. When reaching a point slightly past him, plunge the blade into his kidney area, as shown at the right. Keep on walking, leaving the knife in the victim's body.

not less than 5 feet from the victim and is initiated as soon
as the attacker has arrived at that spot. It is important that
the attack be immediate because of the animal instinct, emphasized by keeping your eyes steadily on him as you approach, which will often warn the victim that some one is
approaching and watching him. The upward thrust of the
knife into the right or left kidney section is executed at the
end of the leap to the attack. At the same time, the free hand
is clasped over the mouth and nose of the victim, pulling him
backward, off balance. The thrust into the kidney area has
initially a great shocking effect, but no outcry will occur if
the free hand goes over the mouth and *nose* at the time of
the thrust. The victim is pulled backward upon the blade continually and after a few seconds the knife is withdrawn, and
maintaining the same grip on nose and throat, the head is
lifted up and the jugular vein slashed.

Another method of knife attack or assassination, not un-
common in some areas of the world, may be encountered. It
is as old as history and was a method taught to certain groups
for use in assassination in German-occupied countries during
World War II.

The assassin spies his victim in a crowd and approaches
him from the front. His knife is held in his hand with the
hilt down and the blade lying flat along the inside of the
forearm, or concealed up the sleeve. The handle, of course,
is concealed by the fingers. The assassin, with the knife in
this position, faces the intended victim, walking toward him.
As he reaches a point directly opposite the victim, a simple
movement of his wrist frees the blade, and a short arm movement, as he passes, plunges it into the kidney area of the
victim. The knife is either left sticking in the wound or may
be pulled out while the assassin walks on through the crowd,
his movement generally undetected.

LIKELY PLACES OF KNIFE CONCEALMENT

The places in which a bladed weapon may be carried are
many. Usually local custom and the type of garment worn
by the individual will determine the places in which it is
most likely to be carried, and from which it is usually drawn
prior to an attack.

Knives have been carried successfully in the following
places: in a sheath at the side; on a string down the back of
the neck; up the sleeve; in a special holster taped to the wrist;

stuck in the top of a boot or legging; with the sheath sewn inside the front pocket; under the lapel of a suit coat; in the crown of a hat; between the belt and the trousers; strapped to the inside of the thigh, beneath the trouser leg; in a sheath sewn diagonally across the chest, on a vest; or in any other place that combines both concealment and the element of surprise.

Small knives or cutting edges, such as razor blades, have been carried and concealed by criminals, sewn in all parts of their clothing and taped to various parts of their bodies, even to the balls of the feet. They have been carried sometimes in special sheaths strapped to the testicles. Even though such weapons may seem inadequate, it must be remembered that, in some body areas, a cut or slash one half inch deep can be crippling or perhaps fatal. Such bladed weapons can also be used in cutting cords, ropes, and other temporary means of restraint. It should be obvious that, in any initial search of a known criminal, or of a suspect from a racial group or criminal element addicted to the use of bladed weapons, the searcher should be cognizant of and most careful of the concealment possibilities of this type of weapon.

KNIFE DEFENSE

A successful knife defense depends upon being able to see the attack coming, or at least being forewarned through knowledge and training. A knife assault is many times launched in darkness, or in such a way that it is impossible to detect immediately the opening move of the attack, such as drawing the weapon.

The soldier, military policeman, or law enforcement officer, therefore, should use the following general precautions in any area where he suspects a knife may be used against him. He should:

(1) Dominate any threatening situation by maintaining a bearing that indicates confidence and aggressiveness.

(2) Keep his back well-protected at all times by keeping well away from dark corners, the sides of buildings and driveways, or by having a wall or some other solid object immediately at his rear.

(3) Keep his own hands and weapons in such position that they are readily available for undertaking immediately the proper offensive or defensive action.

KNIFE DEFENSE

THE MAN WHO ATTACKS WITH A KNIFE THIS WAY IS EXTREMELY DANGEROUS

THIS ARM PARRIES STANDARD DEFENSES WHILE THIS ARM THRUSTS AND SLASHES.

A KNIFE MAN WHO HOLDS HIS KNIFE IN HIS HAND THIS WAY INDICATES HE IS A TRAINED KNIFE FIGHTER.

ARMED — SHOOT HIM . . .   UNARMED — A CHAIR (IF YOU HAVE ONE) PLUS A KICK

OR THROW ANYTHING AVAILABLE — THEN KICK HIM IN THE KNEE AND FOLLOW UP WITH MORE KICKS AFTER HE'S ON THE GROUND.

(4) Prevent being placed in such a position that unknown and suspicious persons are within arm's reach of his body.

(5) Always watch the movement and position of any suspect's hands.

(6) In areas where slash knife attacks may be expected, wear heavy clothing (overcoat, shortcoat, or other), since this will furnish a certain degree of protection.

Even strict observance of these precautions will not always

suffice to prevent a surprise attack. On the other hand, too obvious precautions against possible attack may indicate a lack of confidence and fear which will only encourage an attacker.

If an attack is launched at close quarters and the victim of the assault is unable to employ any of the common defenses, the only thing he can do is try to block or parry the thrust or slash with his hands and arms. Such a reaction is instinctive and is the only one possible under the circumstances. Although inadequate, it is better to sustain a wound on the arm or hand than one on the body, face, or throat area.

A number of *unarmed* knife defenses can be undertaken in certain circumstances, but the soldier or police officer on duty should never be without his weapons. He should rely on them first.

In police usage, certain types of knife attacks, such as those made by demented persons, can be stopped or otherwise restrained by conventional methods. At the other extreme is the cold-blooded attack made by the criminal of the most vicious type. In such a case, few explanations will have to be made if the officer draws his weapon and shoots the attacker down. As in other cases, the degree of force used in knife defense is dependent on the local situation and the judgment of the officer concerned.

If he is carrying a baton or riot stick, the policeman can stop such knife assaults with this weapon alone. A sharp blow to the knife wrist, hand, or elbow will often stop the attack long enough to permit a more disabling blow.

In many cases, if the hand gun is drawn, the mere presence of the weapon will deter the potential attacker. If time permits, a well-placed shot in the legs or shoulder can be used to stop the assault. Other circumstances may justify shooting to kill.

KINDS OF KNIFE DEFENSE

The following knife defenses are designed for situations in which the individual is *unarmed,* or for some other reason cannot use the weapon which he normally carries. It is here, especially, that knowledge of the ways in which a knife attack can be made is valuable in estimating the capabilities of the opponent. For example, the man who holds his knife diagonally across his palm and carries it close to his side while advancing to an attack in a crouch is obviously to be re-

CHAIR DEFENSE AGAINST KNIFE ATTACK

spected, and defenses such as the *parry* and the *block* (shown under "Defense IV" and "Defense V" on the following pages) cannot be used as effectively as those discussed first.

Defense 1. Throw anything that is within reach, a handful of dirt, a hat, a piece of clothing, furniture. Follow up by using any object at hand for striking a blow; or use the feet in offensive action. Once the aggressor has been momentarily stopped or disconcerted, a counterattack must be launched immediately.

STICK DEFENSE AGAINST KNIFE ATTACK

Defense II. Use a chair. The chair defense against a knife man is good, provided you have a chair handy. Grip it by the back and point the legs at your attacker. Advance toward him, making short jabs as you advance.

The principle involved here is the same as that used in lion taming. The knife man cannot possibly watch all four legs of the chair at once when they are moving. He becomes confused and is susceptible to blows from the feet, which can be directed towards his body in coordination with a thrust of the chair.

Defense III. Kick out the opponent's knee. When he is down, follow up with an attack on other parts of his body. Stamp on his knife hand when he goes down, or kick him in the ribs or the head. In some cases, a block of the thrust, followed by stamping on his shin or top of the foot, will suffice.

If you find yourself outnumbered and facing attackers who

KNEE KICK

The kick to the knee is one of the best of the unarmed defenses. Note that the body of the kicker is bent back and is away out of range of the knife wielder. Delivered properly, with the element of surprise, the knee kick will stop any knife or club attack.

are apt to use knives, back into a corner and use your feet to keep them out of arm's reach. Never discount the value of the feet when facing an opponent who is unarmed, or armed with a club or a bladed weapon.

Defense IV. The parry is a good defense against the downward knife thrust. It diverts the initial direction of the thrust as it sweeps downward. This is better than the block defense, because the whole length of the arm can be used. By using the right arm to parry to the right, the hand holding the

THE "PARRY" KNIFE DEFENSE

UPWARD THRUST

DOWNWARD THRUST

IN BOTH OF THESE DEFENSES DIVERT THE PATH OF THE KNIFE BLADE BY STRIKING THE KNIFE ARM TO ONE SIDE AWAY FROM THE BODY AREA.

AS SOON AS "PARRY" CONTACT WITH THE KNIFE ARM IS MADE, STEP IN FOR A <u>TRIP</u> AND A FACE <u>BLOW</u>, GRASPING THE KNIFE WRIST WITH THE RIGHT HAND, FINISH HIM WITH YOUR FEET.

knife will follow down along the outside of the body. Even in case ·the parry is not entirely successful, a flesh wound in a non-vital area will result. Here again, the defender takes advantage of the instinctive movement of thrusting his master hand above his head in order to protect himself from the downward blow. The only difference is that the movement of the right arm is a sweep to the right across the front of the body in place of a block. Conversely, one can parry the downward blow of a right-handed man, by using the left arm to parry to the outside; but in this case the chance is greater of the knife crashing through if the parry is unsuccessful. This is because the defender's body is directly facing the knife man; whereas when he uses his right arm, the trunk of his body is turned away from danger.

When you are faced with a knife held in the hand of an enemy for an upward thrust into your abdominal region,

PARRY DEFENSE

The parry defense can be used even after the downward motion of the knife arm has started. By using a sweeping motion with the right arm across the body and knocking the knife arm aside, so as to divert the path of the blow, the attack is foiled. The picture on the right above illustrates knocking aside the arm of the knife wielder by the parry method. The defender must step in toward the attacker the instant the path of the blade is diverted to the side, as shown. A trip, arm lock, or blow can be used as the follow-up.

Better knife defense, using the right hand and twisting the body so as to escape a blow if the grip misses.

Applying arm lock after grasping wrist in the right hand.

Arm parry of a . . .

downward thrust

KNIFE PARRY AND ARM LOCK

Parrying an underhand thrust, using right, or master, arm.

Using the left hand to parry a
right-handed thrust to the outside.

KNIFE PARRY (Continued)

Usual knife defense, initiated with the left hand. Note the danger if the hand misses the wrist.

KNIFE PARRY (Continued)

the parry again is a good means of defense. The parry can be executed either with the right or left arm as follows. As the attacker makes an upward thrust, sweep your right arm across the front of your body and catch the upward moving knife arm on the outside of your arm. This will divert the direction of the thrust to your right, or outside, of your body. The left arm also may be used to parry the weapon to the right, but better timing is necessary if the left is used.

Any forceful cross sweep of the arm in any direction, such as in a parry, causes the body to pivot naturally out of line of the thrust. Once the parry or block has been successfully completed, you must move in close to your man and attack.

Defense V. The block knife defense. Almost all the knife defenses involve a block of the descending knife arm by grasping the wrist or by using the forearm. However, these do not take into account the extreme force of the downward thrust and its resulting momentum, which may cause the blade to crash through such a defense and penetrate a vital body area.

Arm Lock Defense. The most common knife defense is the one which utilizes a grip of the knife wrist by the left hand, followed by an arm lock. In this, the momentum of the knife

PARRY DEFENSE, UNDERHAND THRUST

An underhand thrust, shown above on the left, can be diverted by the parry—as well as the thrust of the attacker who strives to thrust from the arm-raised position. In this instance the right arm is brought across to knock the knife arm aside, as shown above on the right. Either arm can be used to parry, depending on which is the more instinctive action of the defender. Again the parry must be followed by closing in for the attack.

arm may crash through the thumb to the knife's objective. Another danger in using the common block-type defense—of grasping the knife wrist with the left hand—is that such a method depends upon good light and perfect timing to make possible a grip on the moving knife wrist. If the blow is sweeping down with great force and the recipient tries to grip the wrist in his left hand, the force directed toward the body area may be such that the thumb side of the gripping hand is liable to give way, thus allowing the thrust to continue toward its goal.

Block Defense. The block defense is best employed when the gripping hand grasps the knife wrist while it is still cocked above the head, prior to the time when the momentum of the downward thrust is initiated.

A block defense against the downward thrust, which is more certain to stop the momentum of the stroke is executed by crossing the arms and placing them above the head, with the body in a slight crouch, so that the arms are in the path of the descending knife arm. An attack may be initiated when the knife arm is stopped. The same procedure is workable against the upward thrust to the mid-section. In this case, the body should be bent forward, so that the crossed arms divert the thrust away from the body. A straight block of the downward knife-thrust, by the forearm with the arm bent, is not advisable, since the momentum and power of the blow are usually sufficient to cause the elbow to bend and allow the blade to continue in its original direction. Block defenses are best used against individuals striving to strike overhead blows with clubs, and similar weapons.

The key factor in concluding an unarmed encounter with a knife wielder is immediate attack, moving in close to the attacker's body, once the thrust has been parried or blocked. If the knife man is allowed to withdraw and recover, the

FOREARM BLOCK

If the club, or knife, arm can be grasped as shown, before the momentum of the downward sweep of the arm is started, this block knife defense will work. It can be followed by an arm lock, by using the right hand to reach up under the knife arm, grasping the knife wrist and pulling it back and down.

FOREARM BLOCK

This is another block defense, successful only before momentum is achieved. In this type of forearm block, as well as that illustrated in Block Knife Defense and Arm Lock, there is always the danger of a miss, which will allow the blade to penetrate the chest area. Poor light, surprise, speed of attack, and slow reflexes will always interfere with the one-hand or arm block type of knife defense.

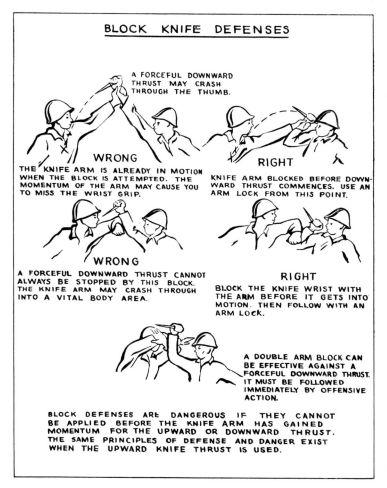

whole procedure will have to be repeated. Either type of knife defense, parry or block, involves a certain amount of risk. This risk can be decreased only by the increased proficiency achieved in practice.

Instruction in knife defense must be preceded by a thorough demonstration of the various types of knife attack. Afterwards, trainees may practice the techniques against one another. For this purpose rubber knives, wooden knives, or pup tent pegs, as issued in the Army, are ideal substitutes for knives.

KNIFE WRIST BLOCK

If the right hand is used to block the knife wrist, the follow-up can be as illustrated, retaining the grip on the knife wrist and using the left hand to knock the attacker backward to the ground. There the feet can be used to finish him off.

Training Aids

For training aids in knife tactics, see page 127.

Chapter 5

COMBAT USE
OF THE HAND GUN

COMBAT shooting with a pistol or revolver is a type of shooting that occurs frequently in certain types of military service and between police and criminal elements. It is neither target shooting nor defensive shooting. It is *offensive* shooting, and is the quickest way to insure the successful conclusion of a gun battle with a shooting enemy.

The hand gun is the basic weapon of many military and police units. Like other skilled craftsmen, members of these organizations must be trained to use it as a tool of their trade. When a man is faced by an assailant who has a gun in his hand and murder in his heart, he must be able to use his firearm instantly and effectively. Only his superior speed and accuracy will enable him to come out of most combat situations alive.

Some persons carry their sidearms for years without actually having to fire them; while others, by virtue of their assignments, have to use them frequently. Regardless of the number of times a shooter has to use his weapon, he should always employ it so as to get the maximum result from its offensive, combat potentialities. To do this, he must have had thorough training in its *combat* use. Training and skill in target shooting alone will not make him proficient in actual combat. This is especially true when he is under combat tension and is faced, at close quarters, by a *target that shoots back*.

HISTORY OF THE USE OF THE HAND GUN

The hand gun made its appearance upon the American scene in the days of our pioneer West. At that time it was considered primarily a weapon for use in personal combat. "Six-gun" experts, such as Hickok, Hardin, Holliday, and

Wyatt Earp, regarded their revolvers as tools of their trade, not primarily as "game getters," or for use in the sport of target shooting. The person who carries a pistol or revolver professionally should consider his sidearm in a like manner.

It has been almost four score years since gunmen of the pioneer West fought—and lived or died according to their individual skill in the combat use of the revolver. From then until World War II, military and law enforcement agencies gradually came to consider the hand gun a target-type shooting and training weapon rather than a close combat weapon.

In World War II, contrary to early predictions, there was a reversion to close-quarter, individual combat. It was evident in street fighting, in house fighting, and in the jungles, woods and mountains. And there was an increased emphasis on night attack and night combat. All this underscored the need for skilled, close-quarter combat use of the pistol or revolver.

Early in World War II it was found that target shooting skill with the hand gun was not enough for the soldier in combat. It was proved that a man trained only in the target phase of the hand gun was proficient up to the point where he could kill an enemy only when he had *time* to aim and fire, and providing he could see the sights. Unfortunately, such ideal conditions were found to be the exception in most close combat situations. For this reason, military training with the hand gun and with other basic weapons changed from the formalized "by the numbers" target style of the prewar days to more realistic training. Battle and infiltration courses, where live ammunition and demolitions were used, were constructed. These simulated, as nearly as possible, the terrain conditions, tension, physical exertion and realities of actual combat. Such courses are now prescribed as standard methods of training. The rifle and bayonet are used on them as they would be in battle. In a like manner, combat training with the hand gun has been improved, so as to enable the soldier who carries a hand gun to get the most from its offensive potentialities.

Early in World War II, American and Allied authorities were inclined to discount the pistol and revolver as first-line combat weapons; but this trend did not last long. Due to military necessity, combat firing training programs, stressing the use of the hand guns without the aid of sights, were soon instituted, and millions of hand guns were issued and used with deadly effect. The British and Canadian armies purchased many hundreds of thousands of Smith & Wesson revolvers, which were used by their troops.

The United States Army began the war with the theory that the hand gun should be replaced by the new carbine. It was found that most soldiers who carried sidearms had little skill or confidence in their combat use. It was recognized, however, that most of the poor performance with the pistol or revolver by our troops in combat was due not to the weapon itself but to the old concept of it as a defensive last-ditch weapon, and to the type of training which concentrated solely on aimed fire at stationary targets and bobbers. Toward the end of the conflict pistols and revolvers were again issued in quantity; and combat training courses, films and training techniques were instituted to make up for previous training deficiencies.

THE HAND GUN AS A CLOSE-QUARTER WEAPON

The hand gun is indispensable in law enforcement and in the Armed Forces, because a small firearm is needed that can be used at close quarters. It is always present in its holster and presents no carrying discomfort or inconvenience. The soldier, or police officer, thoroughly trained in both the aimed and non-aimed phases of a sidearm, has a weapon that is superior to a club, knife, blackjack, or other type of individual weapon in close-quarter fighting.

The average individual will always be a little skeptical of his prowess if he has been trained only in the target, or aimed fire, phase of hand gun employment. There is a vast difference between the training and formalized atmosphere of the target range and the scene of a gun battle or other combat situation. In reality, after the target, aimed-shot phase of training has been completed and the shooter becomes familiar with his weapon, he is only about 50% combat efficient, because the conditions under which most combat shooting occurs are entirely different from those presented in the bulls-eye type of training. In a gun battle, the utmost speed, confidence, and ability to use the hand gun from any position—usually without the aid of sights—are paramount. The man who can instinctively handle his weapon quickly and accurately, in varying degrees of light, under all terrain conditions and while under the physical and mental stress and strain of actual combat, stands a good chance of avoiding becoming an object of interest to the stretcher bearer.

Visualize the first-class target shot in the following combat situation: It is dark, he is in an alley, a poorly lighted street, or a room in a building. He can hardly see his gun at arm's length, to say nothing of the sights. His muscles are tense, his nerves keyed up to a fighting pitch. Suddenly the enemy starts shooting at him from an unexpected quarter. Even if he could see the sights, *would he take time to line them up and fire at the enemy's gun flash?* Does he *take up the trigger slack* and *squeeze off the shot* as he has been taught to do in target shooting? Will he make sure that his feet are *properly positioned* and that he is *breathing correctly?* He certainly will not! He will grip his gun convulsively, raise it, point or shove it in the general direction of the enemy, and pull (not squeeze) the trigger. That is the natural, instinctive thing to do. Most of the formalized styles he has been taught, for making good scores on paper targets, are dropped by the wayside and forgotten. In daylight he will do exactly the same thing, for it is still a matter of "getting there fastest with the mostest lead." Of course, when there is time, when the enemy is moving away from him, when he is lying in ambush, or when the range is great, the sights should be used; but when being fired upon at close quarters, few men, unless they have the attributes of a superman, will take time to use their weapons as they are trained to do on the target range.

DEVELOPING THE ALL-AROUND COMBAT SHOT

Few pistol shooters, whether they are expert or only fair at regulation bull's-eye targets, are good all-around combat shots. The kind of training that makes fine scores on bull's-eye targets does not produce skill in the kind of shooting most frequently needed for man-to-man combat. However, to say that skill with a hand gun acquired in the usual kind of target shooting is not desirable for the man who principally carries his gun for use in combat, is a mistake.

To be the ideal all-around combat shot, the shooter must first have the necessary knowledge in the loading, maintenance and capabilities of his weapon; and he must be competent in the use of his weapon when deliberate sighting shots are possible. While target shooting skill is being acquired, he naturally becomes familiar with his weapon; and after considerable training, he is able to score hits at a considerable range. Consequently he can use the weapon effectively against an enemy when he can take a deliberately aimed shot.

The average hand gun user can do a much better job, when using sighted shots against a live enemy, if he uses *both* hands, or a *rest*, to steady the weapon. In some circumstances, of course, time and local considerations may prevent him doing so. The use of these expedients to enable the shooter to hold his weapon steadier may be severely criticized by the better-than-average pistol shot, who can shoot as well in the customary one-hand position; but the psychological factors of combat and the strain upon the muscular and nervous systems of the shooter must be compensated for by the best available means. In cases of extreme physical exhaustion, or in situations in which there has been sudden physical exertion, the pistol shooter, no matter how good he is, cannot use his weapon and make an aimed shot as well with one hand as he can with two, regardless of how well he does under ideal conditions on the target range.

In many training programs, the average trainee is not given the time, nor does he have the money, inclination, or opportunity, on his own, to perfect a high degree of skill, even in target shooting. Usually, he fires only the course required by his department regulations and puts his gun back in its holster. Such a concept eventually costs lives.

POLICE DEPARTMENT TRAINING

The law enforcement officer must be trained in the same technique as the soldier, and under like conditions, if he is to realize the most from his hand gun. A pistol or revolver in the hands of a confident, well-trained policeman will cause more respect and be much more effective than any other weapon of similar size he can carry.

Those police departments that provide a financial incentive to increase shooting efficiency are on the right track; but again too much emphasis is placed upon bull's-eye or silver cup shooting and too little on the more practical training techniques, programs and ranges which will develop, not an occasional crack-shot who can kill an enemy at 200 yards, but an average officer who can use his sidearm quickly and accurately in most man-to-man combat situations.

If the trainee is not interested in target shooting as a sport, he will not show much enthusiasm in developing his target skill with his sidearm, once his rookie training days are over.

He will always question in his own mind the need for increasing his score from 80%, or whatever his organization requires, to 90 or 95%. He will realize that such an increase in his target shooting ability has little relation to how he will use his gun against an enemy who shoots back. However, the same trainee, who shows little interest in developing himself as a target shot, will readily see the advantages of a training program that will enable him to use his gun in a practical manner in tense situations. Practical combat firing training will enable him to use his gun effectively at close quarters, under conditions which demand skill and accuracy, without recourse to the sighted or aimed shot. Knowing this, he will apply himself accordingly, because he can see the personal benefit to be derived from such a method of shooting.

Many police and military police departments encourage and develop fine pistol teams, which in target competition gain fame for their organizations. It is argued that the reputation and attendant publicity given these teams will increase respect for the law enforcement agency in the eyes of criminal elements. This may be true, but organizational or individual reputations of a few men are of little help to the average officer when he is actually involved in a fire fight.

Nearly every large police department has on hand records of shooting affrays with criminals in which an incredible number of shots were fired at close range by both parties with few if any casualties resulting. Despite this conclusive evidence of something lacking in the training programs, relatively few departments have taken steps to improve the combat efficiency of the individual officer with his sidearm. Although target shooting, beyond a certain point, will not fill such a need, many departments still try to adapt *the sport of target shooting to the realities of combat.* Actually, combat firing training is needed, to enable the officer to shoot his weapon without the need of sights. Only thus can he become proficient with the hand gun.

In the past decade, a few of the more advanced law enforcement organizations have instituted training programs that have stressed to some degree the combat-type hand gun shooting, without the aid of sights. The only criticism that can be made of these departments is that they have not stressed it enough, that in some cases the training and shooting techniques have not been the best, and that the *average* officer does not achieve real, *lasting* proficiency.

Some departments have called the courses in the combat use of their sidearms "defensive shooting"; yet the very word "defense" is a misnomer when applied to any type of close-combat shooting in which the enemy returns the fire. A pure definition of the term "defensive shooting" is: "fire returned by an individual after the enemy fires the first shot." The individual is then considered to be shooting in defense of his life. This often occurs in law enforcement, without any intent of the officer involved. In some cases, such instructions—that is, to shoot only when shot at—have actually been issued to law enforcement officers in combating known desperate men. The result has been casualties among those who have faithfully tried to follow them. Fortunately, in most cases, the criminals involved have been even less skilled than the police in combat firing.

THE FALLACY OF DEFENSIVE SHOOTING

We must recognize that there is no such thing as "defensive" shooting where lives are at stake. This is as true in police circles as it is in the armed services. When a weapon is primarily carried for the elimination or subjugation of an enemy it ceases to be defensive. Neither wars nor individual combat can be won by a defensive spirit. Rather, the all-important offensive spirit must be developed in the training for any type of combat work. This is true of hand guns. Courses in the combat use of these weapons should be called just that: Combat Shooting.

Once a man has a pistol or revolver in his hand, it should be considered that it is there for immediate use against an enemy. There should not be any hesitation in using it if conditions require its use. If the gun is in the hand, it should be there for the purpose of shooting. Otherwise, it should be left in the holster. If this seems to be too strong a statement, it should be remembered that a gun in the hand implies that the trigger will be pulled—if the mere presence of the weapon is not enough to stop the criminal. If this implication were not understood by the criminal, there would be no reason for the appearance of the weapon in the officer's hand. If the police officer considers his revolver principally as a sporting weapon, a badge of authority, or something to be used only in self-defense, he does not appreciate the capabilities of his basic sidearm. This deficiency must be made up in training.

COMBAT SHOOTING

What is meant by close-quarter combat shooting? It is a matter of record that the average hand gun shooting affray takes place at a distance not exceeding 20 feet. Any distance not exceeding 40 feet can be considered as close quarters in the combat use of the pistol or revolver. Beyond that distance the capabilities of the average individual and of the weapon show a marked decline.

This applies either when the sights are used or when they are not. It must be remembered that the enemy will seldom remain stationary and that many times the light and other external conditions will be very poor, making shooting conditions far from ideal. Muzzle blast from an enemy gun at close quarters will also have a decided effect on the shooter and his accuracy, particularly if he is using aimed fire.

A study of the records of military and police combat use of hand guns shows that use of these weapons falls into one of the following categories, listed in the order of frequency:

(1) *Close quarters,* where the firing is done without the aid of, or without time for, the sights.

(2) Instances where the *deliberate type of aimed shooting* is employed.

(3) Instances where the enemy fires the first shot without warning and a draw of the weapon has to be made prior to firing. In this category of shooting incidents, many men lose their lives without being given the opportunity to shoot back. If the enemy's shot is a miss or is not incapacitating, the draw is made and either combat type or the deliberate aimed type of shooting is used, depending on the situation.

(4) Circumstances where the shooter and the enemy "go for their guns" at the same instant, the one making the quickest draw placing the first shot. There are not many instances on record where a situation such as this, reminiscent of the gunmen of the old West, has occurred; but there have been enough to justify, in varying degrees, the amount of training given in quick draw to selected categories of military and police units.

Principles of Combat Training. *By proper training at combat ranges, man-killing accuracy, without the use of sights* *and with extreme speed, can be acquired by the average sol-dier or police officer.* This can be done in less time, and with less expenditure of ammunition, than is required to become even a fair target shot.

The training course must be balanced, with equal emphasis on the aimed shot and on combat type training. The combat phase should not consist of shooting 50 shots every 12 months at silhouettes hanging in the target range, then no further training until another year. After initial familiarization and training on the target range, the shooter should be required to shoot regularly a balanced program of both types of shooting as long as he remains on the active list. This kind of shooting program will enable him to do the most effective job when called on to shoot his weapon. At the same time it will give him the confidence in himself and his sidearm that will carry him through emergencies successfully.

The training and combat shooting techniques described be-low have stood the test of recent battle and are based on results achieved by all categories of troops in all imaginable close-combat situations.

It is assumed that in the vast majority of cases involving use of the sidearm, the policeman, or soldier, will be fore-warned and have his weapon already in his hand. This is a sound assumption because, in most situations, he will know approximately when he may have to use it.

This is the type of shooting that is designed to fill in the training gap between the aimed shot and the close-quarter use of the hand gun without aid of sights. Its objective is to present a method of shooting and training whereby the average man, who is not too interested in becoming a good target shot, can learn to use his hand gun more effectively as a tool of his trade. It is a type of shooting based on a simple common sense approach and is adaptable to the realities of combat. A quick, offensive shooter can be developed by using this technique, with little expenditure of money, ammunition and training time.

The best descriptive term for using the hand gun in com-bat without the aid of sights is shooting by "instinctive point-ing." This is a close-quarter method and should not generally be advocated for distances greater than fifty feet. Combat proficiency at ranges of fifty feet and less will be attained by using this technique. Almost all pistol shooting affrays will take place within this distance.

Combat Firing vs. Target Shooting. Three basic differences exist between combat firing and target shooting:

(1) *In close combat work, the sights will not ordinarily be used,* due to lack of time, darkness or poor light conditions, enemy fire, or other considerations. To shoot without the sights, consider the frame of the gun merely as an extension of the hand, and the barrel as an extension of the forefinger, which you are able to raise and point instinctively, accurately, and naturally at any close object. In other words, all that is being done, is to add a gun to the hand, the barrel being an extension of the forefinger. If, when looking at an object, you instinctively raise your hand, point the finger toward the object and sight along your finger, you will find that the forefinger is pointing at it accurately. This is a basic principle in combat shooting of the hand gun without the aid of sights.

(2) *The basic position for all combat firing is with the body in an aggressive forward crouch.* When a man is in combat or subject to enemy fire, he will instinctively crouch. This is especially true when he is stealthily moving forward. No one will have to tell him to assume a crouching position when he is being fired upon or expects to be fired upon. In practice, however, he will have to be forced to assume this basic firing position.

The crouch which he assumes should be natural, with the knees flexed and the trunk bent forward aggressively from the hips. The position of the feet must be natural, and although he may ordinarily pause when actually firing, he must be able to take another step in the target direction in a natural manner. Unnatural and forced positions assumed in practice are not desirable. Many shooters, when firing from a crouch, neglect to put one foot in front of the other in a natural manner. They are inclined to place their feet in a straddle-trench position which, although seemingly more ideal in practice, will not be instinctive or normal in combat. There will be times when immediate circumstances will not allow the shooter to use the crouch, but in most cases this will be his basic firing position. The instinctive pointing method, however, can be equally accurate and effective from an upright standing position.

(3) *The grip on the weapon in actual combat, when firing, is extremely tight and convulsive, and double action is always used when the revolver is carried.* When a man is in combat,

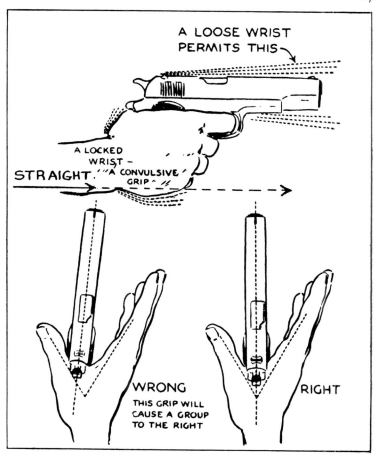

PISTOL OR REVOLVER GRIP

The grip on the weapon must be extremely tight, as it is in combat. The wrist must be locked, since any flexing will result in extremes in elevation, even at close range. The pistol or revolver must be gripped in a vise-like manner in order to have control when more than one shot is fired.

his muscles and nerves are tense, because of the excitement and danger to which he is being mentally and physically subjected. There will be no inclination to take a stance, raise the weapon, line up the sights, and squeeze the trigger when the enemy is firing or about to fire at him. The shooter will grip his weapon, exerting great pressure when he fires it.

The Convulsive Grip. The extremely tight grip used in combat has a decided effect upon the accurate application of the weapon in the fire fight. This is due to different pointing qualities of various weapons when gripped convulsively. There are two general classifications of these weapons. The first is the .45 Colt Automatic Pistol, the official Army issue. It is in a class by itself with respect to pointing qualities. In the second category will be found the two well-known makes of revolvers, Colt, and Smith and Wesson, both of which are generally favored by our law enforcement organizations. Then there are two popular German military pistols, the Luger and Walther.

The .45 cal. pistol has pointing qualities unlike those of any other weapon and it is because of these pointing qualities that inaccuracy often results in combat. When the .45 pistol is gripped in a vise-like manner by the shooter, the structure of the weapon affects accurate firing. The combination of the convulsive grip and the general structural design causes the barrel to point down when it is forcefully shoved out at the target, as it will be in combat when used by an untrained combat shooter. This fact, although long known in sporting circles, was not considered until recently in training for its combat use.

CONVULSIVE GRIP

Note how the muzzle of the .45 automatic is pointing down, not straight. This is what happens when the average shooter, engaged in combat firing, shoves the weapon at the target and instinctively uses a convulsive grip.

INCORRECT READY OR CARRYING POSITION

From this carrying position, the weapon must be shoved toward the target in order to bring it into action. When the weapon is shoved *forcefully*, as is done under combat conditions, the barrel will point *down*, not straight.

For the proper position see page 113.

Shoving Weapon at Target. When the hand gun user carries his weapon at any degree of a raised pistol position, which is a habit he acquired on the target range, and he is suddenly confronted with a target at close quarters, his natural reaction is to *shove* the weapon at the target and pull the trigger. When he does this with the .45 automatic, the barrel

RAISE PISTOL READY POSITION

From the raise pistol "ready" position, the revolver will point horizontally if not shoved forward too forcefully. The pistol points down—
unless the wrist is cocked. Inaccuracy will result, with either type
weapon, if the arm is shoved forward forcefully, to bring the hand gun
into action from the raised pistol position.

points down and a miss usually results, sometimes even at
distances of less than 10 feet.

Any shooter can test this fact for himself by grasping the
.45 convulsively as he would in combat, holding it in a
raised pistol position, picking out a target a short distance
away, closing his eyes, and shoving the pistol *forcefully* in
the direction of the target. Upon opening his eyes, he will
see that the barrel is pointing down at a decided angle.

This structural effect of the weapon must be counteracted
from the outset. It can be done in two ways: One is by equip-
ping the gun with an adapter which will cause it to point
straight when shoved forward forcefully, and the other is by
developing a slight upward cocking of the wrist to compensate for the barrel slant. The latter method is used in target
shooting when the arm is outstretched, but will not be used
instinctively in combat without a great amount of practice.

Neither of the above expedients will be necessary if the weapon is carried pointing toward the ground at about a 45 degree angle from the body. Then, if the individual will have his arm extended and will raise the weapon to a level with his eyes and fire it, he will do so accurately, without having to compensate in any manner for the gun type.

When the Colt or Smith and Wesson, and the two German automatics mentioned, are tested by the convulsive grip, raised pistol, shoving method, they point more squarely at the target, and the barrel remains more nearly parallel to the ground. These weapons will point satisfactorily, if not shoved *too forcefully* toward the target. This does not mean, however, that they should be fired in combat by the raised-pistol, shoving method, although this method is commonly accepted as a way of firing without the sights. It is not always accurate and results in loss of control, particularly when the target is in any position except directly in front of the shooter.

When the gun arm is shoved forcefully to the front, the structure of the arm itself and the effect of the momentum of the forward shove upon the wrist, when the arm becomes fully extended, will cause the wrist to drop and the barrel to point downward, regardless of the structural design of the weapon. This effect in firing will occur with most individuals, regardless of the good pointing qualities of any hand gun. However it is not so apparent with the revolver, as with the Colt .45 pistol. The combination of the convulsive grip, the structural design of the various weapons, and the effects produced when shoving the weapon forcefully forward, are such that few men can use hand guns instinctively and accurately in combat, when firing them in the above manner, without a prohibitive amount of practice.

The size and structure of the shooter's hand and arm and the design and size of the grip of the weapon will also affect accuracy when the weapon is fired by the point-shoving method. If possible, all weapons should be selected so that they fit the individual's hand, whether it be large or small. However, in the Army and in large police organizations, such practices are not always feasible. Rather, the hand must fit the gun, not the gun fit the hand.

Position of Wrist. Because one of the basic fundamentals of combat firing is shooting with the weapon grasped convul-

In combat firing, *DON'T* carry your hand gun at any degree of a raise pistol "ready" position.   *DON'T* shove it toward the target.

Under combat tension, the <u>forceful</u> shove toward the target from the raise pistol ready position results in this — not this —

A combat (tight) grip.

Use a downward "ready" position; have a <u>locked</u> wrist and elbow when you raise pistol to eye level to fire.

READY POSITION, COMBAT FIRING

sively, the position of the wrist will exercise great influence upon accuracy. At the time the trigger is pulled, whether it be a single shot or a burst, the wrist must be in a *straight locked* position and should not be flexed or "cocked." The slightest variation of the wrist up or down from its straight locked position creates a difference in elevation of the barrel of the weapon which is translated into extremes at the impact point of the bullet, even though the target is very close. Any cocked and locked, up-and-down position of the wrist,

SHOOT FROM A FORWARD CROUCH, FEET IN A NATURAL
POSITION ALLOWING ANOTHER STEP. WITH A LOCKED
WRIST AND ELBOW, AND THE SHOULDER THE PIVOT POINT-
RAISE WEAPON TO EYE LEVEL AND 'LET GO

PROPER READY AND FIRING POSITION

which is developed to compensate for the effect of the convulsive grip upon pointing qualities of a particular weapon,
such as the .45, is not advisable because it cannot be used instinctively in combat without an extreme amount of practice.

Another disadvantage of the habit of cocking the wrist to
compensate for the downward pointing qualities of a specific
hand gun, such as the Colt .45 automatic, when it is fired
by the pointing method, is that all guns do not react in the
same way to the cocked wrist position. Once a certain style
of wrist cock has been developed for use on a particular

weapon, it will instinctively be used on all types of hand
guns thereafter. Because of different structural characteristics
of hand guns and the effect of the convulsive grip on them,
their pointing qualities react differently to a certain wrist
adaption or "cock," developed for use on one particular
make and model of gun.

Forward Crouch. The best all-around method for combat
firing without the aid of sights is as follows: the body is in a
forward crouch; the feet are in a natural position, permitting
another step forward. To fire the weapon, the shooter will
grip the weapon convulsively and with a straight *locked*
wrist and *elbow* (the pivot point being the shoulder *joint*),
raise the weapon from the ready position to a level with the
eyes, and fire. The weapon always should be raised high
enough so that, at the time the trigger is pulled, the gun is
directly in the shooter's line of vision to the target. Do not
let the shooter pause before firing, once the gun is at eye level.

The weapon should be carried in the ready position, with
an extended arm pointing downward at about a 45-degree
angle from the body. This does not mean that it will always
be carried with a convulsive grip and the arm rigidly extended. It will ordinarily be carried with the arm and hand
relaxed and the elbow slightly flexed; but in all cases the
arm and elbow should be well out in front of the shooter.

**ARM POSITION IN RAISING
GUN TO EYE LEVEL**

After initial practice, the hand
gun should be carried in this
"ready" position. The elbow is
slightly flexed, to prevent tiring.
It is an easy matter to straighten
the arm to the straight locked
position while the gun is being
raised to eye level.

From this natural, relaxed, carrying position it is very easy to assume the straight-arm, locked-wrist position before or while raising the weapon for firing. This will be done naturally by the shooter; no special emphasis will have to be placed on it after initial training.

At the outset, the straight, locked-wrist-and-elbow ready position should be emphasized, so that the student can develop accuracy and will understand the shooting principles. Later on, after proficiency is acquired, he can be allowed to carry his weapon in the more relaxed ready position in which he will normally carry it in potential combat areas when not actually firing.

Looking at the carrying or ready position from the front, it will be noted, in the training stage, that the gun arm ideally

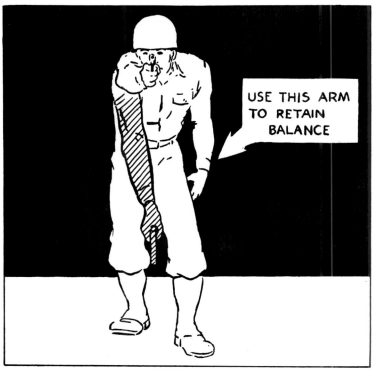

PROPER "READY" POSITION. WEAPON IN PROPER
RELATION TO THE BODY CENTER AND EYES
The gun is carried toward the body center and, when raised, it is at eye level and between the eyes.

should be swung in toward the body center and that the wrist of the gun hand should be flexed slightly to the right, so that a perpendicular line could be drawn from the belt buckle, through the muzzle of the weapon, the tip of the nose, and exactly through the center of the forehead between the eyes. If the shooter carries his weapon in this basic ready position and raises it straight up until the gun is between his eyes and the target, as he would in raising his hand to point

RIGHT

LET THE MOVEMENT OF YOUR BODY TAKE CARE OF CHANGES IN DIRECTION ·

CHANGE OF POSITION

If the weapon is always kept in the same relative position to the eyes and body, you will shoot where you look. From the basic "ready" or carrying position, the shooter wheels his body for angle shots. The gun is brought up to . . .

at an object, windage automatically takes care of itself. The elevation will always be accurate as long as the shooter raises the weapon so that it is at eye level when it is fired.

The basic position, with the gun held in body center and the wrist slightly flexed to the right, should be maintained throughout the early training stage. Later, as proficiency develops, the shooter will adapt his own particular ready posi-

CHANGE OF POSITION (Continued)

the eye (firing) level during the time that the change in body direction is made.

To hit angle targets without changing direction, don't swing the arm; point the body at the target.

tion, which may not carry the weapon as near to body center as the ideal. However, if he still gets the weapon up to the firing position so that it is in line with the eyes and target, and if he is making hits, no correction need be made.

Pointing the Body. The individual who shoots in this manner is directly facing the target and firing in the direction his *body is pointing.* In other words, with the wrist and elbow locked and the arm extended and maintained in the same relationship to the body center and eyes, he will shoot where he looks. In firing at a target directly in front of him, it will be necessary only to raise the weapon from the ready position, using the shoulder as a pivot point, and fire.

Whenever the shooter is forced to fire at a target which is not directly at his front, he need only wheel his body so that he is directly facing the target; then fire. In other words, *the body points the weapon,* and as long as the same relationship between the weapon, the body center, and the eyes is maintained, accuracy will result. He will shoot where he looks if he points his body at the target instead of swinging his arm.

When the shooter wheels his body to make an angle shot, the gun hand should be brought up to eye level while the body is changing direction. The shooter should not raise his weapon to eye level and then wheel; nor should he wheel and then raise it. To make either of these movements prior to, or after, the actual wheeling of the body complicates the action and makes the shooting more difficult, since a separate movement must be mastered. Most shooters, when making angle shots, will automatically raise their weapons gradually upward in a curve so that the gun is at eye level at the time the body comes to a stop in the new direction. It is usually not necessary to stress this in practice since most shooters do it automatically.

Naturally, a correction will have to be made for those who are observed trying to make two separate movements (body and arm) when the change in body pointing direction occurs. A few shooters, when they change body direction, will force the arm separately, so that the body and arm are not synchronized. When this occurs, the basic body-center weapon relationship will not be maintained.

To demonstrate the desirability of wheeling the body instead of swinging the arm, to shoot at a target which is at a right or left angle, place yourself so that your body is facing

The firing position with the slightly bent and locked elbow can be used, but more practice will be needed than when using the straight arm method. The position shown by the shaded arm is best for the average shooter.

at a right or left angle from a chosen target. Instead of turning your body to face the target, and raising the weapon to fire, merely turn the head and swing the arm forcefully from the right or left toward the target. It will be apparent that it is very difficult to swing your arm horizontally in a new direction and stop it in time to obtain the proper windage for accurate firing. This is especially true in combat. Ordinarily, two-thirds of the shots will be fired at the target either before the weapon reaches it or after it has passed across it and is on the other side. You can't make your arm stop in the same place twice without excessive practice. After this simple demonstration, the advantages of using the body to do the actual pointing of the weapon at angle targets should be apparent.

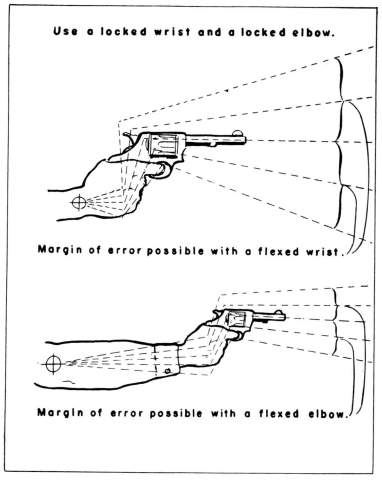

Use a locked wrist and a locked elbow.

Margin of error possible with a flexed wrist.

Margin of error possible with a flexed elbow.

The elbow and wrist must be kept *straight* and *locked* for consistent shooting. A slight movement of the wrist from the locked straight position will result in extremes of elevation, even at close range. To a lesser degree the bent elbow has the same effect.

There is another slight variation of the method of shooting by instinctive pointing which is used successfully by a number of shooters. However, it takes considerably more practice to acquire the same degree of accuracy and proficiency. The only difference between it and the method discussed above is that at the time of firing the arm is not in a straight locked position, but rather the elbow is *slightly* bent and locked. The arm is still well out in front of the body. This method is favored by certain shooters because it brings the barrel of the weapon to a horizontal position at a point half way between the ready position and eye level. This allows the shooter to bring the weapon into play a fraction of a second sooner than if he raised it the remaining distance, as he does in the straight arm method. Although some shooters favor this method because of the time element, the fraction of a second saved in bringing the weapon into play is not enough of an advantage to justify its adoption by the average shooter.

Shooting from the Hip. Although the method of shooting by instinctive pointing has been called hip shooting, it is not. A pure definition of the term hip shooting is: "the type of shooting done when either the wrist or the elbow is pressed or held tightly against the side or center of the body at hip level at the time of firing." There are many who can shoot accurately at targets on a horizontal level from the hip position, but it is not a method by which the ordinary individual can achieve proficiency without a prohibitive amount of practice.

There are numerous disadvantages in the hip method. Facing the man who fires from the hip, it will be noted that the barrel (gun hand resting on hip) is usually pointing about eight or 10 inches to the right of the body center, hence to the right of the line of vision. This does not help accuracy and will have to be compensated for in practice. The hip shooter will also be unable to fire at targets above his natural eye level from this position. He will be forced to extend his arm and raise it to shoot at high targets. It is awkward and impractical to shoot from the hip position when the body is in a crouch. In this position, the shooter is forced to extend his arm. Bulky clothing, ammunition belts, and such, interfere with placing the elbow or wrist firmly against the hip in the same place each time the weapon is fired. All such minor considerations cause changes in elevation which will influence accuracy, especially at distances greater than 10 feet.

Using Your Own Weapon. Although, above, the .45 pistol has been mentioned specifically, the principles and the system of firing discussed are the same regardless of the kind or caliber of weapon, whether it be automatic or double action revolver. It is only common sense to advise that it is always

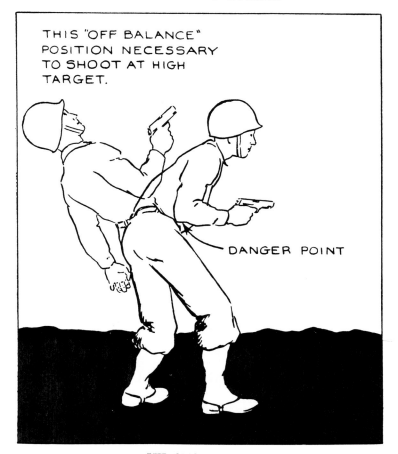

THIS "OFF BALANCE"
POSITION NECESSARY
TO SHOOT AT HIGH
TARGET.

DANGER POINT

HIP SHOOTING

You can't shoot accurately from the hip at targets *above* or *below* the horizontal. Except when firing to the front, the arm will usually have to be extended in order to get accuracy, as in the instinctive pointing method.

best to practice with the weapon which will be used and carried in actual combat, if it can be determined. A gun is like a favorite golf club. Different makes of guns and revolvers, like various kinds and sizes of clubs, feel different in the hand of an individual. The balance and feel of one particular weapon will usually appeal more than any of the others. Whenever possible, let each shooter choose his own

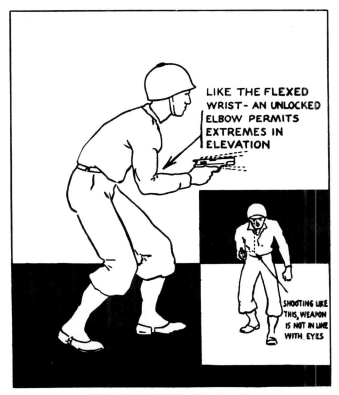

LIKE THE FLEXED WRIST- AN UNLOCKED ELBOW PERMITS EXTREMES IN ELEVATION

SHOOTING LIKE THIS, WEAPON IS NOT IN LINE WITH EYES

HIP SHOOTING (Continued)

There are too many danger points affecting accuracy in this type of firing. A prohibitive amount of practice is necessary to achieve any degree of combat proficiency by this method.

weapon. For psychological reasons, a man will have more confidence in a weapon of his own choosing; hence the weapon will have a direct bearing on his proficiency in practice and in combat.

TRAINING METHODS

In training groups of men in combat firing, it is very important that the proper introduction be given. In the introductory phase, the differences between target firing and combat firing must clearly be defined. Each must be put in its proper perspective. It must be stressed that each way of firing complements the other, to make the ideal hand gun user.

HIP SHOOTING (Continued)

It is difficult to master this method of shooting, where the elbow is bent as much as shown above, or when it is resting on the hip. It is hard to achieve, through practice, the ability always to bend the elbow at the same angle under combat conditions.

It is advisable to show the various methods of combat firing and to explain why one method is superior to another. American shooters, more than those of any other nationality, have to be shown the whys and wherefores of anything they use personally, especially when it is to be their basic combat weapon.

Define the term "instinctive pointing"; then let each student raise his arm and point toward any object, sighting along his finger to see the accuracy with which he instinctively points at the object. Then explain that this is the basis of combat firing.

Ideally, before a group of men is introduced to combat firing, they should have completed the target phase of instruction and be familiar with the weapons which they are going to use. The three basic differences between target work and combat work must be clearly explained and demonstrated. If the men are to use the .45 pistol, the effect of the convulsive grip upon the weapon's pointing qualities must especially be emphasized. Each student should make for himself the simple test described above, so that he can see the effect of the tight grip on the weapon when it is shoved toward the target. It should be brought out that, from the raised pistol position, other hand guns, when shoved at the target, will react in the same manner in lesser degree.

All members of the group will not have the same degree of familiarity with hand guns and their firing, but all, including the dyed-in-the-wool target shooting advocates, must be convinced of the limitations of sighting methods in close combat.

Every possible means must be used to develop an aggressive spirit in the hand gun user. In the "fire fight" the shooter should always be going in toward the enemy. If he remains stationary, he is a better target. If he fires and keeps advancing, he is harder to hit, and the psychological effect on the enemy is great, even if he misses. Tell him, right off the bat, that he can get shot just as easily backing away from an enemy as walking toward him.

The Safety Habit. As in any type of shooting, the safety factor must be stressed. However, in combat work the emphasis can not be too great, because training methods and practice will include pointing the gun at other individuals, as is necessary in combat. It must be impressed upon the student that he must never point his gun at another student until so instructed. The importance of automatically checking the weapon for live ammunition each time it is picked up must be drilled in from the very start. The student should do this until checking the firearm, whenever it comes into the hand, is instinctive. Impress upon the student that he is checking the piece not only because of the safety factor, but also because, prior to possible combat, he should be sure that the weapon he will use is loaded.

One of the most direct methods of ingraining the safety habit in men who have not previously been associated with weapons of any type is the following: Get a large leather paddle, such as is popular in a college fraternity house, and hang it where every one can see it. Make it a rule that any man who carelessly or thoughtlessly points his gun at another without being told to do so by the instructor, will have it used on him in the traditional manner by the man at whom he pointed the gun. Such a method is direct and is much better than a mere reprimand by the instructor. It will serve to make the shooter safety-conscious in a short time.

Combat Shooting. A very successful means of introducing combat shooting is to line the students up against the butts and have the instructor, from a distance of not more than 10 feet in front of the group, fire a foot or two to either

side, or above their heads. This will demonstrate the effect
of muzzle blast and will give a picture of what a gun looks
like from the receiving end. Naturally, this must be carefully executed by reliable shooters; but it will serve better
than anything to put the student in the proper frame of mind
for an introduction to combat shooting. Then it is only
necessary to ask any dyed-in-the-wool target enthusiast in the
group if he would have deliberately raised his gun and used
the sights against an enemy who was shooting at him from
close ranges in such a manner.

The question of how he would react in the face of firing
directed toward him, and of whether his reactions would be
the same as in practice, has often arisen in the shooter's mind.
The answer is Yes; the reaction will be the same, because
practice will make firing instinctive and he will not realize
that he is actually being fired upon. This is best shown by
the following example: A spectator watching one of the
famous Army infantry assault courses—in which live charges,
live grenades, and live rounds of ammunition are fired around
the men participating in the course—asks himself if he would
actually be able to take such a course. From his viewpoint,
it looks very spectacular; and the element of danger thrown
in by live ammunition striking close to his feet, charges
bursting around him, and all the other battle effects, is very
real. The same spectator, once he enters upon such a course,
is so intent on firing his own weapon, throwing his own
grenades and reaching his objective, that he does not notice
the various charges bursting around him. In general, this ex-
plains a man's reaction in combat. He is so intent on his own
job that, after the initial effect, he is not bothered. He does
not think about what is going on around him but concentrates
on his mission.

During a demonstration of the right and wrong way to
shoot without the aid of sights, a small toy gun, which can
be purchased at most toy counters and which fires a wooden
dart with a rubber suction cup on the end, can be used to
illustrate the effects of various body, arm and wrist positions
upon accuracy. It will give the student visual proof at the
outset. Such toy guns, or small BB pistols, can be issued to
students during the dry-run phase and will help speed up
individual proficiency. Using the suction tipped darts against
a full length mirror, where the student can see his own mistakes and can aim at the reflection of his own body, will
help a great deal. The darts will stick on the mirror at the

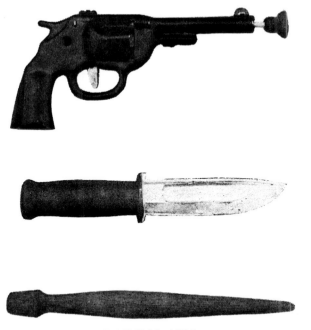

TRAINING AIDS

These are valuable and readily procurable training aids. The toy gun with the rubber-tipped dart is available at most toy stores. The rubber knife and the military-type tent peg also are easily obtained and are useful in teaching knife defense.

point of impact, showing where the bullet would have hit if a gun had been used. Basic errors are much more easily corrected with training of this type. Even after actual proficiency has been achieved, the toys can be used for practice with or without the mirror. Shooters can also use them when ranges are unavailable. Practically all basic firing principles can be proved with these toys.

Actual practice for the student should proceed in somewhat the following manner. He should be placed initially at a distance of not more than 6 feet from a full length mirror, or facing a fellow student who will act as a coach. He should then be told to assume a crouching position. He must be checked to see that he has a natural foot position for a forward crouch (either right or left foot may be forward). To ascertain whether the position is natural, have him advance four or five steps remaining in the crouch. He should walk

GRIP FOR TARGET SHOOTING

This is the normal grip used by the target shooter. The thumb is extended along the side of the frame, so that the weapon can be held steadier.

GRIP FOR COMBAT SHOOTING

This is the best grip to use in combat shooting, when double action is the only method of firing used. The thumb, in this case, touches the second finger. This is a better grip to use when the gun is grasped tightly.

evenly, without any bouncing effect caused by bending the knee joint and raising the body up and down.

Once the instructor is certain that the shooter has assumed a natural crouching position, he should check to see that the body is bent forward from the hips in an aggressive manner. The student's right hand and arm should be forward in the 45-degree-angle ready position. The right shoulder must not be shoved too far forward; it is as nearly parallel to the left as is natural. It should be explained that this is the basic ready position and that the student need only raise his arm and point in order to fire at the target.

The student should practice about 15 minutes raising his arm (to eye level) and pointing his finger from the ready

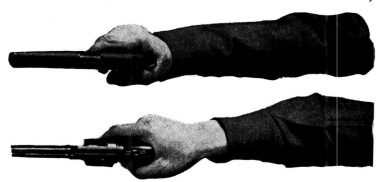

THUMB AND FOREFINGER POSITION

These downward views of the gun hand show the proper position of the weapon with respect to the thumb and forefinger. In both cases the hand gun points straight and the gun bisects the angle between thumb and trigger finger.

position. When the instructor is satisfied that he has mastered the fundamentals, he may be given a weapon and the same type of practice should be continued, with the trigger being snapped when the gun is raised to a point where it is in line with the target. The locked wrist and elbow must be checked continually during this period. If the toy dart gun is used, let the shooter try dropping or cocking his wrist or elbow, so that he may see the effect of this action upon the impact points of the darts.

COLT .38 CALIBER

DETECTIVE SPECIAL MODEL

SMITH AND WESSON
.38 CAL.
SAFETY HAMMERLESS
MODEL

When light, fairly heavy caliber guns of the types above are used on double action, they often are hard to control after the first shot. The grip of the weapon is usually best taken by placing the little finger under the butt, so as help prevent the gun from bucking too much. Guns of these types usually have smaller grips than larger models, making possible the style of grip described here.

After he has mastered these first steps, the student should be made to advance toward the mirror, raising his weapon and firing as he walks, because, in reality, the stationary position is only the pause for firing which he makes if he is walking forward with his weapon ready for any enemy who may appear. Care must again be taken to check for the bouncing habit as the student walks forward in his crouching position. After the instructor is satisfied that the student is qualified and is doing the dry-run properly, he should have him face away from the mirror at right angles and allow him to wheel and snap the weapon at his mirror image.

Movement of the Feet. Any tendency to swing the arm and not point the weapon by the body, when turning to look at the target, should be stopped immediately. The question of how the shooter should move his feet, when using his body to point the weapon, will arise. Because of the different positions in which the feet will be when firing in combat, the shooter should change his body direction by moving his feet in *any natural manner.* To wheel to the right, some men will start off by shoving the left foot forward; others will bring the right foot around to the rear, using the left as pivot. Either is correct as long as the desired change in body direction is accomplished. Stay away from any set method of

SPECIAL ROPER STOCKS

This Colt Banker's Special is equipped with a special Roper Stock. This type of stock affords a better grip on the weapon, because of its design and larger size. A grip of this type on the small hand gun gives better control in double action combat shooting.

changing body direction. Terrain is uncertain, and the actual position of the feet in combat may not always be the same. There may be times when the feet cannot move at all, but the body can still be twisted to get necessary accuracy.

The method used by some instructors, which involves jumping instead of a natural foot movement to change the body direction, is not advisable because of uneven ground and the possibility of losing balance and a sense of direction. You can't jump and always land in the same place.

During practice in wheeling or changing direction of fire, it is well to let the student demonstrate to himself how much better this body pointing method really is by allowing him to face at a right or left angle from the target. Then, instead of wheeling his body, have him swing his arm from the right or left toward the target. The difficulty of stopping the swing of the gun arm, so that accurate windage will be maintained, will then become apparent.

Next the student can be placed with his back to the mirror and made to wheel completely around to fire at his reflection.

After this last exercise the desirability of firing always with the arm extended, the gun raised to a point in line with the eyes and target, and letting the body do the actual pointing of the weapon, should be apparent. The question of what is the proper position for the free hand (left for a right-handed shooter) will be asked. It is best that it be used for maintaining balance or carrying other equipment, such as a grenade or flashlight. Set positions for this hand should not be emphasized, although some coaches do make the student place his left hand on the inside of the left thigh so as to square the body. This will work all right in practice, but it is not natural and will not be used instinctively in combat.

Silhouette Firing. After not less than three hours of "dry" work, in which the fundamentals have been mastered, the shooter may be allowed to fire live rounds at a ¾ silhouette.

In the introduction, or prior to actual firing, the student should be told that the most vulnerable part of an enemy's anatomy is his mid-section. When firing at silhouettes, all shots should be concentrated in this area. If the impact point of the bullet is a little high or low, to the left or right of the navel, it will still be a man-stopping shot. When a hit is scored in the mid-section, no matter how slight, the psycological, as well as the physical, effect is very great.

In combat firing, it is usually advisable to fire either the

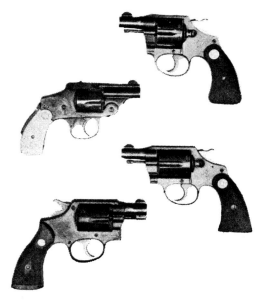

HAND GUNS FOR CONCEALED POSITIONS

These types of hand guns are easily carried in concealed positions, such as coat pockets. The police officer who approaches suspicious automobiles or persons will do well to have his hand on a weapon of this type. These guns are relatively inexpensive and often provide "cheap" life insurance, when shooting starts from an unexpected quarter.

pistol or the revolver in bursts of two, and during the dry run and actual practice the trigger should always be pulled twice. A study of the spacing of the two-shot burst on a silhouette will show that, even when a weapon is fired from a convulsive grip, the shots will be spaced from 6 to 8 inches apart, and on approximately the same horizontal level. This spacing, which is caused by the recoil of the weapon when two quick shots are fired successively, provides an additional hitting probability. This is a good reason why it should be used in combat firing.

It is a good idea to have the silhouette target hanging, or suspended above the ground, so that its center is at approximately the same level as an enemy's stomach area. Place the student, initially, not over 8 feet from the silhouette. Have him assume the crouch position, with his weapon at ready, and let him raise his arm to fire in bursts of two. He should then lower the arm again to the ready position, then raise it to fire another burst. Never allow the gun arm to remain pointing at the silhouette between bursts, because the student can easily observe where the first bursts hit and move his arm accordingly. In combat, it is the first shots that count. There will often be no opportunity to observe a miss and to correct it. This point should be emphasized; the student should consider each time he raises his arm, fires, and lowers it again as a separate shooting incident. In this way he will achieve proficiency with first bursts.

Common Errors. The following are common errors which must be corrected at the outset:

(1) If the groups of shots are consistently hitting the lower portion of the silhouette, it indicates that the shooter is not raising the weapon high enough, so that the barrel is parallel with the ground surface; or that he is shoving the weapon at the target, causing the barrel to point down.

(2) If the shots are scattered over the silhouette, a loose wrist is usually to blame.

(3) If the group is consistently to the left, the shooter's grip on the weapon is wrong, or he is shoving his right shoulder too far forward when he raises his arm to shoot. If he is using a double-action revolver, he may be slapping the trigger on the right side, causing the gun to point left when it fires.

(4) A loose grip on the weapon, as well as a failure to lock the wrist or elbow, will also result in the shots being widely scattered.

(5) Some shooters may bounce up and down by springing at the knees every time they fire. This is not a natural movement and must be corrected.

(6) When bringing the weapon back down to the ready position after firing, many shooters let the weapon swing down until it is pointing directly at the feet. This is dangerous. The coach must check to see that the gun arm stops at no less than a 45° angle in practicing the ready position.

Advanced Training. When the shooter has mastered his first firing lesson and is consistently placing his shots in the center of the silhouette, so that the group is no larger than ten inches, he can be gradually moved backward until he has reached a distance of not over 50 feet. This increase in the range must be gradual and done in not less than three steps.

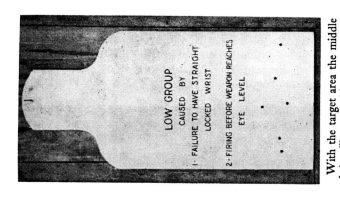

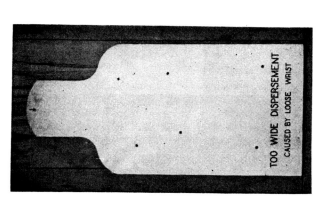

With the target area the middle of the silhouette, this group would have hit there had it not been for the reasons stated in the picture.

DISPERSION OF SHOTS

Here again a loose grip, as well as improper wrist action, caused too wide dispersion.

A loose grip will cause too wide a dispersion of shots.

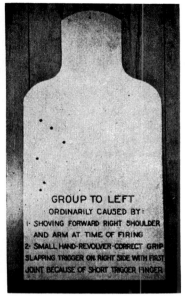

DISPERSION OF SHOTS (Continued).

Whenever possible, the hand should fit the gun. The shooter with a small grip, who carries a hand gun with too large a grip, often overshoots to the right. This is because he cannot so grasp the weapon that the tang is in the V of the thumb and forefinger.

Point 2 above applies here. The man with a small hand who shoots a weapon, the grip of which is too large, is often unable to get his trigger finger far enough around the trigger to pull straight back on double action. He then "slaps" the trigger with the tip of his trigger finger. This results in a shot group to the left.

Consistent hits in the center of the silhouette must be made each time before he moves further away from the target. From the maximum 50-foot distance, a group which can be covered by the spread of two hands is very satisfactory. After the strictly frontal firing stage has been mastered by the shooter, move him back to the eight-foot station and have him practice firing at the silhouette from right and left angles, each time making a complete body turn, to get his windage. The wheeling action should be begun from the ready position. The weapon should be brought up naturally, so that it is at eye level, and the trigger should be pulled at the time when the body faces its target. After the shooter can consistently place the bursts in the body center from both right and left angles, repeat the process of increasing the range.

In actual firing, the speed with which the arm is raised and the weapon is fired from the ready position must be slow in the beginning. It can be increased as proficiency grows. However, after considerable practice, each individual shooter will find out for himself the speed with which he most accurately brings his weapon into play. Naturally, this will increase with practice, but the average shooter will do well not to try to force himself to get his weapon into play so fast that he loses control.

To repeat, combat firing and target firing are different types of shooting. This difference must be strongly emphasized. The objective of target shooting is to be able to achieve a good score on a bull's eye target and to be able to use an aimed shot in combat. Its training methods and practices are principally directed toward this goal. On the other hand, the objective of combat firing is to shoot the enemy before he shoots you. It is difficult to draw a clear-cut line between the two types of firing, but the well-rounded shooter should be trained in both phases. Each complements the other.

Training Suggestions. After basic combat-firing training has been completed, variations and more advanced shooting problems can be given to the shooter. Additional training suggestions and techniques, which will be of practical use in combat, and the completion of which will increase the combat proficiency of the shooter, are as follows:

(1) Place two or more silhouettes 8 or 10 feet apart and let the shooter fire first at one and then at the other, using his body to do the actual pointing.

(2) He should be able to shoot and hit any man-sized object as long as he can see its outline, regardless of the light. Make him shoot in all degrees of light. Targets which should be used include: silhouette targets—which come up from the ground, out from behind corners, over the tops of walls, out of windows, from behind trees, from places higher and lower than the shooter; and running-man targets.

(3) Through repeated experiences in night shooting with the hand gun, it has been found that the shooter instinctively fires at gun flashes of his enemy. This provides a real reason for moving, rolling, or otherwise getting out of the area of your gun flash the moment you fire. If, in darkness, a gun

flash looks oval (the shape of a football) you will know that the enemy is firing directly at you from your front. If on the other hand, the gun flash is a streak, you will know that the shooter is firing from an angle and that you are not directly facing each other.

(4) Teaching a man to reload his weapon quickly is often neglected. Skill in reloading can be attained only by practice and by establishing competition among students, to see which one reloads the fastest. This should be practiced slowly at first, with the tempo speeded up after proficiency has been reached. This practice should also be done in pitch darkness.

(5) Students should be instructed in two-handed firing for

TWO-HANDED GRIP

The type of two-handed grip used by the shooter should be the one that fits and feels best. Each shooter should experiment to find the one best suited to his weapon and his hands.

KNEE REST

In this position, the arm resting on the knee is far forward, so that the elbow is not the point of support. Some shooters find this position more satisfactory.

PRONE SHOOTING

Prone shooting at long range should be practiced by all law enforcement officers. Each officer should do enough shooting to know his limitations and capabilities, in accuracy and range.

long, deliberate, sighting shots. They should be shown how to take advantage of such cover as telephone poles, posts and windows. They should be shown the proper method of prone firing in a two-handed rest position. The student also should be instructed in, and allowed to practice, firing with his left hand (that is, the hand not naturally used). Sometimes the right hand is put out of action and it should then be possible for the man to use his gun at close quarters in his other hand.

(6) Give the student all sorts of practical problems, in which he is walking in one direction and is forced to fire at a right or left angle from his line of march. Change the size of the silhouettes from ¾ to head and shoulder size as his proficiency increases.

(7) Place rubble and all types of debris in his path, such as he would find in a dirty back yard or alley. Over this uncertain footing, let him advance toward the target, firing. This provides good simulation of combat conditions. Even here his eyes should be constantly on a possible target and not on his feet.

(8) Give him firing problems where he will not be able to turn his feet, but must twist his body to change the angle of fire.

FIRING FROM SITTING POSITION

Range practice like this, which simulates firing from the seat of a car at an angle target, is a good addition to any practical combat training program.

SHOOTING AROUND A BARRICADE

Range practice such as this is valuable, to simulate shooting around the door or edge of a building. The thumb of the hand against the wall forms support for the gun hand.

(9) Give shooting exercises where he will fire at sound in complete darkness. Teach him to fire and roll, arm extended, when shooting from the prone position under these conditions.

(10) In the initial phases of instruction, when live rounds of ammunition are used, a large dirt bank against which silhouettes can be placed is useful, because misses can be spotted

on the bank. If silhouettes are unavailable, boards, boxes, or other objects can be laid against the bank.

(11) Night training can be accomplished against a dirt bank by using a flashlight. Have the lens of the flashlight specially covered, or adjusted, so that it throws a clear-cut spot about 18 inches in diameter. The coach should stand directly behind the shooter and flash the spot on the bank at various places. The shooter will fire at the center of the light circle on the bank. The bullet impact can be observed without too much trouble. This is a simple but valuable form of practice which does not involve too much in the way of training aids.

(12) Don't ever try to teach a man the combat use of a hand gun, when only a few practice rounds and limited time are available, by allowing him to shoot at a standard bull's-eye target. Missing the bull's-eye makes him feel that he is not handling the weapon accurately. He will have no confidence in it.

If you have a group which has never previously fired weapons and you have available only a few hours for training in shooting before they are expected to carry and use the gun, the following method is successful. Show them the rudiments of the proper stance for firing from a standing position. Let them grasp the pistol for firing as they would in the instinctive pointing type of shooting, using a stiff arm and a tight, almost convulsive, grip—which will be the instinctive grip in combat. Instead of using a target, let them practice firing using the sights and pointing the gun at silhouettes at a distance of not more than 5 yards. Even the poorest student will score a fair percentage of hits on the silhouette. He will then feel he can hit a man if forced to. His confidence, in himself as well as his weapon, will be greatly increased.

(13) In combat shooting, the shooter should always fire his weapon from a *stationary position*. To attempt to hit a running target while the shooter himself is in motion is foolhardy. It generally would be just as well to throw a handful of rocks. Aimed shots fired at moving targets (such as a man running down a dimly lighted alley) can best be done using any of the various two-handed positions described in this chapter. The free hand and arm can be raised simultaneously to support the gun hand and make for a steadier, more accurate aim. This is particularly true when the shooter is out of breath from running or under the stress and strain of the combat situation.

In training have your men run for a distance of 50 yards and then have them stop and fire immediately an aimed shot at a distant silhouette target *with one hand.* Have them repeat, using the two-handed system. The advantage of using both hands will then be very obvious.

(14) Make a dummy target by stuffing an old pair of coveralls with rags or excelsior. This dummy can be dropped from a concealed position such as a tree or slid down an overhead wire on a pulley to give realism in shooting at moving targets. An old automobile tire, with center filled with a cardboard target, rolled down an incline will also provide a very difficult but practical target. The difficulty in hitting a moving target in contrast to the stationary one will then be more vividly emphasized in training. There are many other variations of moving-type targets, such as the running deer target used on sporting rifle ranges, which can be improvised using inexpensive or scrap materials; these will greatly aid in achieving combat realism. Again don't neglect the use of two-handed shooting techniques in this type of firing.

(15) *Wax bullets* can be used to good advantage in combat training. The empty, *primed* pistol cartridge case can be filled with wax or paraffin and used to simulate duels—or fired against mirrors, etc. The power of the primer is sufficient to propel the wax, as a bullet, up to 15 feet. There is no damage to the weapon or the target. The .38 Special revolver cartridge is ideal for this purpose. It is best to take a small drill and enlarge the primer hole in the case so as to get maximum propulsion. If a duel, quick-draw type of training between individuals is used, plastic goggles, such as worn by industrial workers, can be worn for safety. A little experimenting can develop some very realistic types of training techniques with this method. The method is a new one as far as modern combat training is concerned but it was practiced by French duelling instructors over 150 years ago.

Any practice training method that can be devised by instructors which will fit the student for his particular mission should be included. Such training methods are just common sense. Unfortunately, they are not used to any great extent in many training programs involving the hand gun and its combat employment.

MENTAL ATTITUDE

Most important, in training with the hand gun, is the attitude toward the weapon and its use. The student must never forget that combat shooting is different from shooting at a fixed target. In combat, he is shooting at a target that shoots back. No time is permitted for the precision of the target range. The stance, grip and actual firing taught must be that which come naturally to the man who may himself be under fire.

The individual shooter should be cautioned repeatedly during the training period that he should have a previously fixed

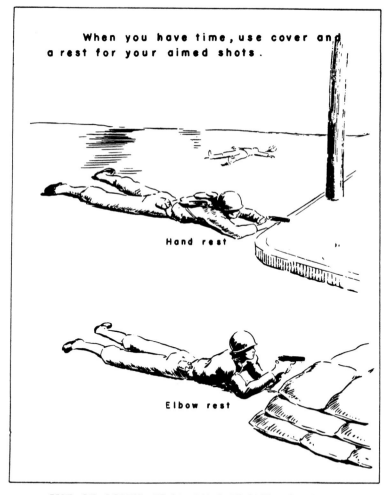

USE OF COVER FROM THE PRONE POSITION

idea in his mind of what he will do in combat. While he is engaged in practice firing his mind as well as his reflexes should be in unison in order to avoid panic. He should in practice, every time he pulls the trigger, visualize in his mind that he is firing at a target that shoots back. In this manner the reflexes of drawing, aiming, or firing a gun at a human target become an instinctive, automatic reaction.

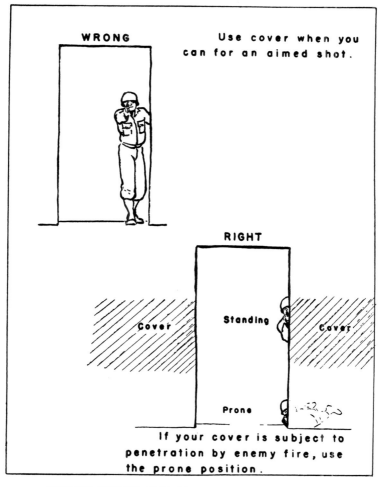

USE OF COVER AND REST FOR AIMED SHOTS

USE OF PROTECTIVE COVER AS A REST

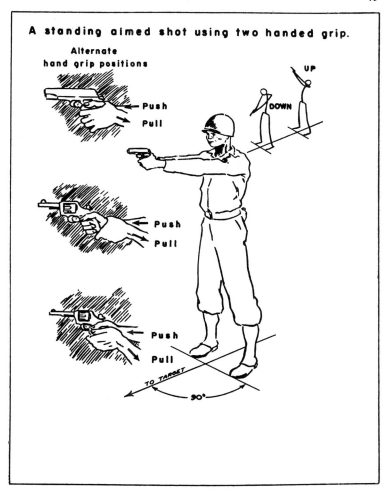

A standing aimed shot using two handed grip.

TWO-HANDED GRIP

The average shooter can shoot much more accurately with aimed fire, when under combat conditions, by using a two-handed grip to steady the weapon.

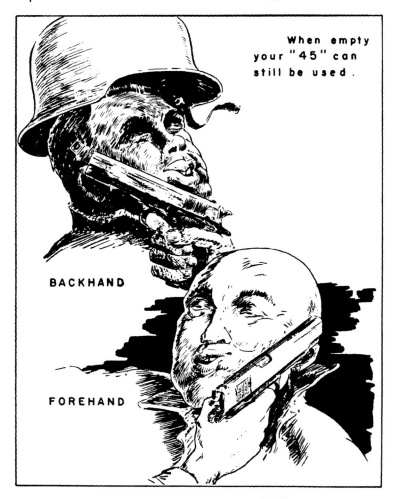

THE HAND GUN AS A CLUB

An empty gun can be used as a club against the face and temple area. Heavy automatics and long-barreled revolvers have been used successfully in this manner.

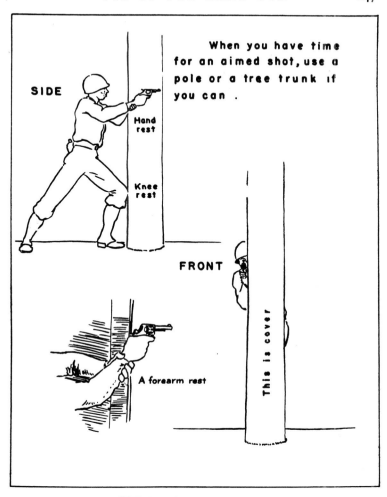

USE OF THE FREE HAND

REVOLVER VS. AUTOMATIC

Much has been written on the merits of the revolver versus the automatic as a weapon of personal defense or offense. In American law enforcement circles, over 90 percent of plain-clothes men and uniformed police carry and use the revolver type. The reasons for their choice are varied, many being attributable to the fact that the revolver is the historic-type

hand gun used throughout the winning of the West. Primarily
they chose the revolver because it has better frame construction for a swift and comfortable grip and draw. It is faster
on the first shot (double action) than most automatics, when
complete draw and firing are necessary. It has better all-
around balance and pointing qualities than most automatics
and, by using various grip adapters, can be fitted to any type
of hand. European arms manufacturers have never put out a
revolver comparable, in shape or feel or shooting qualities,
with those of our country. Their principal manufacture has
been the automatic hand gun. Just prior to, and during
World War II, the Germans began to manufacture *double
action* automatics, the Walther and Mauser. Manufacture of
these guns was discontinued at the end of hostilities. This
year, for the first time, an excellent, commercial model of a
double action automatic suitable for both police and military
use has been introduced by Smith & Wesson.

Another reason for the use of the revolver in law enforcement has been the fact that more powerful calibers could be
used than in an automatic without entailing excess bulk,
weight and size.

The widespread belief that the automatic is not a reliable
weapon and is subject to jams and malfunctions is erroneous.
Well-made automatic weapons, given proper care, will function dependably and efficiently. Where the weapon carrier has no particular liking for the weapon and considers it
in the same light as any other piece of equipment, it is necessary to have periodical inspections and checks to keep the gun
at its top mechanical efficiency. Some of real advantages
of the automatic type weapon are that it is easier and quicker
to reload, and, after the first shot, it can usually be fired with
greater accuracy and rapidity. In the instinctive pointing type
of shooting, groups or bursts may be initially more accurate
for the beginner because the trigger pull is lighter and shorter
than on the double action revolver.

The majority of jams in the automatic type of weapon can
be directly traced to the magazine. On close examination, you
may find that the lips which hold the shell in place under
the spring tension have been dented, bent outward, or forced
from their original position by dropping the magazine, or by
improper loading. Magazine springs should be treated properly. It is inadvisable to leave a magazine fully loaded over a
period of years, causing the spring to lose its tension. When-

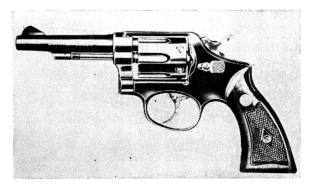

MILITARY AND POLICE .38 SPECIAL

The Smith & Wesson *Military* and *Police* model caliber .38 Special is probably the most popular revolver in its field. Since World War II its makers have concentrated on making many improvements and additions to their extensive line of hand guns. The factory now offers the world's most complete line of hand guns that have been especially designed to meet all conceivable police and military needs.

Good basic design has long made the Smith & Wesson revolver the choice of most experts for double action *combat* shooting. The trigger action is smooth, short, and positive. The trigger guard is large enough to allow fast and positive entry of the trigger finger in the quick draw. Due to the frame and grip design in relation to the angle of the barrel, the gun does not climb during fast, double action shooting. Recoil is straight to the rear.

A strong frame, with locking lug on the barrel, maintains cylinder alignment under the most adverse conditions. Although it is not generally realized, a handgun is frequently used as a striking instrument, blows being delivered by the use of the barrel or the butt. This is an additional reason why strength in the frame and locking mechanism of the cylinder is so important in a revolver.

ever possible, have more than one magazine for your weapon and change magazines frequently. Carry the spare magazine with one or two shells less than its capacity. Magazines should be kept dry and should not be carried loose in the pocket where they will be subject to body perspiration, lint, dust and denting from other objects in the pocket.

COMBAT LIGHTWEIGHTS

Any revolver so small that it can almost be covered by an ordinary man's hand, weighing 21 oz. or less and shooting the .38 Special cartridge, can hardly be considered as the ideal target weapon. Even though creditable scores can be achieved by using their fixed iron sights against conventional targets, such guns are designed, manufactured and intended for use against targets *that can shoot back.*

Recently there has been developed for special police, military, and self-defensive purposes some interesting new hand guns. They are important advancements in the firearms field and are of special interest to anyone who carries a hand gun for defensive or professional purposes. Because of an entirely new design, use of a coil mainspring, and special steels and alloys, the shooter now has available a small revolver that combines the shocking power of the .38 Special cartridge with most of the desirable features of the small automatic pistol.

These new, potent, lightweight revolvers are easy to conceal, comfortable to shoot and to carry, practical and safe in design and also retain the double action feature which enables greater and more dependable speed on the first shot. More shocking power in relation to size and weight places them ahead of present automatic pistol design. Two of these new revolvers, the Smith & Wesson Chief Special and the Smith & Wesson Centennial are about as close to

MILITARY AND POLICE 2-IN. BARREL MODEL

The .38 Special cartridge is generally considered to be the best all-around revolver cartridge for police and military purposes.

Modern metallurgy has made it possible to greatly reduce the size and weight of undercover revolvers, such as the Chief Special, without any sacrifice of caliber or shocking power.

The Smith & Wesson 2-in.-barrel. Military and Police Model shown above was a general favorite before World War II. It is still preferred by some users.

the ideal undercover hand gun as an arms manufacturer can design and mass-produce.

Members of plainclothes divisions of military and civilian law enforcement agencies have a definite need for such weapons. Also, uniformed officers of these organizations often have occasion to use a "second gun" in the performance of their duties. One of these new lightweights in the trousers or overcoat pocket is on many occasions good "life insurance" against surprise attack when the conventional holster weapon is not immediately or conveniently available for action. Unfortunately, most law enforcement officers often have to let the other party make the first hostile move.

Although it is possible to fire a creditable target score with almost any of the new lightweight guns, it does not necessarily follow that they will perform equally well when a rapid sequence of double action shots is fired. Under combat conditions there is usually no time to use the sights or readjust point of aim or impact. Therefore, these recently introduced lightweights must be judged primarily on their merits as combat weapons. They will be used principally, and therefore should be expected to perform best, on double action.

The combination of small size, light weight, recoil, and fast double action creates a condition requiring that special consideration be given to frame construction and design,

THE LIGHT-WEIGHT REVOLVER

On light-weight revolvers, like the one shown here, or like the Colt Detective Special, a man with a large hand should grip the weapon with the little finger *under* the butt. This prevents the weapon from climbing, and prevents loss of control in fast double-action shooting.

particularly of the grip. This is not so evident or seemingly important when the weapon is fired single action, permitting the grip of the hand to be readjusted between shots, or where the size and purpose of the gun permits the use of specially made grips or adapters.

The recent introduction and use of new lightweight metals and alloys has further made it possible to reduce the weight of these guns to a point where it is hard to conceive how the .38 Special cartridge could be contained and fired with effectiveness if the manufacturer made them any lighter in weight. The new lightweight guns were originally manufactured and still are produced using conventional weight metals. Recently, however, in response to special military and civilian needs, and by use of new, light alloys, their weight has been reduced almost 50 percent. Currently some models are being produced which have an overall weight of approximately 11 ounces. The law of "diminishing returns" has just about set in. It is at this point, particularly, that the basic shape of the frame and design of the grip

An excellent position to use to achieve greater accuracy when shooting the short barrel, snub-nosed type revolver.

become so important in relation to the recoil effect on the shooter's hand and his fire control.

Smith & Wesson can be given due credit for the traditional fine finish of their guns, the smooth double action, and eye-pleasing, streamlined appearance, but the design of the revolver grip and the recoil reaction against the shooter's hand of their new lightweights are perhaps the most important features of their new models.

Recoil of any hand gun and its effect can be explained simply by the following illustration: take a book and incline it on a table top at approximately a 45-degree angle, move a pencil forcefully and parallel to the table top in such a manner that one end strikes the under side of the inclined book. The striking end of the pencil deflects down; the other end goes up. This is essentially what happens

Training in this type of support shooting to give steadier aiming position is excellent for women members of police organizations as well as for men.

when you shoot a revolver with a powerful cartridge, especially a lightweight. Because of frame curvature of the upper part of the grip, the butt tends to slip down in the hand and consequently the muzzle goes up. The lighter the gun, the more recoil shock against the web of the shooter's hand. This tends to loosen the grip. When the firing is done on fast double action, the gun butt moves down and the barrel up, in direct relation to design of the revolver grip. For this reason, the shooter who buys a lightweight hand gun should never take it out and test it solely by using single action and aimed fire against the conventional bull's-eye or silhouette target. Primarily he should find out how the gun reacts when he fires it fast double action and if he can control it. There are too many people who buy small hand guns without regard for anything but weight, appearance, carrying ease, and concealment advantages.

Anyone who has fired one of the new .38 Special lightweights will not argue as to the necessity for a strong, hard grip. Instinctively under combat tension, the normal shooter will exert a great deal of grip pressure. In addition to this, because of the cartridge, weight, and size factors, he must grip the new .38 Special lightweights very hard. He cannot expect to control them on double action unless he does so. If the shooter exerts the correct, strong grip on these guns and fires them using a locked wrist, he has done about all he can to control the weapon. From this point on the particular revolver's recoil reaction will be dictated by the shape of the grip and general frame design. It will be evident that revolvers differ from one another and that some models perform better on double action than others.

It should also be recognized that hand gun manufacturers design their guns, grips, etc. to fit the hand of the "average" shooter. Generally speaking, we are writing about this average shooter and must remember that in this, as in all types of mass-produced weapons, the gun must be designed by the manufacturer to fit the "average" hand. Guns obviously cannot be designed for quantity production to fit all varieties, shapes, and sizes of hand.

Ideally, the recoil of any hand gun should be straight back in line with the horizontal center line of the gun. Any climbing tendency after the first shot on double action should be eliminated as much as possible. If a hand gun

The length and size of the shooter's arm and general body construction will determine the most comfortable position in the arm support type of shooting. There is no one best position which will adapt itself to all type of physiques. For a person with long arms the right position is many times the most steady and comfortable. In the left illustration note that the gun butt is resting on top of the left arm and the left hand is grasping the shirt seam on the right shoulder. Generally arm support type aimed shooting should be done with the arms elevated to a high enough position so that it is not necessary to lower the head too much for the eyes to be in line with the sights.

An excellent, steady position with the back supported against a solid object for long range accurate revolver shooting.

were designed only with this purpose in mind, it probably would be better to have the barrel protruding between the middle fingers and to have the body of the gun completely round. Some years ago a freak gun of this type was actually designed. It was called the Chicago Palm Pistol. This

This position, although not as steady as those when fully standing or when the back is supported, has certain advantages if the body physique permits it to be assumed comfortably. Note that the heels are in contact with the ground to give as much stability as possible. This position has some merit when it is desired to present as little a target as possible to return fire while at the same time taking advantage of both arms to achieve greater steadiness and accuracy.

type gun was designed principally for purposes of concealment by a manufacturer who was not concerned with recoil features as the caliber used was small.

The more the grip on any revolver, particularly lightweights, resembles a saw handle, the better for double action shooting. Any design of grip and frame which permits recoil straight to the rear is desirable. It is in this respect that the Smith & Wesson revolvers generally, and their lightweights especially, are effective on double action as combat weapons.

The Chiefs Special is now well-known, having been in production several years. Currently, the gun is also being manufactured with a light, alloy frame giving an approximate overall weight of 13 ounces. Many shooters, by reason of past experience and personal choice, desire a double action,

THE CHIEFS SPECIAL

The Chiefs Special, caliber .38, is designed to meet the needs of the shooter who wants a small powerful undercover gun with an exposed hammer. The gun can ,be used double action or deliberate aimed fire is possible by cocking the piece.

The Chiefs can be fired and controlled in rapid double action shooting by maintaining a hard grip. For those with large hands the little finger under the end of the butt will enable better fire control and help maintain straight-to-the-rear recoil.

The Chiefs and its combat twin the Centennial weigh about 19 ounces in the standard-weight, all-steel model. The air-weight models, a combination of steel barrel and cylinder with light alloy frame, weigh approximately 13 ounces. Both airweight models control excellently when fired fast double action if a tight grip is maintained.

undercover gun with the hammer exposed that can also be fired single action. The Chiefs Special fills the bill.

The combination of the shape of the frame, giving a saw handle effect, plus the Magna type grip, makes a Smith & Wesson pleasant to shoot. When their new lightweights are gripped hard for double action shooting, the violent hand-jarring recoil is changed to a pushing effect against the whole hand. This results in a recoil *straight to the rear* and is one of the most important features of these new guns, because the control and hitting factors are increased accordingly. The control-destroying, climbing tendency is practically eliminated. By the use of the Magna type grip, which was originally developed for the target shooter, the shock against the web of the hand is correspondingly lessened. The Magna grip also fills the web of the hand so that no looseness is present. This prevents any side movement which may result from recoil of successive shots.

Over 60 years ago Daniel Wesson produced a new model Hinge Frame Revolver. He called it his New Departure model. It became better known to the shooting fraternity as the Safety Hammerless. It was manufactured in caliber .38 Smith & Wesson and caliber .32 Smith & Wesson Short and immediately became a great favorite among law enforcement officers who valued it as a hide-away gun. Along the frontier the gun was popularly called the "Lemon Squeezer." Smith & Wesson made many thousands of this model and many are still being carried today by law enforcement officers and civilians who want a small, high-grade pocket revolver for defensive purposes.

The old Safety Hammerless model has long been considered the safest and most dependable kind of a pocket gun to carry or have at home in the bureau drawer. It could not be left in a cocked position and could only be fired by holding it in a shooting position so that the grip safety on the rear was pressed in, permitting the trigger to be pulled. Lacking a hammer, the trigger pull on the Safety Hammerless was intentionally hard and long so it could only be fired double action. There was no possibility of accidental discharge, as the firing pin could only strike the primer when the internal hammer was cocked and released by the long trigger movement.

The Safety Hammerless, being without an outside hammer, could be fired safely and rapidly from the pocket, if necessary, or drawn easily from wherever it was carried without danger of the hammer spur catching on the clothing or pocket lining.

The trigger pull on the original hammerless was in two stages. It came to a definite stop just before releasing the hammer. This permitted accurate firing, using deliberate aim, or, if the shooter desired, he could pull right on through the first stage and fire the gun double action, increasing the volume of fire.

Over the years the demand for the Safety Hammerless has been one which has continually increased. Consequently, the factory has produced the Centennial model, a modern version of this dependable old timer.

The current production model Centennial is just about as fine a short range defensive or combat gun as can be

THE SAFETY HAMMERLESS

Smith & Wesson produced the Safety Hammerless until about 1900, when manufacture was discontinued for unknown reasons. Irrespective of this, their Safety Hammerless model is still one of the most popular and practical revolvers. Many thousands are still in use and carried by men who want a dependable pocket hand gun.

secured. It incorporates more improvements than its famous predecessor and, in addition, it also shoots the .38 Special cartridge.

The new Centennial model fills a long-neglected gap in the hand gun field. It is manufactured using both normal steels and the new lightweight alloys. The two-stage trigger pull present in the early models has been eliminated. However, with a little practice it is very easy for a shooter, if he desires to make a deliberate aimed shot, to use his trigger finger against the trigger guard to make a definite stop just prior to firing.

Unlike the earlier top-break or Hinge Frame model, the stronger swing-out-type cylinder design is used. As a result, the gun is very rugged, as well as pleasing to the eye. From the muzzle to the rear of the cylinder, the frame is similar to that of the Chiefs Special, but because the hammer mechanism is concealed in the frame, the overall grip is longer than on the Chiefs Special, providing a better grip for the hand and emphasizing the saw handle effect. When fired rapid double action under combat conditions, the recoil is straight back. Climbing tendency resulting in successively higher shots is practically eliminated.

The Centennial will probably prove to be the most satisfactory to shoot and practical to carry for the man who carries a gun for business or defensive purposes.

THE CENTENNIAL

The Smith & Wesson Centennial model shoots the powerful .38 Special cartridge. It is the modern counterpart of the Caliber .38 Smith & Wesson New Departure model (Safety Hammerless) which for many years has been considered the ideal undercover gun.

The grip safety, which must be depressed to fire the gun, is a valuable safety feature; possibility of accidental discharge is almost nil. A deliberate grip on the gun plus the need to pull the trigger completely through the double action cycle is necessary to fire. The manufacturer has also provided for the professional who wants the advantage of the hammerless feature but does not need the grip safety. By removing the grips a locking pin may be inserted in a hole through the safety and frame so that the grip safety can be permanently held down in the "OFF" position.

The Smith and Wesson Bodyguard, also a .38 Special snub-nose revolver built on a .32 frame and holding five rounds, fills the gap between the Chiefs Special and the Centennial. The frame of the Bodyguard has been built up on both sides of the hammer, so that it is not exposed as is the case with the conventional revolver. A slight hammer spur protrudes (see bottom illustration) permitting the gun to be cocked for single action firing.

Although the lines of the Bodyguard are not as pleasing to the eye as in other models, the result is a practical sidearm combining the advantages of the Chiefs with those of the Centennial. The built-up side walls on either side of the hammer provide a longer grip and enable more speed on the draw and better control on fast double action. The Bodyguard can be drawn rapidly without danger of the hammer spur catching on the lining of the pocket, clothing, etc. It also can be

THE BODYGUARD

fired from a pocket or other concealed location without fear
of the hammer being blocked during its fall.

Smith & Wesson have a new 9mm automatic pistol which
has about all the desirable features possible. The man who
carries it has all of the quick draw and speed on the first shot
advantages that were formerly available only to the revolver
user. The gun is simple to strip, the safety is positive, and it
performs well under all combat conditions. The design and
angle of the grip in relation to the frame and barrel are such
that it does not climb in rapid fire as is the case with many
other automatics. In the instinctive pointing type combat
shooting it performs in a superior manner. Recoil is straight
back and control is easy to maintain.

The revolver type of hand gun is basically popular in the
United States and Great Britain. Throughout the rest of the
world the automatic has been most used by police and military units. This new double action automatic should find
ready acceptance in all of those areas where the automatic
type of hand gun is most popular.

THE SMITH AND WESSON CAL. .357 MAGNUM HIGHWAY PATROL MODEL

This caliber hand gun is manufactured in various models and barrel lengths by Colt, by Ruger, and by Smith and Wesson.

It has long been a favorite among law enforcement officers who have desired a more potent cartridge than the standard .38 Special which can also be fired in the same gun.

Until the recent advent of the .44 magnum, the .357 caliber was considered the ultimate in long range, peneration, and shocking power.

SMITH & WESSON DOUBLE ACTION 9mm AUTOMATIC PISTOL

During 1955 Smith & Wesson announced deliveries on a new line of 9mm automatic pistols designed for military and police use.

The 9mm Luger or Parabellum (European name) is used by military and police units throughout the world. Ballistically it is considered to be one of the best all-around pistol and submachinegun calibers. Although there were double action automatics, such as the Walther, manufactured and used by the Germans during World War II, there has not previously been available a good commercial automatic.

This fine combat-designed automatic has a magazine capacity of eight rounds. With one round carried in the chamber half again more firepower is available than in the standard revolver. Most sales of this arm have so far been in export but recently some U. S. police agencies have begun to use it.

Many police officers prefer to carry a second small "hideout" gun is addition to their regular service arm. These guns are carried in wrist, ankle, groin, leg and armhole holsters and other places where they are easily concealed but accessible. They are many times also carried as "off duty" guns. (Reading from top to bottom) No. 1 is the original Remington .41 caliber two-shot Derringer favored by gamblers during the American frontier period. No. 2 is the American manufactured copy of its famous predecessor, the Great Western caliber .38 S. & W. Derringer. No. 3 is the German manufactured caliber .22 long rifle Derringer type currently being marketed in the United States. No. 4 is the Colt Astra Cub Automatic. This and others of similar type are also favored as "hideout" guns. The small automatic type weapon provides more fire power and is available in caliber .25 and caliber .22 short and .22 long. Although the shocking power is limited, the .22 caliber cartridge is, contrary to popular belief, considered to be more effective than the .25 caliber auto cartridge.

COLT. OFFICIAL POLICE CAL. .38 SPECIAL

This model revolver has been a favored sidearm of the uniformed police for many years throughout the world. It has a smooth action and trigger pull and is a rugged heavy-duty hand gun.

THE COLT COBRA CAL. .38 SPECIAL

This is a lightweight version of the well known Colt Detective Special that has been manufactured and used for many years. It weighs less than a pound and retains the six shot capacity of its heavier counterpart. It is an excellent undercover weapon for those who prefer a lightweight handgun.

THE COLT AGENT CAL. .38 SPECIAL

This is a six shot lightweight revolver for plain-clothes and concealed carrying. It is like the Cobra model except it has a shorter grip, which is suitable to those shooters with smaller hands.

COLT PYTHON CAL. .357 MAGNUM

Colt produces this fine revolver with either four or six-inch barrel. It will also shoot all standard .38 Special cartridges. It is recommended either as a target or service weapon. The .357 magnum is still favored by many officers over the more powerful .44 magnum.

THE SMITH AND WESSON CAL. .44 MAGNUM

Many modern police officers, where personal choice of their sidearm is possible, prefer calibers greater than the standard .38 Special.

Double action revolvers that will handle the .357 magnum, the .44 special, or the new .44 magnum are deservedly popular. Their greater initial shocking power and "man stopping" ability is well known.

Under combat conditions, a criminal who is under stress of extreme rage or excitement has so much extra adrenalin pumping into and through his system that many times he is temporarily immune to normal shock. It is for this reason that many combat experienced officers prefer the more powerful caliber hand gun. A heavy lead bullet, moving at high velocity, has great shocking power and will usually knock down the criminal and put him out of the fight if it hits him almost anywhere in the head, body, arms or legs.

Many officers feel that the extra barrel length, weight and bulk of the larger caliber hand gun is more than compensated for by the increased "knockdown" potential.

The new .44 magnum cartridge has far greater shock power than any other hand gun cartridge commercially produced. It is replacing the less powerful .357 magnum that has been a favorite for the past two decades, when it was known as the most powerful revolver cartridge in existence.

S & W manufactures the .44 magnum revolver in barrel lengths from 4 to 10 inches. The same gun will also shoot the less powerful .44 S & W Special and .44 S & W Russian cartridges.

THE QUICK-DRAW

The ability to get his hand gun out of his holster and into action quickly and accurately is a desirable asset for any soldier or law enforcement officer. However, quick-draw training should not be undertaken until the more important types of shooting—aimed fire and combat firing—have been mastered. Incidents calling for the quick-draw are relatively infrequent, but they have occurred often enough to justify the training of selected individuals—those who are likely, by the nature of their assignments, to have to start hand gun shooting by drawing the weapon from its carrying position.

The amount of emphasis placed on the quick-draw varies greatly in the thousands of police and military organizations. In some instances, it is neglected entirely; in others it is given too much time and emphasis in a limited training program. It is difficult to determine just where and when this specialized type of training should be initiated, and exactly what type of officer should receive it. Generally, plainclothes law enforcement officers are the ones who are most likely to need skill and training in quick-draw. Situations in which they become involved more frequently require speed. The uniformed officer also will occasionally encounter some situations in which he should make a quick draw.

Holsters. Uniformed police normally carry their sidearms in holsters that are not designed to facilitate quick-draw. Safety straps are used to prevent accidental loss of the weapon, or a

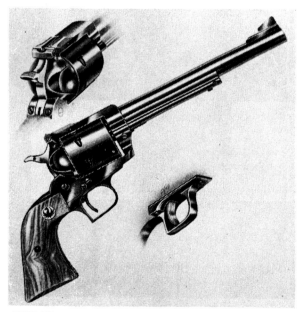

RUGER .44 SUPER BLACKHAWK REVOLVER

This modern single action type revolver is one of the finest produced. It is available in 6½ barrel lengths and longer. Many Western peace officers still prefer to carry single action hand guns of this and the Colt Frontier cal. .45 type. Their longer range and greater potential accuracy, combined with great shocking power, make them preferred.

QUICK-DRAW FROM THE CONVENTIONAL HOLSTER

After the weapon is grasped it must be lifted enough to clear the barrel from the holster. At the left is shown the wrong way to do this. Note the hunched shoulder and the elbow way out from the body. As shown at the right, the draw is much easier because the elbow is well in toward the body. The lifting of the gun is accomplished by bending the elbow instead of lifting the shoulder. More speed and greater ease in drawing and firing will result by observing this fundamental principle.

flap holster completely covers the butt. An increasing number of police departments now issue holsters which are designed to fulfill the two most important requirements: first, a holster that will protect and safely carry the weapon; and, second, a holster so designed that the officer can get his gun into action quickly and easily. The needs of each police department, and the viewpoint of officials in charge of equipment and training, will usually determine what type of holster is carried and how much emphasis is given to quick-draw training.

By practice, it is possible to become proficient in the quick-draw, even with a hand gun scabbard not basically designed for that purpose—but it is more difficult.

COMPLETING THE QUICK-DRAW

The quick-draw s h o u l d be finished by raising the weapon to the eye level, then firing. Greater accuracy will result than when firing from the hip level. The short time lost in raising the weapon high will be more than compensated for by greater ac- curacy. To the man who has been trained in the instinctive pointing technique this will come naturally.

Safety Speed or Clam Shell Type Outside Holster. This holster is now available for the Standard .45 Colt automatic, the Super .38 Colt automatic, and standard police models of Smith & Wesson and Colt revolvers.

It is built on a base of light steel and is covered with high quality leather. It weighs only slightly more than the con- ventional all-leather type. The difference in weight is not noticeable when it is attached to the belt. At the present time it is replacing the older type holsters in many uniformed state and city police organizations. It is also being tested and studied for possible adoption by the United States Armed Forces and by the military departments of many Latin-American countries.

This holster is spring activated; it "splits open from the front." Many additional advantages make it superior to the conventional types of holsters. It must be seen and tested to be fully appreciated.

Quick-Draw—with the clam shell holsters. After a few min- utes practice, the average shooter is able to draw his weapon from his holster and get off his first shot—with revolver or

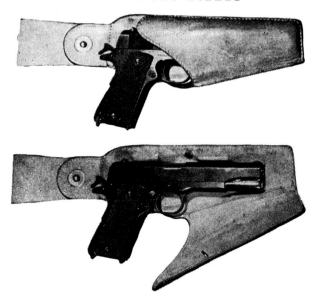

SAFETY SPEED, OR CLAM SHELL, OUTSIDE HOLSTER

At the top is shown the Colt automatic, cocked but not on safety. Below, the open holster is shown, after the release in front of the trigger has been pressed.

automatic—in about half the time it would take from a holster of the conventional type. In the old standard type holster, now generally in use, two motions are necessary to draw and fire. The first motion draws the gun up and out of the holster; and the second points and extends the gun to the firing position. With the new type holster it is not necessary to draw the gun up and out. The holster permits the gun to be raised and fired from the original holster position, in the same way a person would raise and point his finger at an object.

By its design and construction, the holster aids in the technique of combat hand-gun shooting that was used by the United States and Allied forces during World War II. This method of firing was based on the gun being carried in the hand of the shooter in a barrel downward position. Firing was done by raising the gun and arm to eye level and firing. The same type of combat shooting from the holster position is now possible.

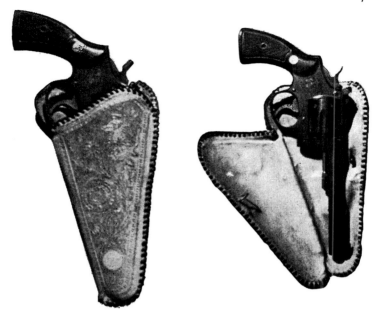

SAFETY SPEED, OR CLAM SHELL, OUTSIDE HOLSTER

At left is the Smith & Wesson target revolver, in the holster. It is locked in position but is available for instant drawing and firing.

At right is shown the open holster after the release has been pressed. Notice how the high, square-type, target front sight is kept from contact with the leather lining.

With the new holster, the Super .38 and .45 Colt automatics are immediately in firing position. They can be carried cocked and *not* on safety with perfect protection and security. A metal prong on each side of the cocked hammer prevents accidental discharge while in the holster. When the weapon is drawn it can be fired instantly without having to release the safety or cock it, or without having to pull back the slide, as is the case when the gun is carried in the standard holster. This feature alone makes it superior to any other type of automatic holster. The shooter who carries a Colt automatic, can now do so safely and will be able to get his gun into action immediately, with no extra movements. In speed of drawing and firing, this puts him on an equal basis with the shooter who carries a double action revolver. It eliminates one of the biggest objections to the police use of the Colt, or

TYPES OF HOLSTERS

At the upper left is shown a good basic-type, quick-draw holster. It is made of heavy, stiff leather that will not bind at the time of draw. Notice how it tilts forward to facilitate the draw. The trigger guard is exposed, to permit easy entry of the trigger finger. This style holster is favored by many plainclothes men.

The Myers Detective Special holster, shown upper right, is a good one. The gun hangs, butt down, and no encumbering shoulder straps are used.

Spring shoulder holsters, as shown below, and the Myers type, are much superior to the conventional under-arm type, where the gun is carried in the barrel-down, butt-up position. A quicker draw can be made, with the hands starting from a more natural and less suspicious position. In the conventional under-arm type, where the gun hangs barrel down, it is always necessary to start the draw by raising the hands high, so as to get them near the gun butt. This motion is a give-away to an alert enemy; it telegraphs the draw before it actually starts.

These holsters are very practical for use with a sport shirt of the type that is open at the bottom. Their design makes them ideal for use with the new small lightweight undercover revolvers such as the Centennial and the Chiefs Special.

most other makes of automatic pistols which lack the double action feature.

Safety. The holster securely locks the revolver, or automatic, in place. The gun cannot fall out of the holster or be snatched out by another person. It cannot be accidentally discharged. The weapon is released from the holster by pressing a concealed trigger on the inside of the trigger guard. The release mechanism is so placed that when the gun is grasped naturally for the draw, the holster trigger can be pressed by the trigger finger without any fumbling or additional motion. On the revolver-type holster, between the gun trigger and trigger guard, is a raised metal projection which prevents the revolver trigger being pulled or the weapon being fired while in the holster.

The objection raised against this holster—that anyone knowing the location of the special release that opens the holster could approach and easily steal the weapon—is without foundation. This same thing could be done just as easily when the person is wearing any other standard type of open holster. In fact, a person wearing this new holster will always know if his gun is being stolen. The noise and movement of the holster when it opens will tell him. With the old standard types, the gun could be stolen without the wearer knowing it.

Protection. The light steel metal base, with the leather lining inside and out, provides a protection for the hand gun that is superior to leather alone. In addition, an automatic or revolver equipped with target sights can be carried in and drawn from the holster without any damage to the sight, or to the leather of the holster. The holsters also are made to fit exactly the various models and sizes of Colt or Smith & Wesson revolvers, and the gun is so securely locked that no movement takes place in the holster. This also prevents the gun blue wearing off.

The uniformed law enforcement officer wearing this holster can draw his gun easily and fire while seated in a car. He cannot do this with most conventional types of holsters, because his elbow is against the back of the car seat and he is thus prevented from drawing his gun up and out until he changes his body position.

Faster speed of draw, and prevention of loss of the gun by its falling out, or by someone snatching it from the holster, has made the new type holster a favorite among uniformed state and municipal law officers in the United States.

THE CROSS DRAW

When carrying the holster on the left side (gun butt foremost), as advocated in some law enforcement departments, the cross draw should be made by grasping the gun and bringing it straight *out* and *up*—in a swing to eye level—as shown at the right. In the illustration at the left, the gun is drawn and the swing is made too far out to the side or too wide. This results in the gun being swung into action by a horizontal swing instead of a vertical one. Inaccuracy results, because it is difficult to stop the horizontal swing when the gun comes into line with the target.

TRAINING IN QUICK-DRAW

Quick-draw training is highly personalized and depends largely on the individual. He must have sufficient interest to practice on his own time. A departmental desire to improve this phase of pistol or revolver employment can be realized only by organizing quick-draw practice and competition, as is done on the target range.

To get men to practice the quick-draw—in the complete movement of pointing, drawing, and snapping the trigger—the following method has been used with success. Pair off

EXECUTING THE QUICK-DRAW

In the quick-draw from the hip holster, the method now practiced by most is to bend forward, then slap back the coat tail with the backward swing of the hand to the gun. The draw is then made and the shooting is done from the aggressive, forward crouch. This is the best and most instinctive shooting position for combat. The holster shown is the Clark, a spring type favored by many police officers and shooters.

trainees who will be working together for several hours. Have their weapons double-checked for safety. (It is best to fill the cylinders with wax and cut off the firing pin, or by some other means make it impossible for a live round to be fired in the weapon.) Let the trainees carry their guns in their holsters and proceed about other training in which they may be engaged. While they are proceeding with their duties, have one of them, when in contact with the other, give a previously arranged signal (such as "reach" or "draw") at an unexpected time. The student receiving the command will execute a quick draw, point his gun at the one who issues the command and pull the trigger. This gives the student the closest thing to actual combat drawing and firing that can be devised. The element of surprise—having to draw from any position and follow through with pointing the weapon; pulling the trigger as if an actual shot were fired—closely simulates the real thing. A similar quick-draw situation can be injected into the practical combat range training that is described in the chapter on ranges.

The actual quick-draw and firing of live ammunition should always be preceded by plenty of dry practice, which must be closely supervised. The speed of the draw should be slow at first, so that the initial grip on the weapon is correct and so that pull on the double action makes the hammer fall at the instant the gun is pointing properly. Quick draw can be learned properly only by starting at a slow tempo. Through practice, speed will increase; but, once the peak of speed for the individual is reached, it can only be sustained by frequent periods of practice.

Each shooter will learn the speed at which he can draw and fire his weapon most rapidly without losing control and accuracy. Thus, actual drawing and firing speed will vary with individuals; but the average, well-coordinated officer can make the complete movement of drawing and firing in a half second or less without having to devote excessive time to practice. Quicker draws can be made if the gun is fired from hip level after it leaves the holster. However, although it may take a fraction of a second longer, the ordinary shooter will be more accurate or will gain accuracy sooner if he raises the gun to eye level before firing. If he has been trained in instinctive pointing, as previously described, this will be a natural sequence to the draw.

Since the advent of televison with the very popular and numerous Western programs, the quick draw hobby has swept America. Special timing devices, special holsters, and special model weapons have been developed. Most of the quick draw techniques advocated are for use with the Western style (Colt Frontier) single action revolver. Quick draw clubs abound and quick draw competitions are being held throughout the country.

However, the weapon used and the style of holster and quick draw are more historic than practical for law enforcement officers. The principal benefit of this particular style of shooting to the man who carries his more modern type hand gun for professional purposes, is to emphasize the potential speed and possibilities of the quick draw which he may achieve *after extensive practice.* By the use of special timing devices incredible quick draw times have been recorded.

Position of Wearing Holster. As to the position in which the holster should be worn, that is entirely a matter of individual taste or departmental regulations. If you are working with the holster in the open, have it in a place which permits you to move freely, where the butt is easily grasped, and where it can be drawn with speed and fired without unnecessary delay. If it is a concealed holster, always bear in mind that it should be in such a place that, regardless of the type or state of your clothes, you can get at it with little delay and unnecessary movement. Once having chosen the spot for carrying a weapon, do not change. Practice drawing the gun a few minutes daily.

Reading References. Various techniques, types of draws, and holsters are well documented in books, such as those written some years ago by Ed McGivern *(Fast and Fancy Revolver Shooting)*, and by Fitzgerald *(Shooting)*. A very fine coverage of the subject has also just been written by Chic Gaylord *(Handgunner's Guide)*. This new book gives a complete and current treatment of guns, holsters, and quick draw methods. Any serious student or instructor, in this phase of shooting, will do well to use these books for reference. The above texts also will furnish adequate authentic information on holsters. Individuals and firms such as Heiser, George Lawrence, Myers, and Gaylord can make and furnish almost any type holster to fit any gun, individual, or situation. Their products are well known. Information concerning them can be obtained from any large sporting goods dealer. A holster should be made of the best leather. A cheap holster of flimsy, lightweight construction, may cause the gun to stick when a draw is attempted.

LOOK AND LEARN

The pictures on this and the preceding page show features in an object lesson training course in combat shooting during World War II.

Chapter 6

COMBAT FIRING WITH SHOULDER WEAPONS

THE actual combat life of the soldier or police officer who may carry a shoulder weapon is often measured in seconds—split seconds. In close-quarter combat, or in-fighting, he must be able to use this weapon quickly, accurately and instinctively. Close-quarter firing, in the case of shoulder weapons, is presumed to be any combat situation where the enemy is not over 30 yards distant and the elements of time, surprise, poor light and individual nervous and physical tension are present.

In street and jungle fighting and in police work, the opportunities for skilled, close-quarter work with the rifle, riot gun, carbine and submachinegun are becoming increasingly frequent. It follows, then, that a method of shooting these weapons so that they can be brought into action with the least possible delay should be emphasized in training.

The aimed shot always should be made when the *time* and *light* permit. However, in close-quarter fighting there is not always sufficient time to raise the weapon to the shoulder, line up the sights and squeeze off the shot. Consequently, training only in the aimed type of rifle fire does not completely equip the man who carries a shoulder weapon for all the exigencies of combat. As in combat shooting with the hand gun, he should be trained in a method in which he can use a shoulder weapon quickly and instinctively and without sights.

Some authorities attribute the failure of certain known target-shooting experts to hit an enemy who is shooting at them at close quarters entirely to a lack of the fighting instinct. The real reason usually is that the target expert has not received the most effective type of training. A lack of moral qualifications, guts, and courage will always contribute to poor close-quarter rifle or hand gun shooting, but lack of combat training is the principal cause. It should be evident enough to most shooters that the formalized techniques learned on the rifle range cannot always be applied 100 percent in battle.

Rifle marksmanship training teaches the correct use of the sights and the aimed shot. These principles are correct when time and light are present, so that the rifle, carbine, riot gun and submachinegun can be used in combat as on the range. However, dark alleys and streets, night raids, poor visibility, and street and house fighting—all create combat situations where the opportunity for the aimed shot will not always be present. The soldier or law enforcement officer must be able to shoot a shoulder weapon in these situations *without taking time to sight*. First hits are the ones that count.

SNAP SHOOTING

There are two methods of close-combat firing with shoulder weapons by which satisfactory man-hitting accuracy can be achieved. The first is called *snap shooting*, the other *instinctive pointing*. Snap shooting is a technique of weapon pointing in which a great amount of practice is needed to achieve individual proficiency. As in skeet shooting, the butt of the weapon must be snapped to the shoulder prior to firing, and the firing must occur at almost the exact instant that the butt of the piece comes to rest. The construction, balance, weight, mechanical characteristics and general design of various shoulder weapons differ greatly, and these variations affect their "snapping" qualities. A carbine is more adaptable to this type of shooting than a larger rifle. Submachine guns, such as the Thompson, are much less adaptable, because of their design, balance and weight. The snapping technique takes a great deal of practice and must be largely self-taught. It follows, therefore, that it is not adaptable to the training of large groups. Comparatively few men have been adequately trained in it.

For those individuals with the time and interest to devote to the instinctive type of shoulder or snap shooting, a very interesting and effective new training system has been developed by B. L. McDaniel, which is clearly described in his book *Instinctive Shooting* (Dodd, Mead & Company, New York).

A special practice kit, built around the use of a Daisy air rifle, under the trade name "Lucky McDaniel Instinct Shooting Trainer Outfit," is now commercially available. The basic idea of the system and kit is to develop with a rifle the proficiency and ability *instinctively* to hit small, moving, aerial targets without the use of conventional sights. It follows that this system once mastered would naturally be directly related to the use of more deadly shoulder weapons in combat.

INSTINCTIVE POINTING

Instinctive pointing, sometimes called *hip-shooting* or *body-pointing*, is the best method of shooting shoulder weapons in close-quarter combat, when the time or light element is not great enough to permit the conventional use of the weapon from the shoulder position. Reports from recent combat theaters continually refer to hip-shooting in close-quarter fighting. In World War II, the Allies trained their men intensively to use instinctive pointing when they reached the combat theaters. It is an effective method of combat shooting and its principles should be understood by all shooters, civilian and military, who are likely to engage in close-quarter combat.

This style of shooting, which can be mastered in a relatively short training period, is adaptable to all military and sporting rifles, and to shotguns and light automatic weapons, such as the M3, Thompson and Reising submachineguns. With these or comparable weapons, a man-killing single shot or burst can be fired. Instinctive pointing is not an indiscriminate spraying of lead in the general direction of the enemy, as some of its critics have declared.

Instinctive Pointing Technique. To fire a rifle, or any of the shoulder weapons mentioned above, by instinctive pointing is simple. The body is used to do the actual pointing of the weapon. The barrel is so placed and held that the muzzle and the eyes are in the same perpendicular plane. As long as the relationship of barrel and eyes is kept the same, the shooter will hit where he looks and his body points. He may not be able to hit a 4-inch bull's-eye at 20 yards, but he will be able to hit the center area of a man-sized silhouette. Changes in direction of fire are made by shifting the feet so that the body points at the target.

The position and technique which the shooter (right-handed) should practice are the same as those under which he would use the hand gun. The body should be in a forward aggressive crouch, the feet in a natural position, and the

INSTINCTIVE POINTING TECHNIQUE—FRONT VIEW

This is how the gun looks from the front when the instinctive pointing technique is used. Note that the muzzle is in line with the eyes. The
shooter will hit where he looks so long as the gun is kept in this relationship to the eyes and the body center.

POSITION FOR CLOSE COMBAT FIRING

At the left is shown the correct position for close combat firing of the shoulder weapon. The butt rests on the hip, elbow tight against the stock. The grip of both hands is convulsive. The barrel is horizontal and parallel to the ground. The body does all the pointing of the weapon, which is never swung independently by the arms. Changes in body position, using the feet, will enable the shooter to hit where he looks and in the direction in which his body is pointing. At the right is shown an alternate position favored by some shooters. The stock of the weapon is in the armpit instead of on the hip. Other shooting principles are the same.

weapon gripped very tightly. The butt of the piece should be pressed firmly against the right side of the body just above the hip bone and should be held there by the elbow and right forearm, which should be pressing in toward the side. The grips of both hands on the stock and forearm of the weapon should be tight. In the case of the shotgun, submachinegun, or rifle, the forearm of the piece should be lying flat in the palm of the left hand, the elbow of the left arm swung in as far toward body center as is comfortable. In this position, the eyes, the muzzle, and the belt buckle are about in the same vertical plane. From this position, the gun is automatically in line, so far as windage is concerned. As long as the barrel of the piece is maintained in the same eye-body-center relationship, the shooter will hit where he looks.

There will be no need to look at the gun while firing,

SUBMACHINEGUN HELD INCORRECTLY

Canting to the side causes the gun to shoot high and to the side.   Submachinegun is not held in line with body center or eyes.

and the direction in which the body is pointing and the eyes are looking should be the same. Generally, the barrel of the weapon should be parallel with the ground. With a little practice, elevation can be controlled for targets up to 30 yards. This position can be taken with any shoulder-fired weapon, slight modifications being necessary in the case of some submachineguns, for example, where the left hand grasps the magazine housing instead of the forearm. The M-3, Thompson and the Reising submachineguns can be fired by instinctive pointing with the stock collapsed or detached, by placing the end of the bolt housing in the middle of the body and resting both elbows firmly against the sides of the body.

Alternate Position. There is one alternative butt position which should be mentioned. All principles are the same except that the shooter crouches even more over his weapon. His head is lowered until his line of vision is on a plane about 10 or 12 inches above the barrel. The butt of the weapon is placed under the pit of the arm instead of resting above the hip bone, as in the first method. This position has the advantage of bringing the eyes closer to the line of fire of the weapon. Consequently some shooters, whose physiques are best adapted to this style, can fire with more initial accuracy.

Some instructors have advocated placing the butt of the piece in the center of the stomach instead of on the hip. This position will give accuracy but it is not a natural one. It is difficult to assume correctly when in combat and carrying full equipment. It is particularly difficult to place the butt of the weapon in exactly the same place in the body center every time, since it must be placed there quickly.

Foot and Body Positions. The stance should be a natural one. The feet should be placed so that a forward step can be easily taken, since the weapon may be fired either from a stationary position or while moving. Unnatural foot positions and set stances, such as a straddle-trench position, should be avoided in practice, because they will be hard to assume in combat. Changes in body direction, in order to shoot at angle targets, should be made by changing the position of the feet. Pivoting should be done in any manner which comes instinctively. No rigid set foot position should be forced upon the shooter in practice, and when firing at angle targets he should be allowed to change the position of his feet naturally. If he is unable to move his feet, he still can get accuracy by twisting his body for gun pointing. As with the hand gun, jumping to change body direction is not advisable.

The normal "ready," or carrying position, of a rifleman who expects to use his weapon at any time, lends itself to quick adoption of the instinctive pointing type of firing. Most shooters carry their weapons in some degree of a port position or with the butt of the piece near the hip; consequently the assumption of the proper position for hip shooting is simple and fast.

TRAINING METHODS

After the instructor presents the need for instinctive pointing and outlines situations in which it will be used, the shooter should be given a weapon and taught to assume the correct basic firing position. This can be done by either the coach-pupil method or the use of a full-length mirror in which the student can check himself.

After he has learned to assume the correct firing position, the student should be made to advance toward the mirror, or toward the coach, with his gun in the correct firing position. This is important, because shooting of this type is strictly offensive. The aggressive spirit must be further developed by having the shooter go in toward his target as he fires. He should be told that he can be hit just as easily going back from a bullet as he can if he were standing still or advancing. While advancing with the weapon in the firing position, the shooter should be checked to see that he moves forward in his crouch, without bobbing as he takes his steps. Most shooters will advance naturally, with the barrel of the weapon held steadily on the same plane, but a few have a habit of bouncing up and down by bending at the knees as they walk. This must be corrected at the outset.

The next step in training should be dry firing at angle targets. The shooter must be watched to see that there is no independent swinging of the arms when changing direction of fire. For this type of training, silhouette targets can be placed to the right and left flanks of the shooter, and he can be directed to wheel and fire at these flank targets, on verbal commands of the instructor. Jumping, to change body direction, should not be permitted.

After the dry work has been completed, the initial firing should be done at a range not exceeding 20 feet against a silhouette target on a paper background, or against a stake target placed in a dirt bank so that the shots can be observed.

To be able to observe the impact points of bullets is particularly important in the early phases of actual firing, so that correct elevation and windage can be learned faster. After the shooter is able to place his shots in the center area of a 3/4 silhouette, he can be permitted to shoot at frontal targets from greater ranges. Ordinarily these ranges should not exceed 30 yards, although accuracy at greater distances can be achieved through practice. After proficiency has been achieved, the shooter should then be made to face at a right or left angle from silhouette targets, wheeling and firing at the targets on verbal commands from the coach. Here again the range can be increased as accuracy and proficiency grow.

The shooter is now ready for advanced work, and all types of practical shooting conditions can be devised. He can be made to advance toward a stationary silhouette over all types of rubble and debris, firing as he goes in. In all cases, his eyes should be on the target. Bobbing targets and other surprise targets should be used in this training period. Courses can be laid out over various types of terrain, with silhouettes hidden at various angles to the path of the shooter, so that

COMBAT SLING CARRY

Assuming the firing position from the combat sling carry.

he is forced to fire at angles and at targets above and below the horizontal.

The ability to do this type of shooting is a prerequisite for the infantry soldier on the battlefield and for the police officer in the performance of many of his combat missions. It is not intended to be a complete substitute for the conventional type of aimed fire, but rather a method of shooting wherein the kill can be made when time and other conditions are lacking for the more deliberate type of aimed shooting.

Combat Sling Carry. At times, a shooter has been unable to get a shot at a target of opportunity because he could not get his riot gun, or rifle, into action in time from the customary carrying position on the shoulder.

When rifle, carbine, submachinegun, or riot gun is carried in the conventionally slung manner, barrel up behind the right shoulder, it is difficult to bring the weapon into action smoothly. It can be done, but it takes an excessive amount of practice. The method portrayed here is a simple, easily-learned sling carry for use in combat and hunting. It is a good addition to the bag of tricks of any shooter.

It has the following advantages:

(1) The muzzle of the piece is down; therefore rain, snow

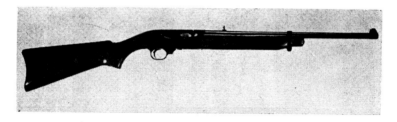

RUGER .44 MAGNUM CALIBER CARBINE

This new semi-automatic carbine is gas operated and weighs less than six pounds. It has a capacity of five rounds when one is carried in the chamber. The gun was originally designed as a short-range powerful brush gun for deer hunters. Police agencies often need a good powerful short-range rifle for special action and emergencies. One of the big objections to the higher powered rifles such as the 30/06 has been that the muzzle velocity and the range were too great, especially when used in crowded urban areas where danger exists of hitting an innocent bystander well removed from the scene of action. Many officers carry from choice the powerful .44 magnum revolver and the new Ruger carbine in the same caliber should be a welcome addition to police armament.

REISING SUBMACHINE GUN MODEL 50 CAL. .45

This is a well-known police and military arm. It has been in production since World War II and is still commercially available. It has a cyclic rate of 500-550 rounds per minute. It can be fired either on semi- or full automatic. Magazine capacity is 12. This gun can be used with the sights with accuracy due to its stock design.

and other types of foreign matter are prevented from entering the bore.

(2) The muzzle of the piece does not extend above the shoulder. It is easier for the carrier to make his way through dense undergrowth without having the weapon catch in branches.

(3) The shoulder weapon carried in this manner conforms to the shape of the body and, by placing the hand on the forearm, the weapon can be carried with more comfort and is in a faster ready position than when carried by the conventional method.

(4) After a short period of practice, the average person can take a slung weapon from this position and bring it into action for a shot faster and more accurately than the ordinary man can draw a pistol or revolver from his holster and fire it.

(5) It provides an alternative to the customary sling-carrying position when the shoulder tires.

Chapter 7

DISARMING

A STUDY of this chapter will enable the soldier and law enforcement officer to handle most of those situations in which he finds himself held at the point of a gun. By proper training and practice in disarming, skill and self-confidence can be developed to a point where the student will become master of any situation in which he is confronted by a gun pointed at him by an enemy who is within arm's length.

Disarming has already been taught, in one form or another, to many men in the military, police, and civil defense services. If disarming and its possibilities are understood more thoroughly it will be given greater emphasis in future training programs.

There are many cases on record in which prisoners of war and criminals have escaped, killed, or seriously injured men who were holding them at gun-point. On the other hand, many military and police organizations have cases on record in which their own men have successfully disarmed armed individuals.

Disarming is a technique that can be successfully used by trained men. Recent military history contains numerous examples of successful disarming. It is a subject which cannot be presented cold to trainees, but requires proper indoctrination and training. If a method of disarming is presented without a proper introduction, the chances are that the pupil will practice it only half-heartedly and will never have the confidence *really* to use it when an opportunity presents itself. The factors which influence disarming must be fully explained before a man can evaluate his chances of success in any given technique.

A study of the numerous techniques being taught in the armed services and police schools indicates that most methods of disarming are not introduced properly. The methods advocated by different instructors are usually too complicated for easy performance and demand too much practice before efficiency and self-confidence can be gained.

The methods presented here have stood the test of actual combat. They come from experience gained during the study and intensive training of several thousand men. The average individual can use them successfully if he understands the basic principles and has had a moderate amount of training and practice. These techniques succeed principally because they are simple.

TYPES OF DISARMING TECHNIQUES

There are two general types of disarming techniques. Both advocate the removal of the weapon from the body area as the first move. The more successful advocates an instant follow-up body attack on the gun wielder. The other one, too generally advocated by law enforcement officers, concentrates on wresting the gun from the hold-up man. If this succeeds, it still is necessary to subdue him before he can be brought in under arrest. How he is to be subdued seems to be left entirely up to the individual. In this type of disarming, there are too many possibilities of something going wrong. What starts out to be a scientific disarming trick can easily turn into just another struggle for a dangerous weapon. *All disarming methods which involve handling and wresting the gun away, while it is still between the bodies of the gunman and his victim, are too dangerous to use.*

The gunman who points a gun at anyone is "asking for it" and should receive rough treatment. Because of this, the student should be trained to disarm and incapacitate at the same time. If disarming is taught and advocated in a police department, it should be a type that will give the officer confidence in its use; and it should be efficient enough to discourage like attempts in the future, by the same or other criminals.

At the best, the disarming of a man who holds a loaded firearm involves a certain amount of risk. If this risk can be calculated, and if the person held at gun point realizes that he has a good chance of success, he will undertake to disarm his opponent. If it has been shown in practice that he can do an effective job without too much personal risk, by a method he has proved to himself during his training, there is a much greater likelihood that he will disarm an enemy if he is given the opportunity. He will also apply himself to practice much more assiduously. *After all, when a man holds a loaded gun at your stomach and you are going to start an action to disarm him, you start something that must be finished, the sooner the better.* Disarming in actual practice is a very personal matter and one that must be undertaken by a person who has confidence in himself and his skill.

No two situations will be exactly alike. Differences in size and temperament of the individuals concerned, light, terrain and other circumstances surrounding the scene of action will cause variations in when and where to initiate a disarming action. It is entirely up to the man with his hands in the air to decide when disarming shall be started.

Some techniques call for a person to initiate a disarming action at the very instant that he is told to put his hands in the air. Such methods advocate disarming with the hands down at the sides. Although there are a few men who might have the skill and the instant reflexes necessary to do this successfully, it is not for the average man to attempt to disarm a man with a loaded weapon in this manner, or at this time. It is much too dangerous and demands an excessive amount of practice in order to achieve only a fair chance of success.

Other disarming tactics are presented with the idea that, if the gunman is armed with a certain type weapon, a specific disarming method must be used. It is easy to see that to recommend the use of a different technique for each of the various types of weapons soon ends in endless complications and results in confusion to the person who is expected to go out and actually to disarm a dangerous man. For example, a double action revolver that is not cocked can be immobilized by grasping the cylinder and preventing it from turning. This technique is all right when used in conjunction with another disarming method, but should not alone be depended upon against a dangerous gunman. Likewise, a .45 cal. automatic can sometimes be immobilized by pressing the hand or stomach against the muzzle so that the slide is pushed back; but again, none but the most foolhardy would attempt this in an actual situation. Not only is the element of chance too great in depending on this type of disarming, but poor light, heavy clothing, gloves, and such would prevent success. A simple disarming technique that can be used against all weapons in all normal situations is much to be preferred.

BASIC PRINCIPLES

When a gunman uses his weapon to hold up another individual he is unknowingly placing himself in a defensive frame of mind and a defensive situation. It is perfectly obvious that he does not wish to shoot; otherwise he would already have done so. The reason restraining him in a simple robbery, for example, is fear of the law and its consequences. The mere fact that he has not fired his weapon indicates that he does not desire to do so. This gives the man with his hands in the air a psychological advantage, if he recognizes it as such, which he may use at the proper time.

We are assuming, at this point, that the average disarming situation encountered by the soldier or the police officer will be one in which he is faced by a lone gunman. There are methods by which a single man might be able to disarm more than one person at a time, but generally they should be used only in extremely desperate situations or by an extremely skilled man. In any case, a very careful evaluation of the chances of success must be made before attempting such a feat. Several practical methods of securing a weapon, for use against its former possessor, will be discussed later; but they are advocated only for specific situations.

Another assumption is that the gunman will be holding his weapon within arm's length of his victim. If he is not doing so at the period of initial contact, he can often be enticed within disarming range by certain strategems. It is only when the gun, or the gunman, is within arm's reach of the victim that most disarming should be undertaken. Usually the gunman will undertake his "stick up" at close quarters, because he wants to emphasize the presence of the weapon in his hand and its authority. The gun muzzle is often placed against the victim's stomach or back. However, if the gunman initially keeps himself and his weapon out of arm's reach, he can often be forced to close in by reacting to his orders too slowly, or by pretending fright or indecision. When the hold-up victim acts in this manner, the gun wielder will often close in, so as to re-emphasize the gun and his authority with it. If robbery or disarming is the motive of the gunman who works alone, he will be forced eventually to come close in order to operate.

With the exception of those who are aware of the special training in disarming given during the recent emergency, most criminals are ignorant of the practicability of disarming and will keep their weapons close to their victims. The average gunman feels that the mere presence of the weapon in his hand will be enough to discourage any opposition. It is a well recognized fact in law enforcement that, were it not for the possession of a firearm, the average criminal would not attempt many of his more violent crimes. The gun is a prop which he must have to commit his crime. If it were gone, he would not attempt the crime. He knows how helpless he would be if it were not for the weapon in his hand, and therefore thinks that his victim should feel and act the same way. Consequently, his complete reliance on his gun and its efficacy makes him more susceptible to surprise attack and actual disarming.

When the command "hands up" is given, the gunman experiences a period of tenseness, during which he is keyed up for possible resistance to his command. This period of initial contact with his victim finds him more alert and trigger conscious. At this time it is not advisable to start any disarming action, since he is more dangerous and less susceptible to surprise attack than he will be later. This is the principal reason why disarming techniques, which start with the hands at the sides and are initiated at the moment of the "hands up" command, are not advisable.

One of the oldest "gags" in the movies is for the victim to say, to a fictitious individual supposedly standing behind the man with the gun, "Don't shoot, Joe." In the movies, the gunman turns to encounter the fictitious character and the hero immediately jumps upon him and disarms him. This, to use a slang expression, is "corny." However, old though it is, in many cases a slow-witted individual may fall for it. One variation, which has been used with success against more intelligent individuals is this: Cast an obvious glance behind your attacker, as though you saw someone approaching from his rear; then as quickly return your glance to him, making no comment. Although he may suspect a trick, he still will be uneasy because a doubt has been created in his mind. He begins to think that it would be entirely possible for another person to come up behind him, and that you are too smart to say anything about it. When possible, a hold-up victim should attempt to keep the thoughts of the gunman on something other than his gun before initiating the disarming action. If he can get the gunman to talk by asking him questions, or by volunteering information, his mind can be distracted and the stage can be set for disarming.

Considering all these factors, which help to lay the ground work for physical disarming, remember that the element of surprise is still the biggest single factor in success. The man with his gun trained upon you may consider the possibility of your trying to escape or of your trying to disarm him, if you are desperate enough; but the longer you wait before attempting your attack, the less paramount this consideration is in his mind, and the more careless he becomes.

By the very nature of the situation, the individual with his hands in the air has an advantage he can and must use. Usually he *can pick the time and stage for his disarming action*. The man with the gun cannot anticipate it, if no give-away indications are made.

TRAINING PROCEDURES

Before going into a detailed discussion of various disarming methods, it is well to consider the conditions under which they must be practiced. The element of uncertainty in an individual's mind, when practicing disarming, must be reduced to the lowest possible point before confidence will develop. All the demonstrations and lectures in the world will not enable a person actually to perform disarming unless he has practiced it in circumstances as close to the real thing as possible. Unless proper training indoctrination is given by the instructor, covering such material as presented above, much time and effort can be wasted.

Practice must be realistic and real weapons must be used. These practice weapons may be loaded with blanks for the more advanced trainee, but, at the very least, they must be in such good condition that the hammer will fall when the trigger is pulled. Most police departments have on hand numbers of cheap weapons which have been confiscated from criminals. They are ideal for this purpose. By sawing off the firing pins and plugging the cylinders or barrels, the safety factor can be increased without reducing the realism. With most of these weapons, it is advisable to saw off the front of the trigger guard, so as to prevent broken fingers during practice, and to cut off any front or back sight blades that may cause cuts or scratches during practice.

Position for Disarming. Disarming with firearms should be practiced with hands upraised, so that the elbows are not be-

**INCORRECT DISARMING
POSITION**

The elbows should not be held
below shoulder height when practicing. Here is shown the improper
position from which to initiate
disarming because, in most cases,
to lower the arms in this manner
would arouse suspicion.

low shoulder height. All disarming methods can be successfully undertaken from this arm position. Although a prisoner
may be allowed, by some gunmen, to let his elbows drop almost to his sides, he may as well practice from the higher
arm position, especially since he probably won't be able to
lower his arms without creating suspicion. The position of
the hands clasped behind the head, as in handling prisoners
of war, may also be used in practice.

Anticipating Movement. The element of surprise is difficult
to achieve in practice, because the man with the gun knows
when you are going to disarm. Anticipation on the part of
the holder of the weapon must be constantly watched and
checked. It can usually be detected: (1) when, at the slightest movement of the man whose hands are in the air, the trigger is pulled. This is not natural and would not occur in
actual disarming; and (2) when, at the slightest movement of
the trunk of the body, the man holding the gun turns the
barrel to follow the movement. This means that he is anticipating, because the holder of the gun, under ordinary circumstances, cannot think fast enough to follow the movement of the body with his gun. He will pull the trigger while

the weapon is still pointing in its original direction; he will not be able to think fast enough to move the gun barrel, following the changes in the position of the opponent, before he pulls the trigger.

In practice, any devices which will enable the student to evolve surprise in his disarming attempts will make him progress that much faster. Unless checked at the outset, the anticipation by the man with the gun will cause the student to lose confidence, and he will not get the full benefit of his practice. If the instructor can't break the person who holds the gun of the anticipation habit, it is best to replace him with another man.

The instructor must watch for evidence of anticipation very carefully and check it at once. It is best to explain to the entire class all the factors involved. Ask the students holding the guns to pull the triggers at the first indication of disarming movement by the victim, but to be sure that they do not try to follow any slight changes in body direction of their opponent by moving the gun barrel before pulling the trigger. This is especially important during the body twist demonstration and practice, which will be described later.

Looking the Gunman in the Eye. In all cases, in practice and in actual disarming, the man with his hands in the air should look the gunman in the eye and keep his eyes off the weapon which is threatening him. This is especially true just prior to initiating any disarming. The body should be kept relaxed, and tensing of muscles prior to any offensive action should be avoided. Many times it is so evident that it acts as a giveaway to the gunman. If possible, the action should be initiated when the gunman's eyes and mind are on something else besides the weapon in his hand.

A difficulty that is often encountered, preceding actual participation in disarming practice, is that, once the introductory instruction is completed, many students immediately become "wise guys"; they fail to hold the gun within arm's reach during practice. This is a natural reaction. It can be largely overcome by the instructor as follows: At the outset, before any introduction or discussion, give half the students guns, pair them off and instruct them to "stick up" their partners. It will usually be found that most of the stick-ups will take place with the gun within arm's reach of the victim. Call the attention of the class to this point; then proceed with the introductory material.

The Trigger Reaction Demonstration. It is only natural that any one participating in disarming instruction will doubt his ability to accomplish disarming fast enough to beat the man who pulls the trigger. Naturally, the first move in any disarming method *is to remove the weapon from the body area* so that, even if a shot is fired, it will cause no injury. But before this first move, the student must prove to his own satisfaction, in practice, the following point: HE CAN MOVE HIS BODY OUT OF THE LINE OF FIRE BEFORE THE GUNMAN CAN THINK TO PULL THE TRIGGER. A small amount of time elapses between the instant the gunman's brain orders the pulling of the trigger, and the instant when it is actually pulled. This time, while the mind is telegraphing its message to the finger to pull the trigger, is sufficient to enable a man to move his body away from the weapon's muzzle, or, as he actually will do later, to knock the gun away from the body area before the hammer falls.

This is the first and most important phase of instruction. It is the basic principle around which all successful disarming techniques must be developed. Without actual knowledge of this fact and the consequent confidence in his ability to beat the man with the gun, the average individual will seldom undertake to disarm a real gunman.

Demonstrate, then let the student practice, the following procedure: Stand facing the class; then have a student press a cocked gun, or double action revolver, against your back. Instruct the man with the gun to pull the trigger the instant he detects any movement of your body away from it. Place your hands in the air and keep them there. Explain to the class that this is only a demonstration of the slowness of the gunman's trigger reaction and that the hands will not be used at this time, as they will be later in the instruction on actual disarming. Execute a body twist, so that the trunk of the body is bent away from the gun muzzle. The twist can be done to the left or right, whichever is easier. In doing the twist, keep the feet in place, flex one knee a great deal, and let the other knee remain almost straight. When this is done, the body will be turned sideways enough so that the muzzle of the gun is pointing past it, not at it. If the gunman pulls the trigger at the first sign of movement and does not follow the body by turning the gun wrist, *he will always pull the*

TRIGGER REACTION DEMONSTRATION

Face the class, with the gunman holding the weapon pressed against your back, as at the left. Tell him to pull the trigger the moment your body moves. Execute a body twist by keeping the feet in place and flexing the right knee a great deal, and by keeping the left knee almost straight, as at the right. The muzzle of the gun will then be pointing *past* the body when the trigger is pulled. Note the position of the revolver muzzle in relation to your body.

trigger after the body is out of line of fire, even though he is expecting the movement.

After the demonstration has been successfully executed from the rear, do the same thing from the front. Place the students behind your back and let the opponent press the gun muzzle against your stomach. Point out to the class that, even though the man with the gun knows fully what is going to take place, he still cannot think fast enough to pull the trigger and register a hit. In other words, even without the element of surprise, the body can be moved away from the muzzle area. In a like manner, the weapon can be knocked away in actual disarming. It should be emphasized at this point that, if it is possible to keep from being shot and to disarm a gunman when he is expecting you to do something (as in practice), it will be 50 percent easier to do the same thing when the element of surprise is on your side. The gunman's reactions, and the thought processes necessary to pull the trigger, will be considerably slowed when he is surprised.

At this point the same demonstration should be performed by each pair of students.

Let the student practice front and rear until he is satisfied in his own mind that he is actually clearing himself from the bullet's path. Even a slow body twist is fast enough to prevent a serious wound; a crease will be the only result. Although the body twist is used in all disarming, both front and rear, in reality it is not a separate movement of the body. It occurs naturally in conjunction with the downward sweep of the hands in the actual disarming.

Any disarming method or technique will not be successful, from the standpoint of the student having enough confidence to use it, unless he is satisfied in his own mind about his speed of movement and chances of success. This can be proved by the body twist demonstration.

The arms and hands have as yet had no place in the disarming procedure. It is well to emphasize again that the purpose of the body-twist trigger-reaction demonstration is merely to prove to the individual that he actually can move his body out of the path of the bullet faster than the trigger man can think to fire his weapon.

Use of Arms and Hands. After the body-twist demonstration has been practiced, so that each individual has achieved proficiency, the arms and hands can be brought into use. With the gunman facing the student and having the gun within arm's reach, have the man with his hands in the air slap the gun away from his body area; or have him strike the inside of the wrist of his opponent's gun hand, using the flat of the hand to knock the gun away from his body. Again the student will find that he can actually knock the gun away from his body area before the weapon is fired. He must, of course, observe the simple rules, such as looking his opponent in the eye.

METHODS OF DISARMING

Following practice and proficiency in this first procedure, the following disarming methods can be introduced and practiced. Knowledge and proficiency in the execution of these two techniques are all that is necessary to handle *all disarming situations in which the gun hand is within arm's reach of the hold-up victim.* They are effective, regardless of the type of weapon used by the gunman, and they can be used in all normal circumstances by the average individual. They are designed for use primarily against persons armed with hand guns; but only slight variations are necessary to make them equally effective against shoulder weapons.

Frontal Disarming (Hand Gun). *First step.* Facing the gunman with your hands in the air, look him in the eye, be relaxed, and use surprise if possible.

Second step. Swing the arm, which is on the same side as the opponent's gun hand, down *forcefully*, so that an edge-of-the-hand blow is delivered against the inside of his gun wrist. Let the force of the blow and the downward swing of your arm carry the gun as far out to the side as possible.

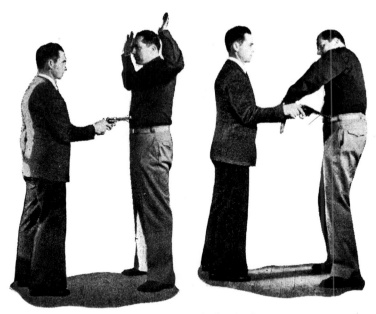

FRONTAL DISARMING

Face the gunman with your body relaxed and look him in the eye, as shown at left. Swing your left arm down forcefully, striking an edge-of-the-hand blow against the inside of his gun wrist, as shown at right. The gun will be knocked away from his body and the fingers gripping the butt of the gun will fly open . . .

FRONTAL DISARMING (Continued)

The way in which the edge-of-the-hand blow should strike the gun wrist, on the inside and on the downward sweep of the arm, is shown at the left. Follow through with a knee to the testicles and a chin-jab blow, as shown at the right. Note, at the right, that the fingers of the gun hand are open. For that reason it is well to use old weapons in practice.

This edge-of-the-hand blow will knock his gun away from your body area. At the same time, the force of the blow on the wrist tendons will cause the fingers of the gun hand to fly open and the gun to drop from your opponent's hand. Usually the trigger will not be pulled; and if it is, the gun will be far out to the side, away from the body, before it goes off.

Third step. At the instant your edge-of-the-hand blow, and the follow-through, carries the gun away from the body, follow up with your knee to his testicles, and use your free hand to give him a chin jab.

This method of disarming combines surprise, attack and other elements previously mentioned, and is practically foolproof when properly executed. The weapon is knocked out of the hand, and the attack, by blows to the testicles and chin, downs the opponent. Even in the few cases where the man retains hold of the weapon, he will not be able to use it because of the pain and knockout effect of the blows to his body. This can be practiced with some restraint by using the flat of the hand against the inside of the wrist, instead of the edge of the hand, and by pulling up short on the chin jab and knee. Its efficiency and sureness will prove itself to the student after a short period of practice.

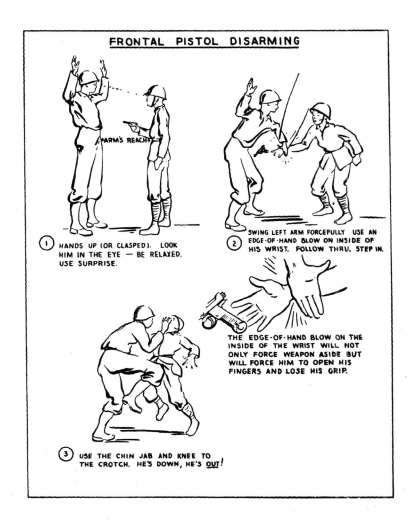

FRONTAL PISTOL DISARMING

1. HANDS UP (OR CLASPED). LOOK HIM IN THE EYE — BE RELAXED. USE SURPRISE.

2. SWING LEFT ARM FORCEFULLY. USE AN EDGE-OF-HAND BLOW ON INSIDE OF HIS WRIST. FOLLOW THRU. STEP IN.

THE EDGE-OF-HAND BLOW ON THE INSIDE OF THE WRIST WILL NOT ONLY FORCE WEAPON ASIDE BUT WILL FORCE HIM TO OPEN HIS FINGERS AND LOSE HIS GRIP.

3. USE THE CHIN JAB AND KNEE TO THE CROTCH. HE'S DOWN, HE'S OUT!

Rear Disarming (Hand Gun). The same general principles apply when the hold-up is from the rear. In this case, however, glance over your shoulder quickly, at the moment of contact, so as to see in which hand the weapon is held. This is necessary to determine whether or not your opponent is using the gun barrel in your back or is using a finger to simulate his gun, while having the gun out of arm's reach on his hip. It is also important to know which arm to use in

REAR PISTOL DISARMING

1. HANDS UP (OR CLASPED BEHIND HEAD). BE RELAXED. USE ELEMENT OF SURPRISE. KNOW WHICH IS THE GUN HAND.

2. SWING LEFT ARM DOWN FORCEFULLY. (FOLLOW THRU) PIVOT INTO HIM WITH MOMENTUM OF SWING.

FOLLOW THROUGH

PIVOT

3. USE THE KNEE AND CHIN JAB FOR A KNOCKOUT. YOU MAY GRASP GUN WRIST WITH YOUR LEFT, IF HE IS STILL HOLDING ONTO IT.

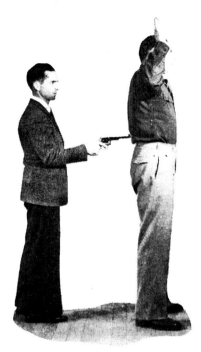

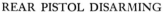

REAR PISTOL DISARMING

After determining in which hand the gun is held, initiate the disarming action. Make a downward sweeping movement across your back with your left arm. Knock the attacker's gun hand out to the right, as is shown in the upper right picture. Then pivot on the left foot, stepping around with the right. End the body pivot with a chin jab and a knee to the groin, as in the lower right picture. Note that, because of your follow through with a striking arm, the attacker's gun hand is way out to the side and is empty.

making the first blow in disarming. Normally, the gunman will carry his gun in his master hand, usually the right, and will keep it there after contact has been made. He may change gun hands while conducting a search, but usually not.

First step. After determining where, and in which hand, the gun is held, make a downward sweeping arm movement to the rear, directed at the inside of the gun wrist. Be sure to use the arm that will strike the gun wrist on the inside and knock the gun out to the side, away from the body. Use the full length of the arm to strike the gun hand. Either clench the fist so as to make the surface of the striking arm hard, or use the edge of the hand. It may not be possible to hit the gun hand exactly on the inside of the wrist, as is the case in frontal disarming; but by striking with the clenched fist, or edge of the hand, on the inside of the wrist or forearm, a stunning blow can be delivered that will knock the gun aside and usually cause the grip on the weapon to be released.

Second step. Finish the body pivot, with a chin jab and a knee to the testicles for the knockout. A complete follow-through, with the arm which strikes the gun hand, will knock the gun way out from the body area. At the same time, the blow to the inside of the gun wrist or forearm will ordinarily cause the gunman to let go his weapon. In some cases, the grasp on the gun may be retained by the gunman, because the blow to the rear is not as well directed as is the edge-of-the-hand blow in frontal disarming. In any event, the gun hand will be far out from the body and the gun wrist can be grasped at the instant the chin jab or testicle blow is delivered.

Disarming Against Shoulder Weapons. It is even easier to disarm a man armed with a shoulder weapon, because the weapon is longer and more unwieldy. The opponent's grasp on the rifle, shotgun or submachinegun is with both hands. All that is necessary in this case (gun held with butt on the opponent's right hip) is: (1) Strike the barrel a hard blow with your right hand, with the flat of your hand towards the left, knocking the gun out of line with your body. (2) Retain a grip on the weapon after knocking it away from your body; then jerk the gun forward, at the same time kicking out his left knee with the edge of your right foot, or kicking him in the testicles. (3) When he receives the blow of your foot on his knees or testicles, depending on position of his feet,

SHOULDER WEAPON DISARMING

Disarming of the shoulder weapon—such as the sawed-off shotgun, submachinegun, or rifle —is easier than disarming of the hand gun. Sweep down with the right arm and use the right hand to knock the muzzle aside, as in the first two poses above. Retain a grip on the piece, as is shown below. Once the weapon is knocked away from the body area, kick the gunman's knee or testicles, as is shown in the third picture. Jerk the weapon away from him at the instant the kick is delivered.

the gunman will release his grip on the weapon. This will enable you to fire the weapon or to use it as a club, because your opponent will go down and be helpless. It is important to strike the weapon away from your body toward your left side when your opponent has the butt resting on his right hip. Striking it from left to right leaves you open for the military butt stroke.

When the rifle barrel is placed in your back, the same

principles and methods apply as in the case of the pistol. With the gun butt resting on your opponent's right hip, sweep your left arm down to the rear; strike the gun barrel on the left side; follow through, pivoting on your left foot, then move in to the gunman, giving him a kick in the testicles and a chin jab.

These methods of rifle disarming can be used equally well against a gunman armed with a sawed-off shot gun, a sub-machinegun, or any other type of shoulder weapon.

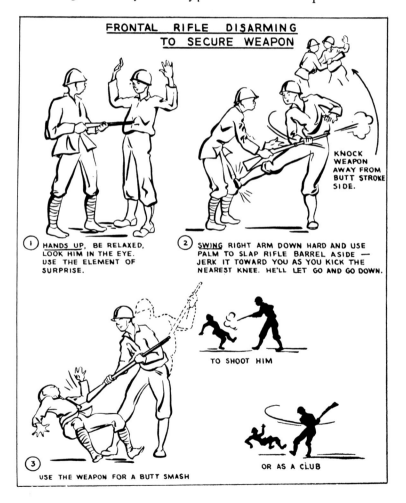

FRONTAL   RIFLE   DISARMING
TO SECURE WEAPON

KNOCK WEAPON AWAY FROM BUTT STROKE SIDE.

1 HANDS UP, BE RELAXED, LOOK HIM IN THE EYE. USE THE ELEMENT OF SURPRISE.

2 SWING RIGHT ARM DOWN HARD AND USE PALM TO SLAP RIFLE BARREL ASIDE — JERK IT TOWARD YOU AS YOU KICK THE NEAREST KNEE. HE'LL LET GO AND GO DOWN.

TO SHOOT HIM

3 USE THE WEAPON FOR A BUTT SMASH

OR AS A CLUB

SHOULDER WEAPON
DISARMING–REAR

After determining on which hip the gun butt is resting, you are ready to start disarming action. It is important that you always hit the weapon on the side that will prevent a butt stroke being used. Sweep down and across the back. with the left arm rigid, and knock the weapon aside, as is shown in the picture above. Pivot on the left foot, stepping around with the right. Step in and place your right foot in rear of the gunman, as is shown in the lower picture. With your right hand, strike an edge-of-the-hand blow to his face or throat area. If he still retains a grip or the weapon, grasp it with your left hand. With your foot in rear to trip, and with the backward blow of your right hand, he will go down on his back and the gun can be jerked from him.

REAR RIFLE DISARMING

1. HANDS UP OR CLASPED BEHIND HEAD. BE RELAXED. KNOW WHAT HIP HE'S HOLDING RIFLE ON.

2. BRING LEFT ARM DOWN FORCEFULLY TO KNOCK WEAPON ASIDE, PIVOTING WITH MOMENTUM OF SWING INTO OPPONENT.

ALWAYS PIVOT AWAY FROM BUTT STROKE SIDE.

PIVOT FOOT

3. IF HE STILL IS HOLDING WEAPON, GRASP IT WITH LEFT HAND — PLACE FOOT IN REAR OF HIS LEG AND SLAP HIM DOWN.

4. USE THE WEAPON OR YOUR FEET TO FINISH HIM.

ADDITIONAL DISARMING TECHNIQUES

There are many kinds of disarming tricks, but the very fact that there are so many is a good reason for limiting training to a few tried and proved methods. Those students who are interested may be permitted to explore other techniques on their own. The inclusion of too many types in a training program will lead to confusion and a lack of proficiency in any of them. If time is available in the training program, the following techniques can be demonstrated

REAR PISTOL DISARMING AND ARM LOCK

First determine in which of your opponent's hands the gun is held and whether it is held close to your back. Then pivot to the right on your right foot, so that on completion of the pivot you are on the outside of the gun arm and are facing the gunman, as in the right pose above. As you pivot, sweep your right arm down, knocking the gunman's arm to his left. Bring your right hand up and under his gun arm, placing your hand on the biceps of his gun arm. The completion of the movement results in your left hand grasping the gun barrel or gun hand, exerting backward leverage and forcing the gunman to release the gun. The movement ends in an arm lock. See lower picture.

after proficiency has been achieved in the methods already discussed.

The Arm Lock. The following method of disarming a man who holds up his victim from the rear is a good one. It has been used with success by various law enforcement agencies. (1) After looking back to see which hand is holding the gun (the right in this case), pivot on your right foot to the right, so that you complete your pivot facing the gunman and place yourself on the outside, or to the right, of his gun arm. As the pivot is being made, sweep the right arm down, outstretched, knocking the gun arm to the gunman's left. (2) Following through with your right arm, bring it up under the opponent's gun wrist, placing your right hand on the biceps of his gun arm. (3) With your left hand grasp the barrel of the piece and exert downward and backward leverage, bending forward as you do so. When this leverage is exerted against the gun hand, the grip on the weapon will be broken and the gunman will find that, not only has he lost his weapon, but also he is the victim of a painful arm lock. This will help in subduing him.

Securing Pistol from Opponent. The following disarming method enables the victim not only to get possession of the gunman's weapon, but also to have it in immediate firing position. If a lone gunman is encountered, the use of the more simple edge-of-hand blow is advisable. However, there may be times when the gunman is accompanied by companions. In this case the method of disarming must result in your having control of the situation and possession of the weapon, so you can use it to shoot, or as a threat against its former owner and the other members of the hold-up party. Naturally, if more than one gun is trained on you, even this method will stand little chance of success, no matter how perfectly executed.

A great deal of practice is necessary to master this particular technique; but skill in its execution, coupled with correct judgment as to when it should be used, has proved it to be successful. It is a more spectacular type and can be used by an instructor to introduce disarming and its possibilities to a group of students. It is not advocated for use against small automatic weapons, but works well against revolvers and automatics having a barrel length of 4 inches or more.

First step. With your hands in the air and facing the

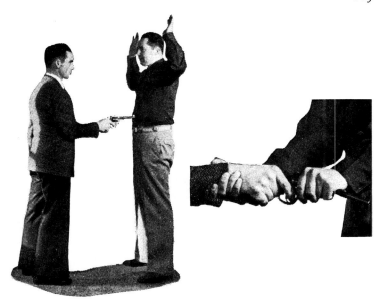

SECURING PISTOL FROM OPPONENT

Facing the gunman, as at the left, bring your left hand down on top of the weapon, grasping it around the cylinder, with your thumb on the inside. Knock it away from the body, to the left, in the same motion. As the gun is knocked away, bring your right hand down forcefully, striking a blow with the flat of your hand against the inside of the attacker's gun wrist. Retain a grip on his wrist, as shown at right. Gripping the wrist tightly, jerk it up with your right hand . . .

opponent who has the gun in his right hand, bring down the left hand so that your left thumb hooks on the inside of the frame, with the thumb of the left hand on the inside of the weapon, and knock it to the left, away from your body.

Second step. Exert downward pressure on the frame and barrel of the gun. In conjunction with this downward leverage, slap the inside of the gun wrist with the right hand. This blow to the inside of the gunman's wrist, together with the leverage being exerted down by the left hand, will cause the gunman to release the weapon.

Third step. The gun, being gripped in your left hand, or initial grasping hand, can be placed butt first into your right hand and is in immediate firing position. It is best to take a

SECURING PISTOL FROM OPPONENT (Continued)

... at the same time, exert downward pressure with your left hand, the one that is grasping the gun, as shown at left. Note that this whole procedure is done, out and to the side away from the body. After the leverage has forced the gunman to release his weapon, the action winds up with your left hand placing the gun butt in your right hand, as at right. Step backward as this transfer is made. The gun is now in a firing position.

step to the rear as the transfer of the gun is made from your left to your right, or shooting, hand.

To Take Over a Shoulder Weapon in Shooting Position. A similar disarming tactic, to secure a shoulder weapon so that it is in immediate shooting position is as follows:

First step. Facing the opponent who has a rifle (butt on his right hip) pointed at your stomach, strike down with the left hand so that your left thumb hooks on the inside of the weapon. Knock it to your left, away from the body area. Grasp the barrel of the weapon with the striking hand as you knock it aside.

Second step. Using the right arm, step in and hook it under the weapon near the trigger guard, and jerk up. With the original grasp on the barrel by the left hand (which is used to push down) and the use of the right arm to jerk the gun upward, the gunman's grip on the gun will be broken by the great leverage exerted.

Third step. As the rifle leaves your opponent's hands, a step backward may be taken, so that the gun can be placed in a firing position. If desired, a knee can be used against

SECURING SHOULDER WEAPON FROM OPPONENT

Face your opponent and look him in the eye, as at left. Strike down and out to the left with your left hand, grasping the weapon on top of the barrel, with your thumb on the inside, as shown at right. By this first movement, the muzzle is forced out to the side, away from the opponent's body. Step in, hook your right arm under the weapon, near the trigger guard, and jerk up . . .

his groin as the gun is jerked from his grasp. In addition to wresting the weapon from him, there is also a good chance that he will receive a knockout blow on the chin, from the butt of his own weapon as it is jerked upwards out of his hands. In practice, this last feature must be watched to avoid injury.

Hand in Back Attack. It is possible to disarm a man who places a hand in the middle of your back and keeps his drawn gun on his hip when he holds you up. When you find yourself in such a predicament, you should realize at once that the man with the weapon has had some sort of training in the proper methods of restraining an individual at the point of his gun. Most attackers, when they have a prisoner at gun point in this manner, feel that if the prisoner makes an attempt to disarm, he will fail. Consequently,

SECURING SHOULDER WEAPON FROM OPPONENT
(Continued)

At the same time, force the muzzle down, as shown at left. The gunman's grip on the weapon will be broken, and the chances are good that the butt of the piece will hit him on the chin as the weapon is released. A knee blow may be made to his testicles. In the final step, right, the weapon leaves the opponent's hands. As you grasp the small of the stock, the gun muzzle is raised to a firing position. At this point a step backward is advisable, so as to be out of reach.

the element of surprise here is much in your favor when you actually disarm your opponent.

The method is little known, but is simple and can be accomplished with practice. The necessity always of looking to the rear when somebody orders "hands up" is very obvious. Once having ascertained that a hand is in the middle of your back and having found the location of the gun, decide for yourself which direction of body turn would bring you into the weapon, or away from the weapon. It is assumed that the gun is held in your opponent's right hand close to his hip, and that his left hand is in the middle of your back. After determining this, start your disarming. Pivot to the outside of the arm held in the middle of your back. Pivot completely around on your left foot, taking a step towards him as you complete the pivot, until you are at a point opposite him. The pivot and step toward him will be so fast that he will be unable to pull the trigger in time. Once beside him, you are naturally out of gun range. A blow and trip, or throw, may easily be applied because, with the first body contact, he becomes off balance. In this particular method, you must be sure of your ground and pick the stage for disarming carefully. If he attempts to shove you forward with the palm of his hand, a good time to initiate your disarming is at the time when he shoves you forward, because at this moment he is most likely to be off balance.

Weapon-in-Pocket Attack. The man who places his weapon in his coat pocket and approaches within arm's reach demanding "hands up" is laying himself wide open for disarming. He can be handled with ease. Facing him, with your hands raised (the weapon being in his right coat pocket and within arm's length), all that is necessary is to shove him backward by hitting him sharply on the point of the shoulder of the gun hand; that is, on his right shoulder. A violent blow will pivot his body to his right, so that the gun barrel points away from you. His hand on the gun is locked in the pocket and is useless. At this point, step in beside him and apply a trip, edge-of-the-hand blow, or other method of elimination. The attacker who carries his gun in his pocket will usually come into arm's reach without being enticed, for three reasons: first, he hides the gun from other people's view; second, he will come close enough to use his free hand for searching; third, since he wants to emphasize to the man being held up that he has a weapon, he has to get close in order to prove it. This type of hold-up occurs daily and is one of the easiest for a trained man to handle.

Attack in an Automobile. There is a distinct possibility of successful disarming when you are sitting in a car, driving or not, with a man covering you with a gun. If you have had a little practice, you can readily analyze your disarming possibilities. Supposing the gun is in the man's right hand, or in any position away from his body and left arm—you can knock the gun hand against his body by a sweeping movement and deliver a knockout punch with your free hand, a chin jab, edge-of-the-hand-blow, or other. This method has many variations. A serious student should practice it with various individuals and try to visualize all possible situations. He should be concerned particularly with how the gun is held in the gunman's hand and its relation to his own body. Practice in this type of disarming will show up your limitations, and the various possibilities of disarming, so that you will soon be able to recognize them as circumstances occur. Knowing the fundamentals of disarming, it will be easy to devise tactics for use against the gunman who points a gun at your head. He should know better; he shows his ignorance in attempting hold-ups of this type.

When the Attacker is Out of Reach. All methods of disarming when the gunman is out of arm's reach and cannot be enticed in should be based on the circumstances of your own situation. *How desperate are you?* Your chances of success are good, but by no means certain. You have a possibility of kicking the pistol out of his hand by a sudden horizontal sweep of the foot, kicking the gun aside, and following right in. Kick with the side of the foot, with the impact being on the inside of the gun hand. Since this kick will place you off balance, follow through with your body and fall forward on the gunman. If he is out of kicking range, your chances are that much poorer, but there is still a 50-50 chance. The best action is to catch him off guard and execute a forward dive or tackle to the side of the gunman on which the weapon is held. This tackle, naturally, should be followed up by bringing the man to the ground and subduing him. Experiments have shown that it is much more difficult for a man to fire at a moving object directly off and down to the right (gun in right hand), than it is for him to fire to the left and down. If the man is holding a rifle on you, your chances are much better, because the larger the weapon the more unwieldy it is for quick, sudden movements.

Another consideration is that ordinarily the gunman will pull the trigger while the weapon is still pointed in a more or less horizontal position. Consequently, by timing your attempt properly and being fast enough, your body will be in a horizontal position during the forward dive, at the time of the firing of the weapon. In this case, unless you receive a head shot, the possibilities of getting no more than a crease are good.

When Moving Forward. Suppose you have started to move forward and the weapon is being held in your opponent's right hand, or butted against his right hip, as in the case of a rifle.

The sweep of your left arm down and to the rear, striking the rifle or pistol aside, and the following blows to his testicles and chin remain the same. The only thing which you have to consider, then, is the way in which you will initiate your pivot.

The best way to do this is to start the pivoting movement when your right foot is just being advanced and your left foot is still on the ground. In this position, by pushing with with the ball of the right foot and pivoting on the toe of the left, a quick and satisfactory pivot into your man will result.

DISARMING WHEN WEAPON IS CONCEALED

When approached and ordered to put up your hands by the gunman who comes in close and conceals his weapon in his coat pocket, watch for the opportune time. Then, with the hand opposite his gun arm, strike a hard blow to the point of the gunman's shoulder, causing him to spin to the right, *away from you* so that your body is out of range. See left above. When your blow pivots him away, off balance, step in immediately. Place one foot, the right, behind him and deliver a blow as shown at the right above. He will go down with his right hand still grasping the now useless gun in his pocket. If need be, your feet can be used, once he is on the ground.

If the weapon is being held in the attacker's left hand or against his left hip, the reverse procedure will apply.

The same method of pivoting will suffice if a hand, or finger, is in your back and your opponent's weapon is held on his hip. If this occurs, remember again to pivot towards the side *away* from the gun hand.

Some instructors believe it is advisable to fake a gun barrel in a prisoner's back by using the stiff forefinger, or knuckle, to imitate the gun barrel. The gun hand is kept back out of arm's reach, so that any attempt directed against the "fake" gun hand will fail. This type of procedure particularly is not one for law officers to use, since it really tempts the victim to try disarming and thus causes him to be shot. A police officer or soldier whose object is to bring in the prisoner, not to kill him, should let the prisoner know that the gun is on his hip. He should use his free hand to shove the prisoner along, not to fake a gun.

Chapter 8

PRISONER HANDLING
AND CONTROL

THE soldier or police officer should avoid getting himself into a situation which would permit an opponent to attempt to disarm him.

HOLDING A PRISONER AT GUN POINT

As previously stated, the man with the gun is at a disadvantage; he does not want to shoot or he would already have done so. This is especially true of the law enforcement officer; his mission is not to kill but to restrain and capture. He must take more chances in handling his prisoner than are necessary on a battlefield.

The man held at gun point is usually an unknown quantity; he may be meek and docile, or he may be so desperate that he will attempt disarming, given the slightest opportunity. Fear of capture, punishment for crimes committed in his past, dope, or just plain viciousness, coupled with the possibility that he has received training in disarming, make every such prisoner potentially dangerous. Therefore, he should be handled carefully. Too much reliance should not be placed upon the mere presence of the weapon in the hand to control or to command obedience and respect.

Generally, police and military departments do not question too closely the man who is forced to shoot an antagonist who attempts to escape; but they certainly hold responsible the policeman or soldier who permits a prisoner to disarm him and escape. The publicity given to a successful disarming or an escape attempt undermines public and organization confidence. Therefore, if it is necessary for the policeman or soldier to use a gun to restrain a prisoner, he should be trained to use it properly as a means of enforcing his authority.

Prisoners who are desperate enough to attempt escape usu-

TAKING A PRISONER AT GUN POINT

Keep out of arm's reach and keep the gun hand well back on the hip. From this position, the prisoner usually should be ordered to turn around, raise his hands higher, and spread his legs apart, before he is searched from the rear.

ally are quick to take advantage of carelessness and overconfidence on the part of the officer. They make full use of the element of surprise and the slowness of the officer's trigger reaction.

Rules for Handling Prisoner. The following general rules should be followed when handling a criminal at gun point.

(1) Give every indication—by inference, speech, actions—that you will unhesitatingly shoot at the slightest provocation. Dominate all the actions of the prisoner.

(2) Keep out of arm's reach until you are ready to search for weapons.

(3) Make the prisoner keep his hands way up in the air and his back toward you, if possible.

(4) Do not allow the prisoner to talk, look back, gesture or otherwise distract you.

(5) If the immediate area of the action is not suitable for

an initial search for weapons move him by oral commands to a more suitable area. Use well-placed kicks, or shoves with the free hand, if necessary to make him move faster and obey orders promptly.

(6) If possible, use the wall search method when searching for weapons.

(7) If no wall is available, make the prisoner spread his legs until he is in an awkward position before approaching from the rear to search for weapons or other items. Do not, alone, search from the front, if it can be avoided.

(a) Keep your gun hand back against the hip and use your free hand to make the "frisk."

(b) Keep your foot that is on the same side as the searching hand against the heel of the suspect's shoe. Search the closest half section of his body; then move to the other side, change gun hands, and repeat.

WALL SEARCH

The prisoner's hands and legs are spread far apart. He is forced to lean forward and support himself with his arms against the wall. The searcher hooks his foot inside the prisoner's foot. At the least hostile act, the foot is jerked out and the prisoner falls. This is an effective way of searching and handling one or more prisoners.

HANDS-ON-HEAD POSITION

The prisoner's legs are spread far apart, putting him in a very unbalanced position. His hands, in this case, are resting on top of his head. The hands-on-head is a good position. It can be maintained a long time without tiring, and the arms are prevented from gradually lowering, as is the case with the hands-in-air position.

CLOSE-IN SEARCHING	SWIVEL-TYPE CUFF

The man with the gun can operate much closer to the prisoner if
he places one foot against the prisoner's heel. The side of the body
is toward the prisoner, so that the
groin area is protected.

After practice, the swivel-type
cuff can be affixed with one hand.
The prisoner's hand that is being
cuffed is pulled way out from his
back, thus increasing his unbalanced position.

(8) After the search for weapons, apply handcuffs, use
a come along, or have him precede you, at gun point, to
whatever destination you select. If there is a possibility of
the prisoner making a break—because of crowded streets,
narrow doorways and hallways, poor light—grasp his belt
in the rear with your free hand. Keeping the gun back on
your hip, control the prisoner's movements by kicks and
the grip on his belt. It is extremely difficult for him to disarm you as long as a strong grip is maintained on the belt
and the gun is held well back.

Trouser and Coat Tactics. There is a variation of this tactic
which permits free movement and still prevents a sudden
break. Cut, or take off, the prisoner's belt or suspenders; rip
the top buttons from his trousers, if necessary, so that he is
forced to use one hand to hold them up. This prevents any
sudden action on his part; the minute he lets go of his
trousers, they will slip down and bind his legs. It is also
very difficult for a prisoner to run if he is forced to hold
up his trousers with one hand. Not only does removing the
trousers support create a physical handicap, it also has a
psychological effect. If a person is partly undressed, it tends

USE OF CLOTHING

When the occasion warrants, the prisoner's clothing can be used to immobilize him. Not only are his arms and legs temporarily restricted, he also is under a psychological disadvantage in his partly dressed condition.

to subdue impulsive moves. Just so, pulling a coat down over the prisoner's shoulders will bind his arms temporarily, while he is being searched, or until final disposition is made.

In emergencies, soldiers and police officers have followed both procedures—they have dropped the prisoner's trousers around the ankles and pulled his coat down over his arms, thus anchoring him in one place until the situation warranted more permanent measures. This strategy is particularly good if a lone individual is forced to stand guard over a number of potentially desperate prisoners.

Occasions may arise when it is expedient to approach the suspect from the front while conducting a search for weapons. This is more dangerous than a search from the rear. The gun must be kept well back; and the body must be kept sideways, hip foremost, so as to protect the more vulnerable spots—groin, testicles—from a hand, foot, or knee blow.

If visibility is good and the situation is otherwise favorable, a suspect can be ordered to lower one hand and unfasten his belt buckle, or other means of trouser support. His trousers will drop, binding his legs and providing an additional precaution while making a frontal search. Likewise, his coat can be pulled down over his arms so as to bind them at the elbow.

Although these methods of prisoner control and contact

from the front are good, they are more risky. There is always a possibility that the more desperate type of prisoner will try to draw and use a concealed weapon, or will attempt a disabling blow and disarming.

THE INITIAL SEARCH FOR WEAPONS

When a desperate man is apprehended and held at gun point, the arresting officer always should search for his weapons. Usually, this search should be made from the rear, so that the prisoner is in doubt about the officer's position and the exact whereabouts of his gun.

This initial frisk for weapons is very important. Although it is often hurried, it should never be done carelessly. The prisoner's hands, feet and legs are sources of danger. The searcher should keep his groin, or other vulnerable parts of his body, and his weapon, out of reach of the prisoner while making the search. However, if the searcher is forced by circumstances to get close to his prisoner, he should get his body so close that any blow delivered by the prisoner cannot be executed with full force.

The "Pat" Search. The initial search for weapons, sometimes called the "pat" or "feel" method, cannot in any sense constitute a thorough body search; but it can detect most weapons and other bulky objects. After this initial "pat" search, the prisoner is usually taken to a headquarters, where he is disrobed and his clothes and person subjected to a detailed examination. The pat search should cover the pris-

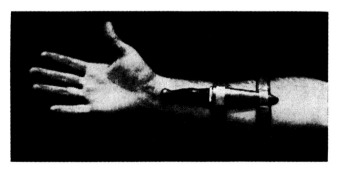

Deadly weapons can be carried in any number of places where a hasty search will fail to locate them. A knife in wrist holster taped on inside of arm when concealed by sleeve of shirt or coat is many times initially overlooked, as is a small "hideout" gun when carried in the same location.

Weapons are many times carried by assassins and criminals in seemingly innocent objects such as a book where the inside pages have been hollowed out.

oner's arms, armpits, waist line and back, his groin and testicle area, and the entire surface of his legs, down to the shoes. In addition to the more obvious places, firearms and bladed weapons have been found on prisoners in the following places: the hat, hair, necktie, shoes, belt; suspended by a string down the back of the neck; tied or taped to the arms; inside the wrists, groin, legs and armpits. The searcher should look with suspicion on such innocent objects as fountain pens, pencils, cigarette cases. Many such items have been adapted to conceal knife blades, or tear gas projectors, or small caliber cartridges which can be fired by manipulation of concealed trigger mechanisms. A collection of items of this type should be displayed in every training school.

If, in the searcher's judgment, the situation is serious enough, the prisoner can be knocked out, or stunned, by a gun butt or edge-of-the-hand blow, so as to permit a more thorough search and provide a better means of handling the situation.

Searching More Than One Prisoner. In some circumstances, a lone individual may be required to search and disarm more than one prisoner or suspect. He should require the prisoners to raise their hands, stand in column about 4 feet apart with their backs toward the officer and their feet spread. The nearest prisoner should be searched first and, on completion, should be directed to proceed to the front of the column; then the next prisoner should be searched, and so forth. By remaining in the rear of all the suspects and keeping them under surveillance, the officer should be able to control the

COLUMN SEARCH

If a lone officer or man is forced to search more than one suspect, the suspects should be made to stand in column, about 4 feet apart, in an unbalanced position. The rear man is searched first, then is directed to move to the head of the column. Then the next man is searched, and so on.

entire group. The wall search method can also be used in cases of this kind.

Searching When Carrying a Shoulder Weapon. Although the law enforcement officer usually carries a hand gun, he may find himself in situations in which he carries only a shoulder weapon, such as a rifle, submachinegun or shotgun. The normal methods of search, employed when using the hand gun, will be extremely difficult. If he has enough confidence in himself physically he can lay down his weapon and search in the same manner he would use when covering the prisoner with a hand gun. If he wishes to keep the weapon trained on the prisoner, he can conduct a search in the following manner. Direct the prisoner to lie on his back, with his arms outstretched close together over his head and his feet close together. Place the muzzle of the rifle in the pit of the suspects stomach and keep the gun upright, with the trigger finger inside the trigger guard. Then, to fire the weapon, it is necessary only to lift the finger against the trigger. The weight of the weapon will be enough to counterbalance the trigger pull, so that the piece will fire with slight movement. Conduct the search with the free hand. Then direct the prisoner to turn over, and repeat the process. The muzzle of the rifle can be twisted in the prisoner's clothing to prevent it slipping off.

In certain situations, the finger has been used successfully by unarmed individuals as a bluff in simulating a gun barrel. The chances of success in a strategem of this kind will depend entirely upon the searcher's force and command of the situation. If the approach is made from the rear and the prisoner is not allowed to turn to see what is pressing against his back, he usually can be controlled long enough to permit a search of his person and the securing of his weapon. The knuckle of the forefinger will be a suitable imitation of a gun barrel when pressed in the middle of a man's back. The forefinger, when applied in its full length, may bend if weight is pressed against it, thus giving away the situation to the more experienced type of criminal.

HANDCUFFS

Military and civil police records are replete with cases in which seemingly docile and subdued prisoners who were not properly secured have escaped, either killing or injuring the guards.

Although each service has its own instructions on the type of persons to be handcuffed, it is still up to the individual officer to rely on his judgment of the potential danger and the difficulty in handling the prisoner. In most police departments the officer is instructed to use handcuffs whenever the status of his prisoner is doubtful, and in other ordinary circumstances. However, the degree of desperation of a prisoner is frequently an unknown factor, and the conventional application of handcuffs will not always suffice to prevent a desperate man from attempting to escape. After the shock of capture and arrest has worn off, an escape attempt will often be made, even though handcuffs have been applied.

The proper use of handcuffs on various types of prisoners requires individual practice and the exercise of good judgment. Although the officer may have been told when and where to use handcuffs, he must have training in applying them so that they perform their function efficiently in all situations.

With his wrists pinioned by handcuffs, a desperate prisoner is still far from helpless. If his hands are cuffed together in front, so that the arms swing free, it is possible for him to

ADJUSTABLE HANDCUFFS

This is the more popular type of handcuffs, with an adjustment that permits a close fit to all sizes of wrists. The method of cuffing shown here permits the prisoner to use his hands for eating and other normal actions. But it also makes him more dangerous, since he can grasp a gun, strike a blow, or use a concealed weapon, even though both hands are pinioned. Prisoners have been known to pick, or otherwise break, locks or links when they are secured in this manner.

deliver a knockout blow using both his hands or the handcuffs themselves. When an officer is alone, it is not advisable to handcuff himself to the prisoner. This leaves the prisoner with one hand free for attack and restricts the officer in preventing any attempted escape. Many officers who handcuff themselves to their prisoners deposit the keys to the cuffs with another officer, in the prisoner's presence. This usually discourages an attempted escape by the prisoner, although it also inconveniences the officer. Generally it is much better to use tHe handcuffs to pinion both the prisoner's hands.

Since there are many methods of using handcuffs, each prisoner can be cuffed in a manner which will prevent him attempting to escape or attacking, according to the officer's estimate of his dangerous potentialities. This is particularly important if the prisoner is being moved from one locality to another.

Types of Handcuffs. There are two general types of handcuffs. One is a cuff of fixed size which is applied to all prisoners, regardless of wrist size. The more popular type is an adjustable cuff, which makes possible a secure grip on any size wrist or other part of a limb that is to be pinioned.

No attempt should be made to apply handcuffs until the prisoner has been subdued, by physical or mechanical means. Handcuffs are often applied after the prisoner has been subdued by the hands, fists, baton, blackjack or other weapons, or when the prisoner is held at gun point. On other occasions, such pressure holds as the arm lock are applied before cuffing.

There are methods of applying handcuffs in a surprise attack on the prisoner, but this procedure is often very risky. It should be used only by extremely skilled persons. If he so

CUFFING TO POST

Using the cuffs to secure a prisoner to a tree, post, or pole until he can be taken in.

EFFECTIVE PLACING OF HANDS

When applied in this manner, with the backs of the hands, not the palms, facing each other the handcuffs are effective. The prisoner is given less freedom, but he cannot use his hands effectively, even though his arms are free.

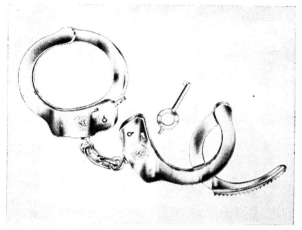

SMITH & WESSON HANDCUFFS

There are many classes and types of handcuffs. They range in price and quality from the cheaper Spanish-made cuff to the very finest which can be purchased for only a little more.

Handcuffs, like the sidearm, should be of the best type and quality. Failure of either one at a crucial time can result in disaster. The best type handcuffs are those that have a rotating jaw, allowing the cuffs to be applied swiftly and fitting the smallest to largest wrist.

These new Smith & Wesson cuffs have great strength and yet are also light in weight. They are so designed that they may be clamped on the wrists with both key holes toward the body and away from the prisoner's hands. This makes picking more difficult. A double lock is another new feature. By using the punch on the handle of the key to depress a plunger, the rotating jaw is secured against travel in either direction, thus preventing increased tightening after application and the consequent loss of blood circulation in the pinioned wrists.

chooses, a prisoner who has not been subdued prior to actual cuffing can be very difficult.

Rules for Handcuffing. The following are good general rules when handling a potentially dangerous prisoner.

(1) When moving the prisoner by car, the wrists should be handcuffed, or tied, and then held to the body by the belt, tied to the outside door handle, or tied to the leg.

(2) The legs and feet are dangerous. Loop a belt around the feet and tie to the cuffs if the situation warrants. The officer should always consider the knees, feet and manacled hands of the prisoner as potential weapons and should restrain them from free movement whenever possible.

(3) Many fanatical prisoners who have been only hand-

cuffed have escaped, while traveling by bus or train, by crashing out through the window. A common dog chain, with padlock, can be put to good use on persons of this type, binding the ankles to the handcuffs. Special leg irons are available for this purpose, but a dog chain will make a satisfactory substitute.

(4) In case of an emergency at the scene of action, use the handcuffs, or any of the other tying expedients, to secure the prisoner to a post, tree, or such. Then proceed with the other elements of the situation. To secure more than one prisoner in an emergency, use an automobile skid chain. Loop it around some stationary object, such as an automobile bumper, then handcuff the prisoner by locking a section of the chain within the cuffs.

(5) In handling and moving a prisoner, always stay a little to his rear and make him precede you. He is then in a position where his every action can be observed, yet he is unable to see what his captor is doing. Always use this procedure when passing through doors.

(6) Firearms must be kept out of possible reach of the prisoner; and the officer's master hand should be kept free for action—the right hand in most cases.

(7) Violent prisoners must first be subdued physically, or held at gun point, before handcuffing. In all cases of this type, the cuffs should be applied with the prisoner's hands behind his back. The arm lock, hammer lock, and similar holds are useful when physical force is used. Force the prisoner to the ground on his stomach. By applying pressure, make him put his free hand back so it can be secured by the cuffs or a tie can be made. If a dangerous prisoner is handled alone and he is held at gun point, arms in the air, make him keep his back to the gun, spread his legs apart and bring one hand at a time down to the rear for cuffing.

(8) In extremely violent cases where time is short, use the gun butt, edge of the hand, baton, or blackjack to knock him out or stun him before cuffing.

(9) When forced to handle dangerous prisoners, either stay entirely out of arm and leg reach, or get in very close, so that an attempted blow cannot be delivered with full force.

OTHER MEANS OF SECURING PRISONERS

When there are no handcuffs available, the officer may have to use emergency means of securing his prisoner. Any of the

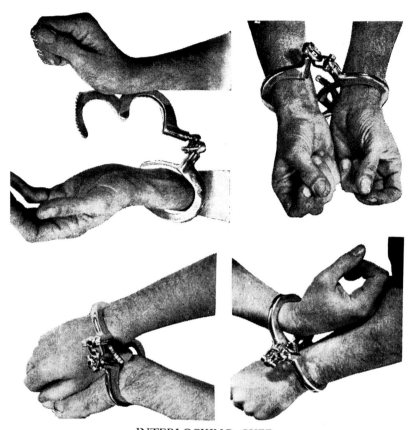

INTERLOCKING CUFF

One wrist is locked and pinioned, with enough room to permit the jaw of the other cuff to be inserted between the cuff and the wrist of the locked cuff, as shown at upper right. The second cuff is then locked. In effect, the cuffs are linked together like a chain while, at the same time, the wrists are kept pinioned in a rigid position. With the interlocked cuff, the use of the hands is greatly restricted, as shown at lower left. Any exertion can be painful if the cuffs are applied tightly.

Dangerous prisoners can be further limited in action by pointing the hands in opposite directions, as shown at the lower right. The restriction here is so complete that, even though the prisoner were given the key, he still could not unlock the cuffs.

following articles may be satisfactory: a piece of rope, the prisoner's shoe laces, adhesive or tire tape, flexible wire, the prisoner's belt, necktie, or handkerchief, a silk stocking, a long, twisted piece of cloth. The effectiveness of these expedients is entirely dependent upon training and practice in their use. Errors in tying procedure are usually glaringly apparent during practice sessions.

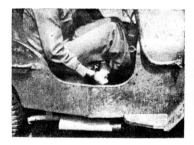

CUFFING BEHIND THE LEG

This method is especially good when a lone officer is transporting a prisoner by automobile. It can be used also to lock a prisoner to a chair in which he is sitting, the links of the cuffs being passed around the rung or leg of the chair. The same method, locking a single leg, may be used in the seat of a car, as shown at upper right. Or both legs may be passed through the loop of the arms, as shown at lower left. The use of cuffs shown at lower right secures the arm of the prisoner that is next to the driver, but leaves one arm free for maintaining balance or smoking.

CUFFING BEHIND THE BACK

Should circumstances warrant, the hands can be cuffed behind the back in this manner. This is a good method to use when forced to walk the prisoner a long distance.

CUFFING TO COUPLING

By passing one end of the cuffs through a trailer coupling or wagon wheel, before completing the cuffing of the other hand, the prisoner can be firmly secured.

CUFFING TO SOLID OBJECTS

When there are two or more prisoners, they can be temporarily secured, under light guard, in this manner. In this case three pairs of cuffs are used. An automobile chain, with one or more pairs of cuffs, also is useful in securing prisoners to any solid object. The chain can be used, together with the cuffs, to wrap around the bodies of several prisoners, thus restricting their movements.

CUFFING THREE MEN

Three pairs of cuffs can be used to restrain three men. Although these men are fastened only by their hands and are free to use their feet, it is difficult for them to move swiftly, since one man must always walk or run backward.

CUFFING TO THE BELT

The wrists cuffed with the link under the belt, as shown in the first picture, will greatly reduce the freedom of arms and hands. This is a good method to use when walking a prisoner a long distance, or when transporting him by car. Ideally, the belt buckle should be moved far enough around to prevent its being loosened by the hands, as shown in the second picture. The belt can also be used to restrict the hands further, when the hands are cuffed behind the prisoner's back, as is shown in the third picture.

Another variation is to remove the belt and force the prisoner to hold up his trousers with his hands. Still another method, when transporting the prisoner by car, is to roll down the window and put both his arms outside, with the link of the cuff over the outside door handle.

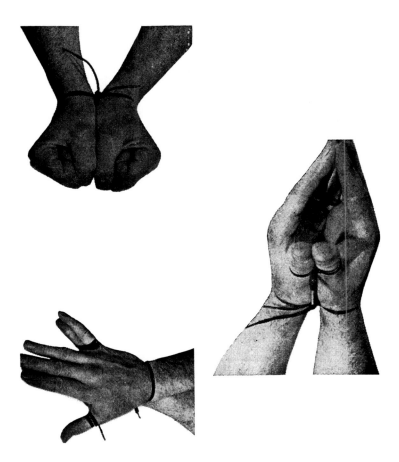

USE OF SHOE LACES, OR LIGHT CORD, TO EFFECT A TIE

Boot or shoe laces can be used effectively, provided they are pulled tight enough and providing the wrists are pulled together, with a wrapping around the cord between the insides of the wrists, as shown at upper left. This method is effective when the thumbs, as well as the little fingers, have been tied to each other, as illustrated at right. This prevents twisting of the hands and possible breakage of the wrist cord by exerting leverage. An outside view of the same method is shown at lower left. If the hands are placed back to back behind the body, an almost unbreakable tie is made.

Tying with shoe lace or cord is most effective when the hands are placed first around a pole or tree. Placing the victim's back to a tree and tying his wrists, little fingers and thumbs, provides an inescapable tie, especially if the arms are placed around a small tree, as shown at right.

CHAIN AND HANDCUFF COMBINATION (Right)

Here is shown a pair of handcuffs used in transporting two prisoners. A 5-foot chain is attached to the connecting links of the handcuffs and a 3-inch ring is attached at the other end of the chain. This combination is available commercially, or can be improvised by using a dog chain with the handcuffs.

HOG TIE

The hog tie, an extremely effective method, is initiated from the arm lock, with your opponent face down on the ground and his forearm bent up behind his back in a painful position. A little additional pressure on his bent arm will force him to place his other hand behind his back, at your order. With a rope, tie his wrists together. Take one end of the cord, run it around his neck, and tie it to his pinioned wrists. There should be enough pressure on the cord to force his hands up high toward his shoulder blades. Cross his ankles and, after doubling his legs up behind him, tie them with the other end of the cord, so that they remain in position. Any struggle to free himself will result in strangulation. When correctly applied, there is no escape from this tie. Various knots have been advocated in making this tie, but any standard tying knot may be used. The essential thing is that the victim shall be unable to make any effort to release himself.

USE OF TAPE TO EFFECT A TIE

A tie using tape, strips of twisted cloth, insulated electric wire, twine, or rope, as shown at left, is always effective. Above adhesive (or tire) tape is used to tie not only the wrists but also the forefingers. By taping the forefinger of each hand to the opposite forearm, the victim is prevented from obtaining leverage and twisting his arms so as to break the tape. Tape is also a good reinforcement of any other material used for tying.

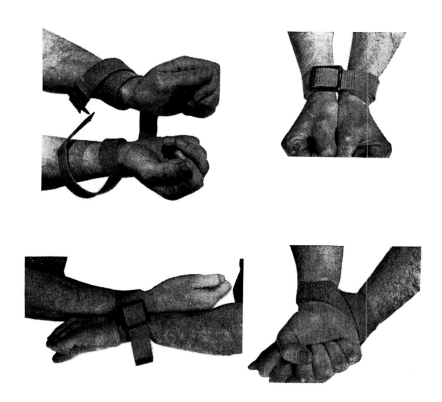

USE OF BELT TO EFFECT A TIE

A canvas or leather belt, or a necktie, makes an effective tie. The belt is wrapped around each wrist several times, as shown at upper left. After tightening, the belt buckle is fastened, as shown at upper right. The buckle should be placed underneath, so that the prisoner cannot loosen it with his teeth. The method shown at lower left is especially effective if the victim's arms are first placed around a post, tree, or other solid object. Again, it is well to keep the buckle out of reach of the victim's teeth. At lower right is another method of belt tie. Here the wrists have been wrapped before tightening the belt. The material used for this tie must be strong enough to withstand the leverage that can be exerted by pushing the elbows in opposite directions.

Chapter 9

RAIDS AND ROOM COMBAT

THERE are many cases on record in which law enforcement officers have cornered desperate criminals or insane persons in buildings and have had to resort to gunfire to subdue them. These cases range from an armed criminal in a room to the planned raid against a building. The latter has its counterpart in combat patrol operations and in street fighting, and the same principles apply.

Properly planned raids will result in the subjugation and capture of criminals with a minimum of casualties. Improper planning, and failure to know and appreciate the many factors involved, have caused many needless casualties, without achieving the desired result. Training—in common sense precautions and in the basic principles of cover, concealment, fire and movement, as practiced by the combat infantryman—should be given every law enforcement officer.

A raid—properly led and executed by well-trained, adequately armed men—will result in success; but police history is replete with hastily planned, poorly executed operations which not only have failed to apprehend criminals but also have resulted in the untimely death of police officers.

Most well-equipped police departments today have gas equipment on hand. When at all possible, it should be used. However, because circumstances will arise when gas munitions are not readily available, law enforcement officers must be able to execute raids which depend solely on prior planning, skilled execution, and firearms. For, if they assume that gas will be available in all emergencies and then are forced into a situation where it is not available, a psychological prop is knocked from under them and failure may result.

The Barrow Brothers Incident. A classic example of what can happen when a raid is poorly planned and executed is the incident involving the notorious Barrow brothers, as described by Colonel Sterling A. Wood in his book, *Riot Control*. Although outnumbered and surprised, they successfully "shot it out" with twelve law enforcement officers and escaped.

On the night of 17 July 1933, the two Barrow brothers, wanted for murder, accompanied by two woman companions, rented a cabin at the Crown Cabin Camp, six miles southeast of Platte City, Missouri. It was a double brick cabin, with a covered garage between the two rooms. Each room had one door facing to the south and one door opening into the garage. After the gangsters had parked their car in the garage, it could be backed out only on the south side.

Late in the next afternoon a tip was received by Sheriff Coffee at Platte City. He posted deputies to watch the cabin and asked the State Highway Patrol and the Sheriff of Jackson County for assistance. The mixed force included four deputy sheriffs from Kansas City in a police squad car, armed with one submachinegun, two riot shotguns, and one revolver; three State Highway Patrolmen, armed with another submachinegun and their revolvers; Sheriff Coffee, with another submachinegun; and four deputies, armed with one rifle and their revolvers.

The cabins were dark as the officers approached. The squad car was driven to within about fifteen feet of the garage door, and the headlights were played on the door of the east cabin. Captain Baxter, of the State Highway Patrol, and Sheriff Coffee, carrying bullet-proof shields in front of them, went toward the east cabin. Captain Baxter was armed with a submachinegun. Sheriff Coffee commanded the occupants to come out for questioning and was answered by a woman's voice, saying "As soon as we get dressed." After a few minutes wait, the Sheriff called that unless they came out the cabin would be bombarded. His answer was a fusilade of shots. The sheriff was hit three times, but the shield protected all vital spots. As he commenced firing, Captain Baxter's submachinegun jammed.

The two officers withdrew. Rifle bullets were now peppering the squad car and the "bullet-proof" glass. After firing about six shots, the submachinegun in the car jammed and, at about the same time, the driver was shot through the legs. The squad car was then backed away from the garage.

Another officer was wounded. Just then the door of the east cabin flew open and a man and a woman ran out. They stumbled under a burst of fire but made the garage, raised its door, and reached their car. Here they were joined by the other pair, who came directly from the west cabin into the garage. The car dashed backward out of the garage and drove off into the night. It was a clean getaway, though a number of weapons were left behind and fresh blood stains indicated that at least one of the group had been wounded.

Despite the complete surprise of the attack, the bandits had fought their way through a cordon of officers and escaped—twelve armed officers against only two men and two women.

The Barrow incident is not an isolated example; there are many others. Not only does a failure such as this cost lives, but law enforcement in general loses prestige and public confidence. Also it increases the arrogance and self-confidence of the more desperate criminal types.

PLANNING THE RAID

In planning a raid, the objective is the first consideration. This may be the apprehension, or subjugation, of criminals or insane persons; or it may be search and seizure of the premises. Next is the element of surprise. If at all possible, the raid should be executed under such conditions and at such times that it will be a complete surprise to the defending party.

A well-planned raid, executed without the benefit of surprise and made in the face of enemy fire, obviously is much more difficult than one where surprise is present. It involves more risk and requires more skillful execution. No raid should ever be undertaken against armed, desperate men without careful planning of the most efficient employment of weapons.

The following discussion should be considered only as a general pattern for the planning of a successful raid. No two raids will be exactly alike. The local situation, the time element, and the nature of the objective will influence the planning and execution of each. Initiative and common sense must be coupled with the experience gained in actual combat, if police operations of this type are to be generally successful.

RAID COMMAND AND PERSONNEL

Any group action which involves the use of weapons and the consequent possibility of casualties must be well led.

World War II reemphasized that there must be a unified supreme command in all military operations, small and large. This holds true in law enforcement. The raid commander, once chosen, must be given authority and his decisions must be carried out explicitly by all members of the raiding party. Innate qualities of leadership, experience and sound judgment are requisites in any commander. In the Armed Forces, the choice of a commander for any given operation is ordinarily dictated by rank; but in civil law enforcement, the selection of the leader and of the personnel to carry out the raid is sometimes not so simple. Raiding parties often are made up of representatives of different law enforcement bodies. Overlapping jurisdiction, and a need for additional strength and experienced personnel, will often result in the raiding party being made up of representatives of State, Federal, county and municipal police forces. Such a mixed personnel situation presents problems in the planning and execution of the raid and in the selection of the raid commander. If at all possible, the major phases of the raid should be carried out by one police organization under the leadership of a man known for his ability—one who has the confidence of the members of the raiding party and who knows the individual capabilities of the men in his command.

Mixed raiding parties often operate under a handicap because of differences in training, experience and cooperation. This handicap must be recognized—and surmounted—in the planning stage. Failure to cooperate or to obey orders, for any reason, after the actual raid has started will lead to possible casualties and failure. Petty or jurisdictional jealousies must be kept to a minimum.

The raid commander should be selected and his authority established; and he should be given his choice, when possible, of the men and equipment necessary to do the job. He must then consider the following factors as they pertain to his mission.

Estimate of the Situation. By observation, information and a study of past records of the individuals involved, the following facts should be ascertained, if possible, prior to the planning and execution of the raid.

(1) *The number of criminals or other persons involved, and their individual characteristics.*

a. Will they surrender peaceably if given the chance?
b. Will they fight it out?

c. What kind of a leader have they?

d. Is the legal penalty due for crimes already committed such that anything other than force is likely to succeed?

e. Are they skilled in fighting? Have they had combat experience against police? Have they been in the Armed Forces?

(2) *Armament.*

a. What specific types of weapons do they have—rifles, shotguns, hand guns, submachineguns?

b. What do their past records, if any, show about their attitude toward the use of weapons?

c. Is their ammunition supply limited? Extensive?

d. Is there a possibility, due to military experience and training, that they may employ trip wires, boobytraps, or explosives?

e. Are they particularly skilled in the use of their weapons? What particular weapons?

(3) *Location and Surroundings.*

a. What type of building are they occupying? Is it constructed of wood, brick, concrete? How many floors?

b. Where are the doors, windows, skylights located? What is their relation to adjoining buildings and to the terrain?

c. Is the roof accessible from adjoining buildings? Is it a possible source of enemy fire, or a likely means of approach?

d. Is there a basement? What and where are its entrances and exits? Does it connect with basements of other buildings? Is it a likely place for enemy fire or approach?

e. Is there a garage? Can it be entered without exposure to gunfire? Could a car from the garage be used to make a sudden break to escape?

f. Where, exactly, in the building are the criminals located? If unknown, can this best be determined by drawing fire or by studying the defense possibilities?

g. What is the exact interior plan of the building? Can this information be obtained from the owner, landlord, tenant, architect, city records?

(4) *Other Factors.*

a. Is it safe to use high velocity weapons (or any firearms) because of the proximity of other residences and civilians? By delaying the action, can gas equipment be obtained? Can it be used to good advantage?

b. What is the attitude of the populace and local civil authorities, toward the use of extreme force, if necessary?

c. Will the death of any of the criminals or their associates, due to police action, bring on undue criticism from the press or the public?

d. Are any women involved in the action? Any hostages?

(5) *Enemy Capabilities.*

a. Considering the characteristics of the criminals involved, what reaction can be expected from a surprise attack?

b. Is a surprise attack possible? Do they have lookouts posted?

c. Should a contact be made with the defending party to try to bring about a peaceful surrender? Is a last ditch fight to be expected?

d. Can contact be made by phone, sound system, voice, or intermediary, if desired?

e. What will be the probable result of an overwhelming display of force and armament?

f. Can the water, light, gas, and other utilities be cut off conveniently? What will be the result?

g. Can a break be expected, once it becomes too hot inside the building? Where is this most likely to take place?

The raid commander who has the answers to these questions should, by the exercise of good judgment and with suggestions from other members of the raiding party, be able to work out a successful attack.

Caution should be exercised during the planning stage to avoid too much high level planning. Persons in higher authority, who are not going to participate physically, should avoid entering into detailed operational plans. Their arbitrary decisions may cause the raid commander and his men to act against their own good judgment.

Members of the Raiding Party. Personnel making up any raiding party should be selected by the officer in charge, if possible, and should be known by him. Men with courage, initiative and ability, coupled with past experience in combat and raids, are most desirable. Men who have had actual combat infantry experience can also be valuable.

The size of the raiding party will depend on the resistance expected. Generally it is a sound plan to use the military axiom which demands a superiority of at least three to one; provided, of course, that the number of the defenders is known. Situations may arise where such a ratio is not possible. In that case, surprise, superior armament and faultless planning and execution must compensate for lack of numbers.

If time permits, it is usually possible to concentrate a sizeable superior force of officers against any group of criminals. Providing the raid commander can maintain control, through his own abilities and through trusted subordinates, he should take advantage of any possible superiority in numbers and armament. If the size of the raiding group is such that the commander does not have personal knowledge of the experience, training and abilities of all the men at his disposal, he should try to assign key missions to men of known ability.

Briefing the Raiding Party. The plan for the raid should be presented to all members of the raiding party and the mission should be stated clearly and in detail, with generalities avoided. The commander must make clear *who* is to do *what, when, where,* and *how.* Each man should be briefed exactly on his duties and also should be given an opportunity to ask questions. The raid commander should, as much as possible, explain the "whys" for certain steps. If each member of the raiding party understands *why,* he cooperates more effectively. This is especially true if the men in the raiding party are inexperienced, unknown to each other, have had different levels of training, or are from different organizations.

If the raiding party is large and has been assembled from various localities and departments, subordinates should be assigned, during the preparation stage, to arrange for weapons and munitions, transportation, communications, equipment, and first aid. If the operation is of considerable size, the leader can issue maps, sketches, written orders and oral instructions. Any action that will eliminate possible error and strengthen control is certainly advisable.

THE ACTUAL RAID

The decision on the type of raid to be undertaken will depend on the local situation and the opposition. A surprise raid, which requires simultaneous entry into the building in order to force immediate surrender, may be one plan. Or it may be desirable to place the men in position, contact the defenders and order them to come out and surrender. Where the defenders have been alerted and have made known their intention to fight, the opening phase of the operation will be a simultaneous, concentrated fire upon the building.

A raiding party, of any size, normally should be split into two sections. One section should surround the area, and the other should make the actual assault, if it has been decided to storm the objective and force a quick decision.

The Party Surrounding the Area. Usually this group will be responsible for cutting off any attempt to escape, for setting up roadblocks if needed, and for covering the advance of the assaulting party by fire or gas. It should also provide for any unforeseen incident by holding some men and special weapons in reserve. Another important function will be to throw up a protective cover, so as to keep vehicular traffic and the inevitable curious public from getting into the area, where they are actually in danger and might hamper the operation. In heavily populated districts, this alone may take as many, or more, men as are in the entire assault group. Fire departments, auxiliary police, and additional police drawn in from other areas, have all been used to control this phase of the operation.

Maintaining Control. In a situation involving a fire fight, prior to a physical assault, the raid commander must have complete control and must be able to direct the actions of his group at all times. The only way he can do so is by having his men well briefed on their exact duties and by having a logical plan which is flexible enough to meet any situation. Methods of communication must be devised during the planning stage. The leader can best maintain control by placing himself where he can observe the major phases of the action. This does not mean that he should lead an initial assault, thus limiting his view. He should select a position that is strategically located for his command post. He should tell all his men where it is located and when and where, in the various phases of action, he can be contacted. As the action progresses, this command post may be changed; but in a limited action, such as a raid on a building, it is usually not necessary to move about until the last assault phase, when the raid commander may move in as he sees fit. Control established by a workable means of communication is especially necessary when the raiding party is large and when the operation takes place at night. In darkness, particularly, the final assault phase must be well-organized and controlled, to prevent confusion and the possibility of the attackers firing on one another.

Means of Control. (1) *Time.* Using a set time to initiate an action is a good method, if all watches are synchronized and if a surprise assault is to be launched. Time can also be the means of launching other set phases. It is well, also, to have a secondary prepared signal for launching the assault, in case something goes wrong before the synchronized time.

(2) *Sound.* Signals, such as whistle blasts, horns, sound systems and voice, can be utilized, but they must be used at times when outside noises (gunfire, for example) do not drown them out. They must be strong enough to cover the entire area of the operation.

(3) *Sight.* At night, colored flares, if available, provide an efficient method of controlling various phases of the action.

(4) *Radio.* The use of radio-equipped cars, walkie-talkies, or other types of portable sets, should be mandatory, especially in a large operation. The recent development and use of tiny transistor type radio tubes and miniature batteries has made the "Dick Tracy" two-way wrist radio an actuality. Before too long a raid commander will probably be able to have direct communication with each man in the action.

(5) *Messengers.* Written messages delivered by hand are better than oral ones. Under the stress of combat, oral messages are subject to distortion, especially if they are lengthy. In planning a means of communication, it is obvious that speed of contact is important. For this reason, messages sent by motorcycle or foot should not ordinarily be used if a swifter means is available.

A few of the basic signals which should be included in the briefing are those for attack, open fire, cease fire, hold ground, retreat, and for the reserves or surrounding party to close in. The character of each raid will determine which of these signals, or others, will be necessary.

The Approach. An assembly point for all members of the party should be designated in the immediate vicinity of the objective. In a surprise raid, this point must be out of sight and hearing. After the members have assembled at a designated time, a last-minute check should be made of plans, weapons, communications, and other equipment. Last-minute instructions should be issued by the leader, watches should be checked (if a set time is to be used), and last-minute questions should be answered. The raid commander should then send the men to their positions. He must be sure to allow ample time for them to get into position. If the attack has been set for dawn, information about the time of daybreak obviously is necessary. Up to the point of attack, the organizational phases of all raids are similar. The scope of the raid and the local situation will influence the initial phases and determine the actual action, once the operation is launched.

Every police department should have on hand specially prepared "canned" plans which are to be used for emergency raids. These plans should be standardized, to take care of all foreseeable situations. They should be taken up during departmental training sessions, just as disaster plans and other emergency situations are covered.

SURPRISE RAID TACTICS

In a surprise raid, calling for entry of a building, the following points should be considered:

(1) A covering party should remain outside to block all possible exits (roof, doors, windows).

(2) A plan of the inside of the building should be studied in advance, and the location of sleeping quarters ascertained, if the raid is to be made at night.

(3) Ordinarily, entry should be made at one point only, especially if the raid is made at night. Simultaneous entry from different directions is apt to cause members of the raiding party to shoot each other instead of the criminals. If it is necessary to enter from more than one point, adequate recognition and cease-fire signals should be prepared. If a plan of the building is available, definite limits of penetradition for each man can be set, to prevent confusion. Men should be placed outside to cover all exits.

(4) Entry from a point where it would be least expected should always be considered. For example, if available and accessible, a skylight in the roof is often a good point of entry.

(5) A signal should be arranged for the covering party outside to close in when the criminals have been apprehended.

(6) In a night entry, at least fifteen minutes should be allowed for members of the party to condition their eyes to darkness. Night sight always must be gained prior to entry of a dark building. In like manner, a brightly lighted room should be entered from darkness only after the eyes have been conditioned to bright light outside; otherwise, the officer may be blinded by the sudden glare.

(7) Entry should be made with gun in hand. Doors and windows should be entered and passed through diagonally, so as to avoid being silhouetted against the sky or outside light. A listening pause should be made after the initial entry.

(8) Each man should carry a flashlight, for possible use after entry.

(9) Once the effect of surprise is lost, by shooting or other noise, it is sometimes advisable to have the headlights or spotlights of squad cars turned to cover the outside of the building. These lights will help prevent possible escape. If this maneuver is desired, it should be planned in advance, so that squad cars are in position.

(10) It is best to stay close to the walls when advancing down hallways or up stairs.

(11) In old wooden buildings, watch out for squeaky floors, steps or doors. Doors with creaky hinges can often be opened more silently by lifting up the door slightly, thereby taking the strain off the hinge.

(12) In advancing through a dark room containing furniture, it is best to keep to the middle of the room, to avoid encountering obstacles that may produce noises.

(13) If a noise is inadvertently made while trying to move silently through a darkened room, a pause should be made until it is certain that no alarm has been given. If the noise alarms the occupants, it is best to drop to the floor in a prone position and face the source of danger. The weapon should be in hand and out in front of the body.

(14) Patience in this type of entry is invaluable. If two hostile parties are aware of each other's presence in the same darkened room, the best strategy is to remain still and let the opponent move first, thus disclosing his location. When under this strain, heavy breathing—which is natural—should be suppressed, as it will give away your position.

If a gun battle is imminent, throw some object carried in your pocket, such as a pencil or comb, into a corner away from you. If the enemy fires at the noise, shoot at his gun flash. It is well to place a shot on each side of his muzzle blast. When you fire first from a prone position, roll over and away, if possible, so as to escape return fire at your muzzle blast. If standing upright when opening fire, drop down the instant the shot is fired.

A position on top of a piano or table is very advantageous in a dark room, especially if it places you above the normal line of fire—and if it can be occupied prior to contact and maintained without noise.

(15) Hand guns are the best weapons to carry in making silent entry in darkness. Shoulder weapons and submachine-guns are too unwieldy and can be noise makers. Parts of the clothing or uniform that make a noise when moving, such as gun and belt harnesses, should be removed before entering. Shoes also should be removed unless they are sneakers or have rubber soles. Luminous dials on wrist watches can be a give away in a silent night entry. They should be removed or covered.

(16) When a lone suspect is finally located in a darkened room and is in bed asleep, shine a flashlight on his face when awakening him. The sudden glare will blind him when he opens his eyes. Hold the flashlight away from the body, to one side or the other if there is any chance of the suspect being awake or opening fire. Desperate criminals often sleep with their weapons under the pillow or under the covers. If possible, make your initial approach from behind the head of the bed occupant. This will place him in a position from which he cannot fire accurately when awakened.

Night entry presents many hazards, especially where desperate men are likely to be encountered. Unless the members of the raiding party have unquestioned skill, training, experience and courage, it is often better to cover the house from the outside, awaken the occupants and demand that they surrender—even though they may not do so without a fight. This is especially true when the building is large, the occupants many, and the exact interior construction and room arrangement unknown.

TACTICS OF AN EXTERNAL ATTACK

(1) The tactics to be used when attacking armed opponents without entering a building depend on local police equipment. Whenever possible, tear gas, smoke, or sickening gas (CN-DM) should be used. See chapter 13 *Chemical Munitions for Control of Mobs and Individuals.*

(2) The capabilities of individual police weapons must be exploited to the fullest. Use the right weapon for the right job.

(3) Fields of fire must be set up that will cover all possible exits. If available, automatic weapons should be concentrated on the area from which the defenders are most likely to make a break and from which most of the gunfire

in the building is being received. Sufficient police, with adequate weapons, should be assigned to cover all possible exits.

(4) Adequate cover should be selected for all firing points. If such cover is not available at close range, where low velocity weapons may be effective, higher-powered weapons should be used from areas further away, where cover is available.

(5) Closed garages and other possible exits of cars should be covered, so as to prevent a break using a vehicle. If a possible escape car is visible, the tires, gas tank, radiator, or other vital part, should be punctured by gunfire.

(6) If men who are in position, or who are advancing while firing, are likely to be subject to crossfire from their flanks, they must be protected by placing additional men and weapons to provide covering fire on these danger areas.

(7) The types of weapons used by the defenders should always be considered in planning an advance and selecting cover. Bullet-proof vests, portable armor plate, shields, and bullet-proof glass will not stand up against high velocity rifle bullets. If a car is used for cover against rifle fire, the hood and engine block will provide some protection. The body of the car will not.

(8) Any attack that has as its objective the entry of a building should be initiated and covered by heavily concentrated fire on windows, doors, roof, or other points from which enemy fire is being received.

(9) A running advance, from cover to cover or toward the defended building, should be made in a zig-zag manner, with the body in a crouched position. Such an advance should be made under covering fire if possible. It should be made in short runs, or bounds, so that the time of exposure to gunfire is short.

(10) An assault in the face of gunfire should be so organized and planned that there are sufficient numbers in the assaulting party to enter the building and subdue the defenders. Single, isolated charges, carried out by individual members of the attacking party, often result in needless casualties.

(11) Well-trained snipers, armed with telescopic-sighted rifles, often can be used to great advantage in combat of this sort; and the use of binoculars by the controlling officer has a definite advantage.

(12) Many buildings have blind sides—with few, if any, doors and windows—so that they can be approached safely.

Once the blind side of a building is reached, the party can follow around the outside walls and enter at a previously chosen section. If accurate covering fire supports the men who are gaining entry in this manner, it is difficult for the defenders to reach them by fire without unduly exposing themselves.

(13) The attackers should always avoid bunching up. Any concerted advance on the besieged area should be made in lines of skirmishers, one man running forward to cover, then another. Since there is always a possibility of criminals possessing submachineguns or shotguns, a concerted frontal assault should be made only after such weapons have been silenced, or made inoperative, by covering fire in volume.

(14) If the number of the defenders is small and their exact location is known, a basic strategy of keeping them and their weapons busy by returning fire, no matter how inaccurately directed, should be used. This will enable other officers to approach and enter the building from unprotected or blind sides.

(15) When armed opponents are barricaded in such a manner that they can only be approached frontally, a truck or automobile, with the rear compartment loaded with a bullet resisting material can be used. Packed newspapers, magazines, firewood and sacks of coal are effective for this purpose. The vehicle is backed up to the desired position in the attack.

Bundles of magazines and newspapers, tied together compactly, will provide a satisfactory shield against small arms fire. Twenty pounds of newspaper tied in a bundle (full sheet size) will stop ordinary hand gun and shotgun bullets— but will not stop high-velocity rifle bullets. Magazines, being a higher quality paper, can be made into even more effective shields. Scoop shovels, heavy planks, the old type folding automobile hood, pieces of furniture, doubled up mattresses, have also been used successfully. In improvising such a shield, it is only common sense to consider the armament that will be used against it, and to test it with a comparable weapon.

(16) In a large raid, especially one that is conducted at night, the protective cordon placed around the area should always include several squad cars, with engines idling,

to be used for pursuit in case the unexpected happens and the criminals make a successful break in an automobile. If there is a possibility of escape by car, and there is a lack of pursuit vehicles or an insufficient force, road blocks can be constructed. These may consist of logs, spiked boards, commandeered cars or trucks, or any other bulky material that will impede a speeding vehicle. A man with a shotgun or automatic weapon, stationed in a covered position near a road block, will make it all the more effective.

(17) An attempt to flush the occupants of a house into the open can be made. If surprise is possible, place men covering all exits. Then, with a squad car, approach a protected side of the building and sound the siren. This may succeed in flushing the occupants into the open in an attempt to escape, especially if the covering party is not visible. Once the occupants are out of the building, the covering party can force a surrender, or can at least be in an advantageous position should a fire fight ensue.

If the criminals fail to leave the building, they can be ordered to surrender. If this fails, the covering party can remain in place; and time can be taken for organizing a concerted attack.

(18) When tear gas, CN-DM, or smoke bombs are not available, police may resort to demolitions. Dynamite sticks with short fuses may be used as concussion grenades, to be thrown through windows; and charges to blast down barricades and walls can be prepared. Of course, men with a knowledge of demolitions should handle this sort of action.

(19) When a criminal is holed up in an outhouse, or some type of building where there is no danger of fire spreading, a fire bomb can be used to force him to come out into the open. Such a bomb can be easily prepared, as follows: Fill a glass container (such as a beer bottle) with gasoline. Plug or seal it securely and tie a strip of soft cloth, about two feet long, around it. Saturate the end of the cloth in gasoline and light it. Throw the bottle against the building. When the glass shatters, the gasoline will be splashed around and ignited by the flaming streamer attached.

(20) In a night operation, all critical areas of the defensive position should be subject to instant illumination by means of spotlights, flares, etc. Cars with spotlights should, when possible, be placed in protected positions to eliminate drawing fire. Portable spotlights should be used in like manner.

Aside from the obvious advantages of being able to light up any given area at will, the psychological effect on defenders is sometimes very great.

THE USE OF POLICE WEAPONS IN RAIDS

The weapons available to a police organization must be used intelligently if the most is to be made of their inherent combat qualities. The use of the right weapon often will make close-quarter physical assault unnecessary. Concentrated firepower, accurate sniping, and the use of arms capable of penetrating the walls and barricades of buildings often will eliminate armed resistance and prevent needless casualties.

The Pistol and Revolver. The combat use of these weapons is practically limited to distances of not over 50 yards. They are most useful at close quarters and inside buildings, especially if the men carrying them have been trained in combat shooting. The hand gun, with the two-handed grip and utilizing a rest where possible, can be effective up to 250 yards, provided the shooter has been trained to use his weapon this way and has had practice.

Sawed-Off Shotguns. Sawed-off shotguns, or riot guns, as used by police, have two principal advantages—one psychological, the other practical. In handling prisoners and mobs, the large bore of the sawed-off shotgun (usually 12-gauge) has a deterring effect on anyone who looks at it from the muzzle end. It is also a most practical police weapon because of its wide shot-pattern and its effectiveness at ranges up to 60 yards.

The normal police load for this gun is Double OO buckshot. In the cartridge, this consists of 9 pellets, about .32 caliber in size.

The pattern diameter of this shot group should be known to all law enforcement officers who are likely to use the weapon. Normally the 9 pellets in the cartridge will spread about one inch to a yard of range. The spread of the pellets is uneven; even at a distance of 15 yards all of them will not hit a man-size target. Depending upon the individual gun, at 50 to 60 yards the pattern will be 5 to 6 feet in diameter, and some of the pellets will hit a man-size target consistently. Beyond this distance, it is quite possible that all nine pellets might miss a man, even though the charge was aimed at him. It is obvious, therefore, that the most effective use of the riot gun and its buckshot charge, at a single target, is at dis-

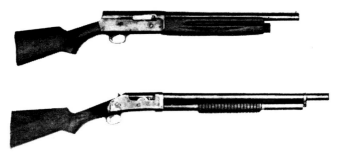

The sawed-off shotgun is one of the most deadly weapons in the police or gangster arsenal. Commercial type 12 gauge sporting weapons can easily be made into deadly short range combat arms by cutting off the barrels and stocks. The shotgun is thereby made more maneuverable and concealable. Cutting off the barrel also eliminates the choke, resulting in a wider dispersion and pattern of buckshot pellets. Tear gas cartridges are also available for firing in this type gun. They are best fired and loaded on a single shot basis due to chambering and ejection problems.

tances of less than 60 yards. At night, when used for guard duty or in covering a designated area, as in a raid, it is a better weapon than a rifle, where a single poorly aimed bullet may miss by 3 or 4 feet.

It is usually effective to use the riot gun when covering a door or window from a distance of 30 to 40 yards, so as to get the benefit of dispersion and cover the entire area. When used against a crowd, or when more than one gun is fired on a specified area, the riot gun naturally can be employed at greater ranges than when used against a single target. Beyond effective range (50-60 yards) the 9 pellets of the charge will spread over an area of about 25 feet at 100 yards, and 50 to 75 feet at 200 yards. Stray pellets have been known to wound or kill up to 500 yards.

After the policeman understands the capabilities of this weapon, he will also better appreciate the danger of using it in areas where its scatter qualities may injure innocent persons.

At close ranges, the lead pellets will penetrate a 4-inch piece of pine; at 40 yards a 2-inch piece of pine; and at 250 yards a ¾-inch piece. Beyond point-blank range, the Double OO buckshot is not likely to pierce the walls of any well-built house or the body of an automobile.

In addition to the many kinds of lighter commercial shot charges, the modern rifled shotgun slug (instead of the round ball) should be considered. In the 12-gauge size, this single slug weighs about an ounce. A shotgun firing it is capable of shooting a 12-inch group at 100 yards. Its extreme range is about one mile, and it is capable of penetrating the average frame house or an automobile body and killing the occupants. When rifles are not available, a supply of this type cartridge for use in the riot gun, in place of the Double OO buckshot charge, will result in more effective all-around use of the weapon.

Submachineguns. Most police departments of any size have one or more submachineguns. This weapon is accurate only at medium ranges, and, in reality, fills in the gap between the hand gun and the rifle. Most American-made guns of this type fire .45 caliber automatic pistol ammunition. In World War II, the weapon was used extensively by all participating armies, the European type being about .35 caliber (9mm). This gun can be fired from the hip or the shoulder. Its accuracy is comparable to a rifle up to 200 yards, depending on the type of ammunition used. It can also be used from the hip most effectively at close quarters, under poor light conditions, or when time is not available for an aimed shot, or burst, from the shoulder firing position.

Although it is possible to use this gun on full automatic and to fire it effectively in bursts of 3 or 4 shots, its best use for police is as a semi-automatic weapon, pulling the trigger for each shot. In ordinary circumstances, the gun can be fired much more effectively, and rapidly enough, on semi-automatic. It is easily possible, after training, for the average officer to shoot one aimed shot a second. To be able to use the gun effectively on full automatic under combat conditions, requires a great deal of firing practice and training. With an untrained man, there is a tendency to spray lead indiscriminately, as though he were spraying water from a hose. This is especially true in combat, when an untrained user will not only exhaust the ammunition supply rapidly, but also may lose control of his weapon, due to recoil.

If a police department has a submachinegun as part of its equipment, provision must be made for instruction and practice. Adequate ammunition must be supplied, and either instruction must be limited to the select few who will be required to use it, or an extensive program must be undertaken to instruct the whole department. Too often a weapon of this type is misused by personnel unfamiliar with it.

Usually the submachinegun is not used or taken out of its

case until a specific situation demands it. For this reason, congealed grease and dust, as well as unfamiliarity with the weapon, have often caused it to jam. On the other hand, proper training, normal care and an appreciation of its capabilities can make the submachinegun a valuable weapon in the police arsenal.

Rifles. A well-stocked police arsenal should always include a number of rifles for possible use in riots, road blocks, raids and other special situations. The caliber of these rifles may vary with individual choice, but they usually will be .30 caliber or over. A police department that is made up of personnel who use not only their sidearms but also their shoulder weapons accurately and effectively, is much respected.

As in the case of the submachinegun, the rifle should only be used by men who have had training and practice with it, even though this may limit its employment to a few selected individuals. From the standpoint of ammunition supply, combat effectiveness and training, it is best to have shoulder weapons standardized so they are all of one type and caliber. This should apply also to hand guns, riot guns, submachine-guns, and all other equipment.

Rifles are very effective when fired by men trained to use their inherent accuracy, range and penetrating power. In addition to having all, or a selected part, of the force trained in use of the rifle, having a few such weapons equipped with telescopic sights and mounts is much to be desired. In most departments, the type of officer who is a "gun crank" can usually be found. In all probability, he will be skilled in rifle shooting and may personally own a scope-sighted rifle. Such

A rugged scope sighted high powered rifle such as this Remington model 721 caliber 30/06 with Lyman telescopic sights is a potent addition to the standard police armory.

an officer, who can serve as a sniper at longer ranges, will be most valuable in a combat situation calling for precision shooting. Accurate long-range rifle fire will often eliminate the necessity for close-quarter work and therefore reduce casualties.

THE BULLET: PENETRATION AND CAPABILITIES

The policeman who uses firearms in combat should know the potentialities of his weapons—in range, man-stopping qualities and penetration of solid substances. Not only that; he should also be aware of the danger of misusing his weapons in areas and situations where innocent persons are endangered. Every training course in weapons should cover this phase of their employment.

An especially effective way of impressing students with the power of weapons is by actual demonstrations of bullet penetration and range. Permanent displays, showing the penetrating qualities of the weapons in such substances as hard and soft wood, automobile bodies, brick, sand, plaster walls, newspapers, mattresses, bullet-proof glass, magazines, bales of straw, and so forth, are most effective in making the point clear.

Another effective demonstration is to use laundry soap, wax, or lard to simulate human flesh, showing the reaction to various bullets. Large sheets of paper can illustrate the pattern of riot guns at various ranges.

Stopping Power of Various Calibers. There is endless controversy over the stopping power of bullets of various sizes and muzzle velocities. Arguments have been long and loud as to whether or not a small-power, high-velocity bullet is more deadly than a large-caliber, low-velocity slug.

Generally, it has been considered that the big, slow moving pellet, such as the .45, is superior to a light-weight, faster-moving bullet. If you hit a man on the chin with your fist, all the force of the blow is transmitted to the recipient. The big, slow-moving bullet functions in this manner; all the energy of the bullet is exhausted at the time of impact and the bullet does not penetrate and go on through. However, when a target is hit with a speedy, light-weight bullet, it generally penetrates the target and sings off into space, wasting a lot of velocity and shocking power. Although this is generally recognized as the standard argument for the larger caliber hand gun, many instances are on record of such large calibers failing to stop individuals in combat. On the other hand, there are instances where small caliber bullets have done the job as well as any other size.

No one caliber is best in all cases, and, although larger calibers generally are better, they are not infallible. The human factor enters in—the position of a man's body at the time of impact, whether he is off or on balance; the spot hit; the size of the man; his resistance to sudden shock; his animal courage and fighting spirit—all affect the stopping power, regardless of the caliber of the weapon or the size of the bullet.

Most police departments have cases on record which will illustrate the stopping power of bullets. Such cases should be covered in the training period devoted to this subject. And students should be informed by lecture and demonstration, of the specific penetrating power of certain calibers of bullets.

Bullet penetration tests are usually based on firing at ⅞" pine boards stacked together to the required thickness at a 15 ft. range. A penetration of one inch in the pine is considered sufficient to give a serious wound. The following calibers will penetrate as follows:

Caliber	Bullet-Weights	In Inches Pine Penetration
.44 MAGNUM	240 gr.	11"
.357 MAGNUM	158 gr.	10"
.30 LUGER (7.65MM)	93 gr. Metal Jacketed	9½"
9 MM LUGER	115 gr. Metal Jacketed	8½"
.38 SPECIAL	158 gr.	6"
.45 COLT REVOLVER	255 gr.	5"
.380 AUTO.	95 gr. Metal Jacketed	4½"
.32 AUTO.	71 gr. Metal Jacketed	4"
.45 CAL. AUTO.	230 gr. Metal Jacketed	4"
.38 S & W	145 gr.	3"
.32 S & W	85 gr.	2½"
.25 AUTO.	50 gr. Metal Jacketed	2½"

Heavy lead alloy bullets are generally carried and used in most police revolvers. Automatics generally fire metal jacketed bullets which increase penetration and better prevent the automatic from jamming. In modern warfare lead bullets are banned as they are considered as "dum dum" and inhumane. The peace officer, however, can take full advantage of the solid lead bullet in his fight against criminal elements.

The heavy lead slug when driven at high velocities expands in diameter on impact and develops much greater shocking and stopping power. The metal jacketed bullet will give more penetration everything else being equal but it holds its shape and diameter due to its construction.

It is easy to see that any such flimsy barricades as bureaus and tables will not necessarily stop bullets. Another fallacy is that a mattress is ample protection against small arms fire.

Actually, the .38 and .45 will penetrate 10 inches or more of solid mattress, not of the box spring type. Either the .38 or .45 will penetrate most plaster walls found in dwellings.

ROOM COMBAT

Combat inside buildings, where one individual attacks or defends himself against another, where criminals and insane persons are cornered in rooms, differs from street fighting. Street fighting, in the "Stalingrad" sense, means heavy artillery, mortars, smoke, grenades, automatic weapons, flame throwers, and similar equipment of the modern army.

Normally, in room combat, the only armament will be small arms such as the police officer normally carries, plus any other weapons he may improvise on the spur of the moment. Naturally, if time and circumstances permit, special equipment and armament—such as tear gas, riot guns, and submachine-guns—should be used; but in most situations it is necessary to get the opponent, dead or alive, in the shortest possible time, and the officer must depend upon himself, his assistants and the small arms he normally carries.

Tactical Considerations. In one respect, room entry and fighting is not unlike land warfare, where the terrain is decisive. Here the construction and architecture of the house and its individual rooms play an important role. A hasty survey of the building and the exterior of the individual room, once it is located, is the standard procedure. Common sense then will usually dictate the course of action. Of course, all possible means of escape should be blocked.

It is well to consider the mental attitude of the individual being attacked. Is he frightened, desperate, cold-blooded? Can he be induced to surrender without a fire fight? Naturally, oral persuasion should be tried before making any physical attempt.

If possible, there should be a numerical superiority of 3 to 1 in an attack of this kind. There will be occasions when one or two officers may be forced to make a room entry and shoot it out; but three or more make a better combination.

It is important to know the gunman's exact location in the room. If you can get him to talk, you may be able to place him. The movement of furniture or a barricade will often give a clue. If the attack is in a hotel, often, by looking at the rooms next door, an idea can be gained as to how the besieged room is furnished. Rooms of many American and European hotels are built and furnished alike.

If unable to get any definite indication of the defender's location in the room, there are some general rules which can be applied. Instinctively, a desperate, *armed* man will take up a position in a room where he can see the door and what comes through it. In other words, he will be on the side of the room opposite the door side. On the other hand, an *unarmed* man, who is hiding and scared, will be on the *door* side of the room, or even behind the door, as it opens. That is why, when searching a house or a room, you should slam each door hard as you open it. If it doesn't bang against the wall, but only makes a thud, cover the area immediately. This behind-the-door technique is an overworked movie trick, but cheap crooks and the like pick up and use such methods.

In actually entering the room, the door itself must first be breached. It will be locked, or have a chair against it, if time has been permitted the defender. It is a simple matter to blow the lock of a door with a couple of well-placed shots. Or fire axes and such can be used if they are available. If the door is heavily blocked on the inside, time will have to be taken to get rid of this block and still avoid being in the line of fire. Care should be taken, at all times, to avoid being in front of the door. Shots from the interior may cause casualties.

Tactics of Entering a Room. Once the door is breached, common sense and strategy enter into the picture. There are numerous strategems that should be employed before physical entry is made. If possible, the defender's fire should be drawn. It will disclose his position and deplete the limited amount of ammunition usually carried by criminals.

If the action is at night, as it often is, be sure that your eyes are conditioned to darkness and that lights outside the room are extinguished. Any movement outside or into the room will cause a silhouette if the light is on. Often the defender, in the room, can look under the door and determine your location.

Improvised dummies, or other larger objects, can be thrown into the room or pulled by a rope across the door, to draw fire. A light bulb thrown into the room, to cause a loud pop; a flashlight on a stick, in a dark room; a bottle of ammonia; burning oily rags; dust from a vacuum cleaner—all will create confusion and often cause a break, especially when accompanied by shouts of fire, or by tear gas. On one occasion, when a fire extinguisher was used through a transom, following up a threat to use tear gas, the defender gave up. These methods are simple and may be improvised from material at hand. They often work because of the nervous condition of the defender. If they don't work, a physical entry will be necessary.

Typical Example. Here is a typical problem of room entry and its solution, oversimplified for instructional purposes.

Situation. A desperate man is cornered in a single room which has no exits except the door. He will shoot it out; all methods of cajolery have failed. All ruses to draw fire have failed; an attack is necessary. The room is an ordinary hotel room. It is dark. His location in the room can not be ascertained.

Attackers. Three men armed with pistols only. Time does not permit getting special equipment, such as tear gas and submachineguns.

Solution. The leader decides on the plan of attack. A leader is necessary, even if the attacking party consists of only two men.

After the lock has been shot off the door and it is found that the door swings freely on its hinges, lights in the hall are put out.

Acting on the premise that the defender is in one of the corners, across from the door side of the room, attacker No. 1 dives from around the side of the door into the center of the room, on his belly. He stays flat on the floor and holds his fire until the defender fires. At the same instant, Nos. 2 and 3, from a standing position at each side of the door, fire into each corner. Chances are good that one of these initial bursts will get the defender. If not, No. 1 must finish him off. No. 1 also must watch the corners on the door side of the wall, in case the defender is holed up there. No. 1 has remained on the floor all this time, in a prone position. His is the position of risk; he should be the coolest head and the best shot. No. 2 will stay outside the room until told to enter by No. 1. No. 3 after the first burst, goes down the hall and covers that avenue of escape, in case a break is made.

It is important that clearly understood signals be arranged for contingencies that cannot be foreseen. Never more than one man of the attacking party should be in the dark room with the opponent at any time. In the dark there is too much danger of firing at a friend instead of a foe.

The solution described is only one of many, but it is sound and has a good chance of success. It is certainly better than the door-crashing technique so overworked in the movies. Plans must be flexible, however. The diagonal method of cross-firing, for example, will often succeed without entry into the room at all. This is especially true in a small room.

DEFENSE IN A ROOM

From the discussion of attack above, the following facts are obvious, if you should have to defend yourself in a room.

1. Don't imprison yourself and limit your mobility by placing yourself behind a flimsy barricade—made up of what is on hand—which ordinarily a bullet will penetrate. If you do place yourself behind such a barricade, you will limit your mobility, for when you want to leave the room in a hurry, you are at a disadvantage.

2. Have the lights out in your room. The longer the lights are out, the more conditioned your eyes become to darkness. This will give you an advantage; for if the lights are out in your room, and if the attackers leave the lights on in the hall, you can easily place them by looking under the door. A few well-placed shots through the walls or door then may solve your problem.

3. There are two places where the attackers will least expect you. Both are good because they combine, with the element of surprise and cover, the factor of mobility. If you lie on your stomach in the middle of the room away from the door, you will make a very small target; and you will be in a good firing position. Or place yourself somewhere near the center of the wall facing the door, on top of a table or any other furniture. This is the last place the attacker will expect to find you; and you also are in a position of mobility, once the firing is over. It is most likely that you will be above the line of fire during the initial bursts.

4. Hold your fire. Remember that, in darkness, you always instinctively fire at the other man's muzzle blasts. You will always know where the attacker is when his gun goes off. So, when you are on the floor, it is wise, if possible, to roll over and out of the area each time you fire.

SHOOTING THROUGH WALLS AND DOORS

A factor not often enough considered in combat inside houses, is the penetrating power of sidearms through ordinary walls and doors. With due allowance for the ammunition factor, certain well-placed shots through doors, down or up through floors, or through ceilings or sections of wall, may finish the attack before it starts. One of the easiest ways of getting a man in a room, if a submachinegun is available, is to shoot a line about a foot above the floor for the length of the room.

The .38 caliber pistol, or larger caliber, is normally carried by the law enforcement officer. He should realize the penetrating power of this weapon, so as to apply it best when the need arises.

For detailed information on the penetrating power of various calibers, see the section on *The Bullet: Penetration and Capabilities*, earlier in this chapter.

BULLET-PROOF VESTS AND POLICE SHIELDS

Police Departments and certain types of military organizations should have available bullet-proof vests and police shields for use against armed individuals in raids and in situations where frontal attack is necessary. Law enforcement supply agencies, such as W. S. Darley and Co. and Federal Laboratories, stock these items. They are relatively inexpensive and help to reduce casualties when they are used properly.

Practice in shooting from behind the police shield should be mandatory during combat firing training. Shooters should not be allowed to stand and use the shield. All shooting should be done from a kneeling position.

Bullet-proof vests, especially, should be available. These vests formerly were either solid metal plate or a chain type of mail, or were made of overlapping steel strips. They were quite restrictive in the body movement of the individual and were heavy, so that they could not be worn with comfort for any length of time. They can, however, be issued for special missions. The overlapping-strip type and the solid-plate type are more satisfactory and more bullet-resistant than the chain mail vest. Newer body armor vests are made of plastic and nylon, increasing the protection to the body, greatly reducing the weight, and making the vest less cumbersome.

Since World War II increasing use has been made of body armor vests. Two types tested by the U. S. Army have proved most successful thus far. Each weighs about eight pounds. One is made of twelve layers of spot-bonded nylon. The other, the Marine Corps model issued to the 1st Marine Division in Korea in 1952, consists of a vest with "built-in" inside pockets into which twenty laminated fiberglass "doron" armor plates, each about five inches square, are inserted, to

A protective police shield can be constructed of bullet-proof steel plate or preferably of the new light weight fiberglass material. Every police department should have on hand this item of equipment for use in combat situations.

Firing position when using police shield. Note that gun is being fired through a firing slot in the upper right hand corner. The shield protects all vital parts of the body. It can be constructed in various sizes by the individual department, if desired. Fiberglass panels can be purchased for this purpose. Steel type shields are commercially available. It is generally a good idea to paint the outside of the shield a dark color so as to more readily conceal the firing position when used at night.

protect the thorax, abdomen, and back; nylon is used in the shoulder areas where flexibility is needed. Such a vest gives great protection against grenade and bomb fragments and against bullets whose velocity at time of impact is not over 1400 feet per second. The Universal Moulded Products Corp. of Bristol, Virginia, is a basic manufacturer of the doron material, which can be made to any thickness needed, depending on the type of protection desired.

This new light weight armor is also being used in armoring police automobiles, bank trucks, and automobiles for important dignitaries; and our military services are continually experimenting and developing new uses for it. Eventually it could replace steel armor plate entirely, because of its lighter weight. Currently it is being used in lining cockpits of airplanes and by the Infantry for protecting body areas that are subject to long range rifle, pistol, and submachinegun fire, and grenade, mortar and artillery shell fragments. The United State Army has a quantity of vests available for issue to selected assault units.

In training, a demonstration should be made of a bullet-

Individual wearing new type bullet-proof vest, holding one of the white curved fiberglass "doron" bullet-resistant panels. A vest for a normal sized individual, giving front and back protection, consists of about 20 panels. It is approximately 75% lighter in weight than the old type vest made of steel plates, strips or chain mesh. Approximate weight is nearly eight pounds. For additional protection double panels can be inserted in the pockets, depending on the desire of the wearer.

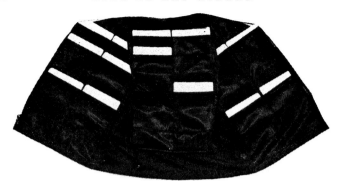

Inside view of vest showing pockets in which protective curved fiberglass "doron" panels are inserted.

proof vest, placed around a sand bag and fired at by conventional police and sporting hand guns. In any firing demonstration involving a protective-type vest, it should be stressed that cartridges developing muzzle velocities greater than 1400 feet a second will possibly penetrate. The chain mail type ordinarily will be penetrated by bullets of much lower velocity.

IMPORTANCE OF TRAINING

Little has been written on the subject of room combat. Too often such combat is left to trial and error—and needless loss of life. It is important, therefore, that consideration be given, in police training, to all aspects of this dangerous type of criminal apprehension. The basic principles, at least, should be deeply ingrained in students. Once these principles are learned, their application in each raid will not be too difficult.

A basic principle is that the leader must take the time to think through his plan to its logical conclusion. Only so will casualties be kept to a minimum. Room entry is a case in point. The movies are prone to show attackers breaking into a room by putting their shoulders to the door. This tactic, except as a last resort, is foolhardy. Because of it there have been too many dead "heroes."

Chapter 10

TRAINING TECHNIQUES
AND COMBAT RANGES

To cushion the initial shock of battle and to provide realistic training and practical tests, the modern soldier is required to participate in an "assault," or "blitz," course before being sent into actual combat. In this course he is subjected to live ammunition, demolitions and other simulated battle conditions. He uses his rifle, bayonet, hand grenades and other personal weapons in a realistic manner.

Similarly, if a soldier's or police officer's basic weapon is his hand gun, he should have a certain amount of a comparable training. When a hand gun shooter becomes familiar with his weapon and can use it accurately for aimed shots, after training on the target range, he should be projected into situations where he will be forced to use his weapon as he will use it most frequently in man-to-man combat. This, of course, applies not only to the hand gun, but also to the rifle or other firearm which he may carry.

Soldiers and law enforcement officers do not carry weapons for the exclusive purpose of shooting bull's-eyes. Primarily, their weapons are for use against enemies and criminals. Those concerned with hand gun training sometimes lose sight of this simple truth and place overemphasis on the bull's-eye target type of training, with a consequent neglect of the other.

Target training and combat firing are both needed to make a proficient, all-around combat shot with the hand gun; but those trainers (and they are legion) who consider pistol marksmanship training the complete answer to training a man in the combat use of his hand gun, are like the proverbial ostrich with his head in the sand.

It is unfortunate that many soldiers and law enforcement officers have an impersonal attitude toward their training in weapons firing. This applies particularly to those shooters who are not interested in weapons and shooting in general

COMBAT FIRING RANGE, WITH BULLET-PROOF ALLEYS

This type is suitable for training with either the hand gun or shoulder weapon. Each shooter is separated from others. Note the silhouette targets.

and to those who subconsciously feel that the technique of hitting an inanimate black dot on a white piece of paper is not closely related to the man targets they will encounter in combat. This leads to an indifferent attitude during training. Consequently, for psychological as well as practical reasons, realistic combat shooting ranges, involving the use of lifelike targets, are especially beneficial. They arouse the individual's interest by injecting the personal element into the use of his weapon. By means of practical ranges and training, the shooter who looks on his hand gun as he would any other piece of equipment, can be made to appreciate his weapon and his capabilities with it. Being able to use his gun effectively on a practical range will develop his all-around confidence—in himself, his ability, and his weapon.

POLICE TRAINING PROBLEMS

The problems of the civilian police department are not always the same as those encountered on the battlefield. Although training in combat firing is essential, there should be additional variations added to the shooting program to meet specific law enforcement needs.

Aimed, accurate fire (single or double action) has a

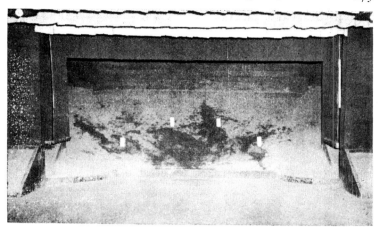

INDOOR COMBAT FIRING PRACTICE RANGE, WITH DIRT BANK AS BULLET CATCHER

The white stakes are used in practice. Bullet impacts are easily observed because of dust created on impact. The dark spots represent places where water has been thrown, to prevent too much dust arising from the impact of bullets.

USE OF BOBBING TARGETS

The same range with bobbing targets exposed. The target in the center runs across the range; the others bob out from behind walls. The curtains hanging from the ceiling reduce concussion.

definite place in police combat training. After bull's-eye target accuracy is achieved, the police trainee should then be projected into practical police-type combat ranges, where he shoots at silhouettes under simulated conditions such as he may encounter during the routine performance of his many and varied duties.

Since World War II, and as a result of combat experience, there has begun a gradual increase in practical weapons training programs and techniques by police departments. There has come about a realization that a few shots a week at a paper target do not qualify the law officer for actual fire fights with criminals.

Unlike the soldier, the police officer is faced with an additional hazard. Once he commits himself and his firearm to action, he must not only hit his man but he must also avoid wounding or killing innocent bystanders. The fear of police departments of injuring innocent spectators is a real and ever-present one. The unfavorable publicity resulting from such an accident is often so great that the department will swing almost entirely away from advocating the use of firearms. Regulations sometimes make it almost impossible for the average officer to use his hand gun with any degree of confidence or skill. His firearms training is cut down to the extent that not only is he hesitant to use his weapon but when he is forced to do so, to perform his duty or save his own life, he becomes a greater hazard to the bystander than ever.

There has to be a "happy medium" in police training. The current trend by progressive police departments has been to give more emphasis to practical range firing and to create a state of balance with the conventional target range firing. One complements the other.

The Federal Bureau of Investigation is doing a great deal to develop and encourage practical police weapons training. Along with the regular training program for bureau personnel, trainees from various city, state and county police departments are invited to participate. A very practical and effective course in shooting has been in a continuous process of development for many years at the Bureau ranges in Quantico, Virginia.

The F.B.I. Practical Pistol Course is one of the finest ever developed to properly train the police officer to defend himself and the citizens of his community. A total of fifty rounds are fired at a man-sized silhouette target in a total time of six minutes and ten seconds. In this period, firing is from the 7-yard line to the 60-yard line; right and left hands are used and many different firing positions assumed. All trainees get sound training in the use of the ordinary police weapons. Those trainees, from outside the Bureau ranks, take back to their various departments training doctrine and information that in many cases are passed on and used in their own local training programs.

One of the most practical and well known civilian police training programs is the "Combat Course" of the Toledo, Ohio, Police Department. This course has a series of targets that simulate the situations under which a police officer may be called upon to use his gun. The range facilities cover approximately 8 acres of ground and include:

The Observation Course—here metal men appear at doors and windows of simulated house fronts and spring up suddenly among trees, disappearing again in 10 seconds. Fired *single* action.

The Bull's-eye Target—a sound recording, optical illusion bull's-eye target set at 30 yards; and fired *single* action.

The Rodeo Course—a series of metal targets strategically placed on a ¼-mile, twisting, up-and-down-hill road; fired *double* action from a moving automobile.

The Running Man Target—a moving figure which threads its way through stationary figures, to be hit without injuring the "bystanders" or be penalized in points. Again, firing is *double* action.

An Anatomical Target—shaped like a man. Four-inch areas are located in six vital areas of this figure, and shots hitting any of them would theoretically make a person unable to proceed. (Three areas would be fatal and three disabling.) Firing, at a distance of 15 yards, is timed, and the target requires the officer to fire *double* action, 6 shots in 10 seconds, simulating actual conditions where he might meet an armed adversary who is ready to shoot or shooting.

Most of the targets are fired double action instead of single, thus accurately duplicating the type of firing that officers would be likely to encounter in actual combat situations.

The importance of the combat type pistol training is finally becoming more and more recognized. The Indiana University Center for Police Training, in combination with the Colt Patent Firearms Company, is now sponsoring invitational police combat pistol matches. Individuals and teams composed of regular members of any organized police department are eligible to compete. Regularly organized bank, railroad, and industrial police along with Federal agencies are also eligible to enter this competition, which is now being held annually in Bloomington, Indiana. The interest and entries are increasing yearly. It is hoped that from this and other type combat training courses a standardization of "practical" firearms training for police officers will eventually be achieved.

Generally too few civilian police departments are using practical range training. Most stick to the conventional bull's-eye training while others emphasize the "safety with weapons aspect" to an almost ridiculous degree. Too many have no training at all, after the badge is pinned on the officer. In almost all cases not enough attention and training is given to the close-quarter, instinctive-pointing type of shooting, even though police case histories show that this is the type of combat they encounter the most and usually under poor lighting or adverse shooting conditions.

SIMULATING COMBAT CONDITIONS

The conditions of actual close-quarter combat with hand guns—which make instruction and training in the instinctive pointing technique necessary—are as follows.

(1) In most cases, the *time* to take an aimed shot will not be available, and the hand gun ordinarily will be used at distances of 50 feet or less;

(2) The light necessary to see and use the sights (if the time were available), is not always sufficient;

(3) The grip on the weapon is a *convulsive* one, because of combat tension; and

(4) The instinctive position assumed by a hand gun user in a fire fight will usually be an aggressive forward *crouch*.

Most or all of these conditions are usually present in every case in which hand guns are used by men shooting at each other. It follows, then, that systems of practice and practical ranges should be developed, to give the shooter actual experience in shooting under combat conditions.

Silhouettes. Silhouettes are facsimiles of men. If the primary objective of hand gun training is to teach men to shoot men, these silhouettes should be the principal type targets used. They should be placed, and fired at, on ranges that simulate all foreseeable conditions under which a soldier or law enforcement officer would ordinarily use his weapon.

After being trained in combat firing on silhouette targets —under all possible light, terrain and other conditions—and after he has had shooting training on a range of the type to be described, the student no longer will harbor doubts as to why he should receive training in combat firing. He will realize that there is a vast difference between being able to hit a stationary bull's-eye target, at a given number of yards and under ideal conditions, and being able to hit a target that shoots back under combat conditions.

Results of Practical Range Training. The practical hand gun range described below, known as the "House of Horrors," was in operation over a two-year period. During this time several thousand hand gun shooters, of all degrees of training and experience, fired over it. A study of the records led to the following conclusions:

(1) That target shooting proficiency *alone* is not enough to equip the average man for combat, where the hand gun is his primary weapon.

(2) That the instinctive-pointing technique of combat firing is the best all-around method of shooting the hand gun without the aid of sights.

(3) That this type range is a reliable test of the combat effectiveness of all the known techniques of hand gun shooting without the aid of sights.

(4) That there must be greater appreciation, by most training officers, of the physical and psychological effects of combat tension upon the hand gun user. In addition to the changes in established techniques which were demonstrated, those shooters who were psychologically unsuited for combat or who had the wrong kind of temperament were discovered.

Constructing a Practical Range. If an old unused basement or a warehouse of medium size is available, a good combat range can be constructed at very little expense, using local materials. The first precaution, naturally, is to make the walls and ceiling bullet proof against the caliber gun to be fired. This can be done by adding 5 or 6 inches of rough planking to the walls or ceiling, or by sand bags, or by a dirt filling· inside a wood retaining wall.

In this range, at irregular intervals, place bobbing silhouette targets, stationary silhouette targets, and actual dummies. These can be painted to resemble men and can easily be set up, using hinges, springs, and trip latches, so that they pop out, or up, by pulling a cord or wire control. Steps, movable floor sections, or similar innovations may be built into this basement. Passageways, made of scrap lumber or burlap hung from the ceiling, can be built in or installed, to give realistic close-quarter effects such as might be found in a house, alleyway, or basement. The silhouette targets may be placed at appropriate intervals, in conjunction with whatever built-in effect it is desired to simulate. The result, naturally, should be that which the students expect to encounter most frequently. General lighting effects should be dim, so that only outlines are visible. A sound effect system of amplifiers and records can be installed, if available, and can be coordinated with the targets. Guns which fire blanks at the shooter can be put into dummies. Other innovations which help to create combat tension and realism can be installed. The possibilities, in building a range of this type, are almost endless, largely depending upon the available local materials and the ingenuity of the builder.

A word of caution here. The tendency to use boobytraps, false floors and other trick devices, such as are found in a carnival "fun house," should be avoided. These trick devices can, in a large measure, defeat the purpose of the range.

Described in the following pages is one such range (The House of Horrors), constructed and used for the successful training of large groups of men for specialized military duty. The basic floor plan took its shape simply because of the original construction of the only available basement, which consisted of three separate compartments. The floor is dirt and the original rock walls and pillars are covered by 6 inches of dirt held in by a wooden form made of 2-inch planking. The training weapons used in this range were standard model .38 Spl. revolvers, the .45 cal. automatic, and the Colt Ace.

In all cases the shooter is accompanied by an instructor, who guides him through the course and makes comments or makes corrections during the shooting sequences and immediately after they occur.

THE COMBAT COURSE—STEP BY STEP

Let's follow a shooter who, in this case, is armed with a .22 cal. Colt Service Ace. First, he is brought into a small room at the head of the stairs, indicated in the lower left in diagram. He is seated in a chair and left alone in this room, which has dim lighting. He is given a knife and sheath to strap on, and is told to read the following instructions, which are posted on the wall:

You are equipped with a pistol, 24 rounds of ammunition, and a fighting knife. Upon these weapons your life depends as you go down into the darkness. Below are twelve of our enemies awaiting you as you make your way along. You will fire at these enemies in *bursts of two shots.* You will use your knife at appropriate times. You will fire directly to your front, to your left, or to your right. *You will never fire to your rear.* A coach will follow immediately behind you to act as your guide and confessor.

Are you one of the quick or one of the dead?

There are no boobytraps, collapsible stairs or trick devices in the darkness below. *Just enemies who shoot back!*

If you come out alive, please tell no one else the details of what you have been through.

While he is reading the instructions, he is subjected to several record sequences (broken English) of typical enemy propaganda newscasts. Interspersed with the records are other sound effects, such as organ music; or morbid symphonic airs may be used. (In this range the extracts from the Firebird Suite by Stravinsky were used.) After not less than 5 minutes of this indoctrination, the student is called into a little annex at the head of the stairs and given his pistol and 3 magazines of ammunition, 8 rounds to a magazine. The instructor tells him to insert one magazine and place the other two where he can get them in a hurry. He is then asked if he has any questions; if so, additional last minute instructions are given. When he is ready, he is told to pull back the slide, loading his weapon, then proceed cautiously down the steps. The instructor follows immediately behind him with one hand in contact with the shooter.

The instructor, aside from acting as a guide and making on-the-spot corrections, trips all targets at the appropriate times. For obvious safety reasons, the instructor at all times maintains contact with the shooter (usually with one hand hooked into the back of his belt) while he is carrying his pistol. The instructor stays out of reach when the knife is used and when the student is in complete darkness.

As the shooter descends the steps, a record sequence (Stravinsky) is started and is interspersed by shots and screams.

When he reaches the bottom of the stairs, the coach pulls target No. 1, which is a bobbing target concealed behind a pillar. It is dimly illuminated by a red light. After firing,

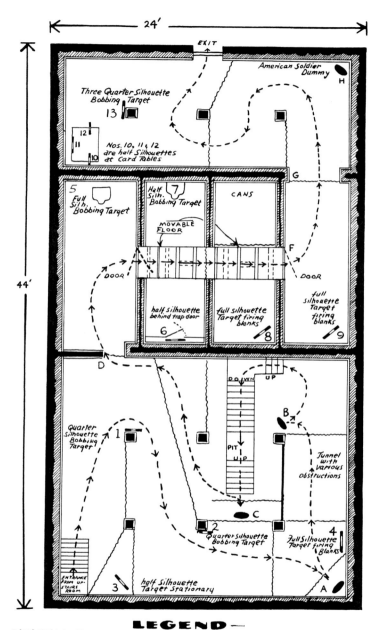

24'

44'

EXIT

American Soldier Dummy H

Three Quarter Silhouette Bobbing Target
13

12
II
10

Nos. 10, 11 & 12 are half Silhouettes at Card Tables

G

5 Full Silh. Bobbing Target

Half Silh. Bobbing Target 7

CANS

MOVABLE FLOOR

DOOR

F

DOOR

full silhouette Target firing blanks 9

half silhouette behind trap door
6

full silhouette Target firing blanks 8

D

DOWN UP

B

Quarter Silhouette Bobbing Target 1

PIT UP

Tunnel with various obstructions

C

Quarter Silhouette Bobbing Target 2

4 full Silhouette Target firing Blanks

ENTRANCE FROM UP-STAIRS ROOM

3 half Silhouette Target Stationary

A

LEGEND

PATH FOLLOWED BY STUDENT - - - → · · ·   SILHOUETTE TARGETS ⬛—

DUMMIES FOR KNIFE TARGETS ⬤   · · ·   CURTAINS ∿∿∿

Tunnel has artificial cobwebs and innertube flooring.

shooter and instructor continue around target No. 1 to target No. 2, which is also a dimly illuminated quarter-size silhouette target popping out at eye level from behind another pillar. Target No. 3 is a half-size stationary silhouette, which is exposed to the shooter's view by pulling aside a curtain. This target is illuminated by a dim green light. Target No. 4 is next, concealed behind a curtain. This dimly-lit full silhouette is exposed when the curtain is pulled. A blank-firing revolver placed in the center of the target fires in conjunction with the opening of the curtain.

At this point, the shooter's gun should be empty, if he has fired the required bursts of two at each target. In any event the gun is taken from him by the instructor and he is told he will proceed alone through the tunnel using his knife at appropriate times. Just as he is about to go down to his knees to enter the tunnel, the instructor exposes Dummy A, which is constructed of old fatigue clothes and excelsior; and the shooter uses his knife on it. While he has been proceeding from Target 1 to Target 4, a locally-made Gestapo-type torture scene record sequence, interspersed with cursing and other sound effects, has been played. While the shooter is going through the pitch dark tunnel on his hands and knees, with his knife in his hand, he is subjected to the Stravinsky music sequence and to ad libs given him over the sound system by the instructor or a helper.

Progressing through the tunnel, he encounters strings hanging from the ceiling to simulate cobwebs, and crawls over partially inflated inner tubes (inclosed in fatigue suits) which simulate dead bodies. While he has been progressing through the tunnel, the instructor has moved to a position where he can see him emerge from the tunnel. Upon emerging, and after stabbing a stationary Dummy B, he proceeds up the stairs to the platform and then down the stairs—into a pit, then up out of the pit by means of another set of steps. The

---

DIAGRAM OF THE HOUSE OF HORRORS (See opposite)

All numbered targets are to be fired at. Lettered targets, with the exception of D, are dummies for knife targets. Dummy H is an American so placed that the student will have to choose between firing at the soldier or passing him. This teaches recognition of U. S. troops. All targets and curtains are controlled by an accompanying officer. These devices are moved by attached strings. Target Nos. 4, 5, 8 and 9 are full silhouette targets with blank-firing pistols attached.

latter procedure imparts an illusion of height and depth, which is emphasized by a lack of light and the artifically developed combat tension.

As the student proceeds, a sentry-killing sequence is started over the record player and a curtain is pulled, exposing a moving dummy which, for a short distance, falls towards him. This dummy is dressed in "aggressor" uniform and is illuminated by a dim blue light. After using his knife on Dummy C, the instructor, remaining out of contact with the shooter, tells him to place his knife on the ground. Then he is given back his pistol, which he loads, proceeding under the guidance of the instructor to Target No. 5. A sound sequence of a dog barking and growling is sent out over the record player at this time.

As the shooter goes through the open door at point D, a half silhouette which rises from the floor is pulled and he fires the first two shots of his second magazine. He then approaches a door which swings in either direction. If he *kicks* the door open and enters the next room, he fires at Target No. 6, which is a quarter silhouette concealed in a window frame. It is exposed when a shutter swings out, as the cord controlling the spring latch is pulled by the instructor. On the other hand, if the shooter *pulls* open the door, he fires at Target No. 7, a half silhouette which rises from the floor and is illuminated by a red light. A discussion of the best ways to enter doors of rooms occupied by an enemy is held at this point.

During the firing at Target Nos. 5, 6, and 7, sound effects over the amplifier have consisted of a whispered conversation interspersed with faint groans and pleas, such as would be made by a wounded man asking for water. Proceeding on toward Target No. 8, over a flooring, sections of which have been placed on pivots so they will tilt slightly to simulate unsteady footing, he enters the area of Target No. 8, which is in total darkness. There he returns the fire when Target No. 8, which is a life-size silhouette of an "aggressor" soldier, illuminated by the muzzle blast of a blank-firing pistol installed in the dummy. At this point, after a short pause, the instructor tells him to proceed and, at the same time, pulls a string rattling some cans to his immediate left. These cans are in complete darkness. If the shooter fires at them, a discussion is carried on by the instructor as to the advisability of shooting at something which he cannot see. He then approaches a door at point (F). He pauses there and a record sequence of a rape scene involving a young woman is played. He is told to kick open the door and get the rapist. As he goes through, a life size silhouette fires at him; and he returns the fire. These are the last rounds in his magazine (provided he has not fired at the cans); so he is told to reload before proceeding on to a curtain at point (G).

A short music sequence commences over the amplifier at this point, and a conversation is heard involving a number of persons. He is told to listen, and hears the sound of bottles, laughter, and cards being shuffled. The instructor tells him there are enemies in there playing cards and he is to go in and get them. The instructor tells him to jerk the curtain aside at (G) and enter the room. In the corner, under a bright light, is standing a dummy of an American soldier in full equipment—a sergeant with his stripes exposed, to facilitate recognition. If he fires at it, he is reprimanded for shooting one of his own men, when recognition was easily possible (this happens to about 10% of the shooters). He is told that the American (dummy) is there for the same purpose and has been awaiting an opportune time to do the same thing he is about to do.

Proceeding on around the pillar, he approaches a curtain and listens to continued sound effects of the card game in progress beyond it. If he has not fired at the American dummy, he has eight rounds left in his gun. As he pulls aside the curtain, he fires at Target Nos. 10, 11 and 12. These targets are life-size silhouettes of 3 men sitting at a table playing cards by candlelight. After firing at the three seated targets (3 bursts of 2—seldom done—usually one of the card players is missed), he should have two rounds remaining in his pistol. Seeing no other targets, he is allowed to relax. As he does so, thinking he has completed the course, the instructor pulls Target No. 13, which is a three-quarter size silhouette bobbing out from behind a pillar, firing a blank shot as it comes into view. The shooter fires his last two rounds. At this point, his gun is taken from him and he proceeds out through the exit.

A brief, general critique of the shooter's firing technique and his reactions to the targets during his 15-minute ordeal is given.

It is difficult to describe by written words and diagrams the effects of this range on the shooter. All the elements involving the use of the handgun, mentioned earlier, have taken place while the shooter was making his way through the course. He was subjected to physical and mental tension, to the ele-

ment of surprise, and to the unknown. Realistic and difficult
shooting and reloading conditions were caused by poor lighting, unsteady footing, and sound effects; and the loss of sense
of direction, because of his irregular progress, was emphasized.

In this sequence, the shooter learned by his own mistakes.
He also had the opportunity, which seldom occurs in combat,
of being corrected on the spot by the instructor, at the time
and under conditions in which the mistake occurred. There
is no better way to teach and to learn the use of weapons
and their employment than by practicing under conditions
as close to the real thing as possible.

In The House of Horrors there were twelve silhouette
targets at which the shooter fired in bursts of two shots.
None of these silhouettes had been at any greater distance
than *ten feet* from the shooter.

After the period of trial, error and experiment was completed, a careful observation and study was made of the
records of 500 men, who had just previously qualified in the
prescribed course on standard target ranges, either as marksmen or experts. These 500 men, when projected into The
House of Horrors averaged four hits out of a possible 12
silhouette targets. After these same 500 men had received instruction in instinctive pointing, they were again sent through
this range. (Necessary changes in lighting and target location
were made, to provide a fair test by eliminating, to a great
extent, any benefits derived by previous familiarity). The
average number of hits on the silhouettes increased from
four to ten for this group. On this range, or any similar one,
it is not difficult to establish a system of scoring after a number of shooters have gone through and an average number
of hits is determined.

After this test, many more hundreds of men were put
through the range, with the same general improvement noted.
It was particularly noticeable that men who had received
training in instinctive pointing only, and who had never fired
the hand gun previously, did as well as those who had had
previous bull's-eye instruction.

Once realistic conditions and situations are created, under
which men will actually be firing, and after training and im-
proving the ability of the shooter to fire under these conditions, confidence in himself, his ability and his weapon will
be achieved.

Again, the payoff will be in LIVES—enemy and criminal
lives.

BOBBING TARGETS

This type of surprise target is practically fool-proof in operation. It does not contain the usual springs, hinges, and so forth, which are a continual source of trouble and which are commonly found in bobbing targets. These targets can be best installed behind the edges of walls and behind trees, and in ranges such as the House of Horrors.

The counterbalance principle used in their operation is the secret of their success. The "offset" hole, through which a bolt or large spike can be driven into the target support to make the pivot point, is largely responsible for ease and simplicity of operation. This pivot point eliminates excessive weight on the end of the arm opposite the silhouette. The more the pivot point is offset and the more weight added on the end opposite the target, the faster the bobbing action of the target will be.

In the first illustration the release cord is pulled and secured tight, holding the target from view. When this cord is re-

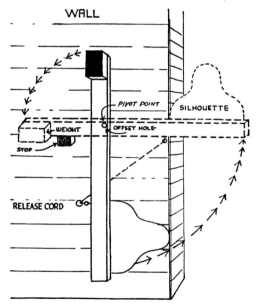

SURPRISE SILHOUETTE, OR BOBBING, TARGET

These surprise targets are foolproof and easy to make. The counterbalance weight and off-center pivot make for smooth, easy operation. Weight on the target, as shown above, swings the silhouette into view when the cord is pulled.

leased, by trip or other mechanism, the weight falls until it hits the stop and exposes the target.

The device in the second illustration works on the opposite principle, the cord being pulled to bring the silhouette down to where it is exposed. The target disappears immediately from sight once the cord is released.

Awning pulleys and sash cords have produced the best results on such target devices.

The silhouette, which can be of any size, is tacked on the end of the arm and is replaced when it is shot up. Likewise, the end of the arm which is exposed to the fire can be replaced merely by splicing on another piece of wood, thus eliminating the replacement of the whole weight and counterbalance system.

Old pieces of plywood are good as a backing for silhouettes, with light paper replacements stapled on the plywood backing when needed. A piece of plywood will take an incredible number of shots before it falls to pieces; and it is not as susceptible to splitting or damp weather as is a solid piece of wood or cardboard.

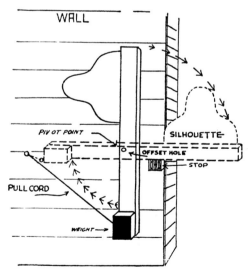

SURPRISE SILHOUETTE, OR BOBBING, TARGET (Cont.)

Here the cord pulls the target down and the weight swings it up. Awning pulleys and cords make the best release devices, and plywood cutouts make durable silhouettes. (Illustrations are from *The American Rifleman*.)

An object lesson course, to impress upon the trainee . . .

Combat shooting is not a sport, but a "deadly" serious business.

Chapter 11

ELEMENTARY FIELDCRAFT

A KNOWLEDGE of the elementary principles of movement and concealment in hostile territory is essential, not only for those who are in the Armed Forces but also for members of state police forces, sheriffs' offices, and civil defense organizations. Army manuals, covering the subject in detail, may be purchased from the Superintendent of Documents, Government Printing Office, Washington, D. C. It is intended here merely to set forth some of the basic techniques that can be covered in a lecture, designed primarily for members of civilian organizations.

Typical Problem. This lecture may be based on a hypothetical situation, such as the one described below, elaborated and localized to lend greater interest. Points in the narrative may be discussed as they arise.

Training aids are suggested, as follows:

(1) If the class is small, a sand table for demonstration purposes.

(2) If the class is large and if the facilities are available, a film strip, or glass slides, in a darkened room.

(3) Or, as an alternative, each student can be issued a map to follow; or a large map may be drawn on a blackboard.

The Situation. Corporal John Thomas, of the State Police, is one of the surviving members of an ill-fated patrol. He has escaped an ambush and at 1700, 15 September, is standing on a ridge above the Jones Farm, in hostile territory.

The Objective. To return to a selected rendezvous point on the outskirts of Blank City.

Rendezvous Time. The patrol members had agreed to stay at the rendezvous point until 2100.

Equipment. Corporal Thomas has a map, a revolver, a carbine, a compass, and his wits.

Preparation. Thomas has devoted considerable time to studying the map, and has located himself on it. He now compares the map with the terrain. He knows that the map may save him many mistakes.

After locating landmarks and choosing a tentative route, Thomas then divides the ground into sectors, with a recognizable landmark in each sector. He rules out of consideration all paths, trails, and roads, which might be covered by the enemy and selects the most difficult and wildest route—because it is least likely to be covered. He realizes that the sun is in front of him and may shine on him; so, to make the

CONCEALMENT

When possible, your clothing should blend with the terrain and not be in contrast with it.

best of the situation, he darkens his face, hands and clothing. In this way, his figure will blend with the background. To escape detection, he must use every ditch or depression, and every dark or shadowed piece of terrain.

Technique. At 1830, Corporal Thomas leaves his observation post near the Jones Farm and proceeds north about 800 yards through the woods. As he takes cover and observes around a rock, he sees a herd of sheep in his front. He does not want to disturb them, because that would indicate to any one watching that something is wrong. Thomas decides that it will be easy to go below them and keep out of sight.

Before he proceeds, however, he checks on the direction of the wind by wetting his cheeks. The cheek is extremely sensitive to moisture and wind. The wind, he finds, is coming from the northeast; so it should be safe to pass below the sheep, who have a keen sense of smell. After he is well past them, he checks the terrain with the map and finds that his detour was too long and that, if he were to continue, he would walk into the center of a road net, where enemy guards are certain to be.

Heading east, the Corporal crosses a small stream and begins to climb a ridge. Nothing more happens until he is within 200 yards of a big rock. Suddenly, from behind the ridge, two crows rise and fly quickly about him, cawing as they go. Immediately he is suspicious. A good woodsman is always suspicious of disturbed animals or birds until he learns the cause of their alarm. The Corporal knows that something, probably a man, has frightened the crows. He takes cover and looks around for a line of retreat, if that becomes necessary.

Ten minutes later, three sheep come trotting onto the skyline. They stop every now and then to look behind them. Since the sheep are still frightened and continue to trot on, Corporal Thomas is even more certain that a man is somewhere on the ridge. If the man were a sheepherder, he would undoubtedly have a dog with him.

The Corporal tests the wind, finds it from the right direction and remains concealed. After ten minutes of cautious waiting, he continues uphill toward the rock. The rock proves to be an excellent landmark. From his present site, it looks quite different, but its distinctive size enables him to recognize it and locate himself on the map.

From his map he finds that he is now near the Hanson Farm. Looking around, he is able to see a good deal of the

COVER
To be effective, cover must shield the user from enemy fire.

country he had not seen before. To observe from the top of
the rock would give him an excellent view, but it would also
silhouette him against the skyline. A place in the grass beside
the rock, although it restricts his vision, gives him more
security.

He looks around—very slowly, for he knows that quick
movements are easily seen. To his rear he sees a bright flash,
several hundred yards above him. At first he is dazzled, then
identifies the glare—a man with fieldglasses. The Corporal
thinks to himself, "It is lucky that the observer does not know
he should shade his glasses, to keep them from flashing a
message over the hillside."

The observer seems to be looking directly at Corporal Thomas, but Thomas does not move. His safety lies in perfect stillness. After a few minutes, the observer gets up and starts walking toward the Blank City road.

The Corporal continues his observation and makes a mental note to avoid all houses as he goes forward. One of them might have a dog that would bark and give him away. He remembers that the same warning applies to farmyards; there is always some animal which will make a noise. Alarm noises of domestic animals are better known than those of wild animals; people recognize them for what they are.

DECEPTION

An old Indian trick that often draws fire and discloses an enemy's position.

OBSERVING FROM COVER
Never look over an object when you can look around the side of
it. This holds, also, when firing a gun from cover.

At this point, he sees a shepherd only 100 yards away. Since
it will soon be dark, he does not want to waste time. Keeping
his head down, he crawls on his stomach for about 30 yards
to a deep ditch, down which he makes his way unobserved.

After about 300 yards, he rests. His crawling and rapid
withdrawal have tired him. He crawls into some brush, keeping his carbine close by and spending the last half hour of
light observing the countryside.

To the left and below him, the Corporal sees a small stream,
which he knows leads to a road and then joins the main stream.
His plan is to get to the road by moving down the stream
in the water. The high bank will hide his body and the
noise of the water will mask the sound of his movements.
If this were still water, he would avoid it as a plague, because
still water, like dead wood and leaves, is a sound trap. But
this stream flows rapidly because of the sharp decline; so he
proceeds to the stream and follows it to the road.

The stream leads into a culvert too small for him to crawl
through. He must, therefore, cross the road. His point of

crossing gives him a clear view of the road. He sees that the road is gravel and that he cannot move up or down the road because there is a guarded road junction several hundred yards away in each direction. He must then wait for a counter-noise.

After a half hour a car finally comes by, and the Corporal, the sound of his movements covered by the car noise, dashes across the road to the grove on the other side. As soon as he is again ready to move forward, the door of a house to the right of the grove opens and an armed man steps out. Thomas, knowing that the man will be unable to see clearly for a time because he has stepped from a lighted room into darkness, quietly leaves the immediate vicinity, continuing on through the trees.

He then gets back into the stream. He is still too far from safety to risk leaving footprints in the soft mud banks of the creek.

He follows the stream along the edge of the woods, then cuts through the woods to the junction of the creek leading to Blank City. The first 500 yards along this creek are easy enough, but the creek bed becomes so shallow and rocky that he must move forward on the ground. So he walks through the high grass, stepping high and taking each step very care-fully. This avoids the brushing noise of the foot moving through tall grass and keeps him from tripping over low obstacles.

In this way, Corporal Thomas reaches the rendezvous at 2015. He waits in the shadows of the designated building until he is joined by the two other surviving members of the patrol. The three men then return to their headquarters.

Chapter 12

POLICE BATON AND MISCELLANEOUS WEAPONS AND TECHNIQUES

THE police baton in the hands of a guard or police officer is an additional symbol of his authority and implies that he knows how to use it. If he is skilled and practiced in its use, he can cope with most situations where physical force is necessary. Basically, the police baton is an offensive weapon. It is usually used defensively only to enable an officer to survive an attack so that he may retaliate with offensive action of his own. The manner in which he uses his baton depends upon the local situation. It can be used as a club, as a jabbing or parrying instrument, or as a restraint device.

THE NIGHT STICK

The short baton is round and made of hard wood or plastic. It is 1 to 1½ inches in diameter and about 12 to 36 inches long. Generally the short baton, or night stick, is carried by the individual patrolman on his beat, while the long baton, or riot stick, is more useful in handling crowds, mobs, riots. Whether long or short, the technique of using the weapon is much the same.

The Grip, Either Baton. The grip is most important. Place the loop or thong of the stick over the right thumb so that the stick will hang with the thong crossing over the back of the hand. Turn the hand in and grasp the handle so that the thumb points parallel to the stick. Raise the baton to a 45-degree angle—and the grip is complete. The thong must be adjusted in length to fit the hand. When correctly adjusted, the butt of the club should extend slightly below the edge of the grasping hand. If gripped in this manner, the baton will not fly out of the hand when in use; but, if an opponent should seize it so that it can no longer be used as an effective weapon, it can be released by relaxing the grip. The thong should never be looped about the wrist, for then an opponent who grabs the baton and twists it prevents the officer from releasing it and pinions his hand in a painful manner.

Right: Baton grip No. 2. Note that the grip is toward the place where the leather loop is fastened to the baton, and that the leather loop passes across the back of the hand.

Left: Baton grip No. 1. Initial position to enable the baton to be grasped properly. Note the leather loop is hooked over the thumb and passes over the back of the hand.

Left: Baton grip No. 3, inside view. Note that the leather loop does not pass around the wrist as would commonly be assumed. Only the thumb is encircled by the leather loop. In the event that the baton is grasped by a mob member (this is not a likely event if the baton wielder has been properly trained) and the baton is lost to the mob member, the leather loop will slide off the thumb and the policeman's arm will not be pinioned in the loop, with the hand immobilized also.

Right: The WRONG way to use the leather loop on the police baton. If an opponent gains control of the baton he can, by twisting it, immobilize the policeman's arm and take him out of action.

The thong can be fastened to the baton either at the butt end or approximately six inches from the butt end. The length of the thong will have to be adjusted accordingly.

The Blow. A blow delivered by the baton is generally effective in the same body areas as those in which the edge of the hand is best used. (See chapter 2, *Offensive Unarmed Combat.)*

However, the policeman should not, ordinarily, use his baton as a bludgeon to strike blows about his opponent's head. Used in this manner, the night stick is dangerous and fatal injuries can result. Side blows to the temple and throat area also are potentially fatal when delivered with enough force. Blows delivered to the top of the head and forehead are also dangerous, yet at times even this kind of blow has been ineffective. Wild blows, using the full length of the arm in the swing, are not nearly as effective as they seem; they leave a police officer wide open for parry and retaliation by a trained opponent.

Well-directed blows to the following areas are usually as effective as head blows, with less chance of serious injury to the recipient. A man who is moving in to attack can be dropped with a downward blow to the collar bone; or by a shoulder shove, to twist the body, followed by a hard blow across the big muscle in the back of the thigh. This can be delivered with full force and results in cramping the leg muscle so that the victim is temporarily unable to walk. If the opponent's arm is outstretched, a blow to the back of the hand, or the outside of the elbow or wrist, will suffice. Blows to the shin bone will often block an attempted kick and can

BLOW TO TEMPLE

A blow to the temple, the top of the head, or the side of the throat, is potentially dangerous. Concussion, skull fracture, or rupture of the neck artery may result.

BLOW TO COLLAR BONE

A downward blow to the collar bone will break up the most determined attack. The broken collar bone will make the whole arm useless, but will not inflict an incapacitating injury that is potentially fatal—as will blows to the head area.

THRUST TO SOLAR PLEXUS

By using the night stick, or baton, as an extension of the arm, and thrusting at the solar plexus about 3 inches above the navel, an opponent is forced to give way. This is a useful method for clearing a way through a hostile crowd. It does not inflict any serious injury, but causes enough temporary discomfort to be effective.

BLOW TO SHIN

A sharp blow to the shin will discourage an attempted kick. Also, a blow to the inside, outside, or edge of the wrist will prevent use of the hand, or any weapon it may be grasping.

BLOW TO REAR LEG MUSCLE

When an opponent advances from the front, shove him sharply on the left shoulder with the left hand, causing him to spin off balance. Strike him hard with the baton on the big rear leg muscle. This blow can be delivered with all possible force. It will cause the muscle to cramp and will down the opponent. It will not cause permanent injury but will prevent the opponent from walking for a short time.

BLOW TO INSIDE OF WRIST

A blow to the inside of the wrist will cause the opponent to release his grip on any weapon he may be grasping. Like a blow by the edge of the hand, the blow on the wrist tendons forces the fingers to release their grip.

THONG PINION OF WRISTS

The thong of the baton can be looped around t h e wrists. By twisting the baton, the wrists can be so pinioned that a painful and compelling control of the prisoner is effected.

also be used against a kick after it has been launched and sidestepped.

By using it as an extension of the arm, the night stick can be an effective parrying instrument in much the same manner as the foil serves a fencer. A powerful thrust delivered to the solar plexus will temporarily disable the opponent; and short jabs to the plexus and stomach region are effective in clearing away crowds or clearing a pathway through a mob.

LONG BATON OR RIOT STICK

The English peasant in the medieval times of Friar Tuck and Robin Hood fought with a long, stout, round wooden stave called a quarterstaff. It varied in length from six to eight feet and was quite a formidable arm. He used it as a two-handed offensive and defensive weapon. Because he was seldom permitted to bear other arms, such as edged or other lethal weapons, the peasant developed the technique of fighting with the quarterstaff to a high art. Competitions were held at county fairs in somewhat the same manner as we have challenge wrestling matches at county fairs today.

In the Orient, a similar long stick has been used over the centuries. Tradition has it that the ancient Buddhist monks carried the stick on their wanderings, using it as a defensive weapon as well as a cane. Police in Japan and other areas use it in mob control today.

During World War II interest was revived in this type of fighting and many members of the armed services were given instruction in stick and cane fighting. The principles are much the same; only the length, diameter, and strength of the stick cause variation in the technique.

THE LONG BATON

For purposes of this discussion we will use the word *baton*, considering it to be synonymous with the term "riot stick" in modern police terminology. This is a formidable weapon in the hands of a trained man who has confidence in his ability and training.

The long baton, properly used, is an important weapon in riot control. With this weapon, trained men will have no hesitation in making physical contact with the mob members. When it is used in tactical formation so that each man is protected on his flank by other squad members similarly armed, a mob can be split, forced to flee, or be subjected to casualties

Left: Port arms is the position that the policeman armed with the baton will normally use when moving into action and from one area to another. The better the appearance, the more psychological effect it will have on the mob. The baton can be used in various drill formations in the same manner as the rifle. The combination of white baton, white helmet, and white gloves, gives a well-drilled unit a very "snappy" appearance, and has a practical use also. In night actions it enables the leader of the unit to have better control of his men as he can better see them. The gloves—aside from the visual effect—also protect the hands of the soldier against cuts, blows, and thrown objects. The helmet can be plastic or metal. The plastic type safety helmet now used by workers in mines and steel construction is light and tough and will give protection against practically all types of thrown objects.

Right: The parade rest position, aside from the drill aspect, should be used when the unit is facing a potential mob action but there is still no activity.

When standing in the parade rest position it is sometimes necessary to prevent non-aggressive mob members from getting too close to the police line. A sudden series of rapid thrusts with the baton to the eye, throat, stomach, or testicle area will keep the desired interval. The thrusts should be rapid and the withdrawal also rapid to prevent the mob member from grabbing the baton. Note that the thrust is made with the leg extended to the front to give the maximum distance to the movement. The object is to force the individual back and keep his distance, not to hit him.

that may not be fatal but are at least temporarily disabling. The full potential of this weapon and its tactical value in riot control is not yet realized by most police and military organizations.

An examination of various training manuals on riot control written in the years past for civil police and military units, will indicate mention of the riot stick as an issue weapon but little is said concerning its proper use. The baton is not a weapon to be used by each man as he sees fit and to permit him to engage in individual combat with various members of a mob. It is a weapon best employed in mass in attack or defensive formations.

The tip and butt end are used to deliver blows and jabs. Its full length is used in restraint and in defense. Its thong is used as a means of restraining prisoners. In addition its use in drill and dress formation adds much to the appearance of the unit, which in turn has a sobering effect on the mob.

Trained units using the riot stick alone are capable of handl-

Left: A forceful blow or thrust to the testicle, groin, stomach, or solar plexus area will put most mob members out of action. It would normally be followed by advancing with the rear foot and delivering a butt stroke blow to the chin or head area. This is a disabling tactic for use against a violent adversary.

One of the best methods of forcing a mob to break ranks and leave an area into which the formation of baton men are advancing, is to use short thrusts to the stomach and solar plexus area. The force of the thrust can be regulated by the situation. A line or wedge formation moving against a crowd using this technique can often clear the area without resorting to more violent blows.

Right: Blows such as this to the Adam's apple or point of jaw area are disabling and can be fatal. Normally, the same upward thrust to the body area with force will disable the opponent, with much less chance of a fatality.

ing mobs of large size. When the riot stick is combined in the unit with the capability to use gas munitions and firearms, a complete range of weapons is available to apply the principle of "necessary force" against the mob.

Left: A butt stroke to the jaw or temple can cause a fracture or a "knockout." This blow delivered from the parade rest position will normally be followed by a butt smash to the rioter's face on the return to the port or ready position. Note that in this and all illustrations, the leg of the baton man is advanced toward the adversary. Blows are delivered by "stepping in" to the opponent. At the same time the forward leg always protects against a kick to the groin area by the mob member. A return to the ready position so that the stick man is in a forward crouch with stick at port arms is always advocated. In this position the stick man is ready for the next adversary, since he is in a position of mobility and balance and one leg is normally forward making his body area "out of reach" to the mob member.

Right: Baton blow from the chest position that can result in a knockout or other serious injury. This blow would normally be a follow-up to an upward two-handed blow with the baton from the parade rest position.

Blows to the inside or outside of the ankle, shin bone, and knee cap are effective. These blows are given from the port arms position, with the hand on the point of the baton shoving to give more momentum. In the illustration a blow is being struck to the inside of the ankle which is a very sensitive spot and is one that can be used against a rioter launching a kick. All blows are followed up with either a return to the on guard position or followed up with other thrusts or blows until the point is reached where the rioter either is out of action or flees.

A blow from the port arms position breaking the collar bone is very effective in putting a man out of action. The blow is not only painful but will immobilize the whole side of the body and put the most aggressive mob member out of action, with little possibility of a fatality. The blow can also be delivered from the rear. Normally, blows to the head area are dangerous and should not be used when fatalities are to be avoided.

Blows to the biceps, elbow, and inside and outside of the wrist, are very effective. These can be used without danger of permanent damage whether or not the rioter has a striking weapon such as a club.

Left: Blow to and across the large leg muscle—No. 1. The left hand is used to strike a forceful blow or thrust to the point of opponent's right shoulder. This places the opponent off-balance and forces him to pivot, exposing the rear of his leg to a blow with the stick.

Right: Blow to and across the large leg muscle—No. 2. As the body pivots exposing the rear of the leg, a blow of maximum force is given to the large leg muscle. The more the victim is turned exposing the striking area, the better. A blow delivered with all the force possible will do no permanent damage but will be very effective. The blow will normally cause the muscle to cramp and, aside from the pain inflicted, will make him unable to run, walk, or move about. Many times the effect of the cramp is such that the recipient will fall to the ground and stay there until the cramp leaves. The principal after-effect will be a bruise area at the point of impact.

Left: The long baton is very useful when it is necessary to restrain or force back non-violent mob members who are pressing against the police lines. A shoving motion can be changed to a blow at any time, either by bringing the baton upward against the chin or by a forward thrust to the Adam's apple area. The knee will be used against the groin should the mob member try to grapple with the baton.

Right: When the stick man is faced with a passive mob, especially when women and children are in the front line, he can often force a retreat by shoving against the throat or face area. Such a thrust can vary from a forceful one to a "shoving" action. It is usually sufficient to use this type of baton action alone against female mob members and children that are often put in the front ranks against the police by trained agitators and leaders. If this maneuver is not sufficient, or the line can not be moved back by this means due to pressure from the rear, gas munitions are necessary.

COME-ALONGS USING THE BATON

After the rioter has been subdued, many times it is necessary to walk him to a rear area where he can be held for questioning or other purposes. The riot stick is very useful to control the prisoner. Those come-alongs which necessitate the use of both of the policeman's hands are all right for short distances and enable complete control.

Note in both the left and right illustrations that the elbow joint is in such a position that the outside of the elbow or the point is resting against the stick. Downward pressure exerted by the policeman on the hand results in a painful, controlling pressure on the prisoner.

The method at left is only effective for a short distance without tiring the policeman. He is shoving forward with his left hand which is grasping the shirt to create an off-balance position. At the same time he is lifting with the hand on the stick to impose a greater degree of control on the prisoner. This type of come-along is more spectacular than others and puts the victim in a ridiculous position—that can create much humor among onlookers with the definite psychological advantage thus obtained.

LONG-RANGE COME-ALONGS

Many times it is necessary to transport a rioter over a considerable distance to a point where he can be released to the custody of others. This type of prisoner control must be such that, regardless of attempts by the captive to release himself, he has little opportunity. It should also permit the policeman to maintain control with only one hand on the stick, leaving the other hand free if necessary to grasp his pistol, or at least have access to it.

The left illustration shows the rioter with one hand pinioned by the thong on the stick and being forced to hold up his pants with the free hand. The belt should be cut or removed and the buttons on the pants ripped off so that they will fall if not held up by the prisoner.

The right illustration shows both hands pinioned by the thong, which is twisted so as to make a tight bind. In this position the rioter can be kept under control by one or two hands by pulling back on the arms, or by jabs with the butt of the stick to the small of the back or kidney area.

The opposite illustration is very usable for a potentially violent prisoner. Strangulation can be effected by pressure on the throat. Again, the belt can be cut to occupy his hands.

MOVING A PRISONER

This method of moving a prisoner with the baton is a good one when the prisoner must be taken a long distance. A firm grasp on the rear of the collar with sharp thrusts to the kidney area with the tip of the baton will normally be sufficient to keep a prisoner under control once he has been subdued enough to permit the application of the come-along in the first place. If he gives trouble a kick to the back of the knee joint will put him on the ground and subject him to further forceful handling.

HOLDING A PRISONER

Many times in a general riot there will not always be calm in the back areas in the rear of the main action. Attempts may be made to liberate prisoners. In this case the prisoner can be controlled by having both wrists pinioned by the thong of the baton. At the appearance of possible trouble the policeman can force the prisoner to the ground with jabs to the kidney area and a kick to the back of the knee. With one hand he can still control the prisoner and at the same time have his side-arm available for instant action against a rescue attempt.

Stick release—1. If a mob member grasps the riot stick it usually can be forcibly retrieved by quick counter action, that can be followed by offensive tactics.

Stick release—2. Step quickly toward the adversary and grasp the end of the stick in the rioter's hand, either above or below his hand.

Stick release—3. Exert full strength and jerk the end of the stick from the rioter's grasp and step backward. As the point of the stick is released, a follow-up can be made to the point of the jaw with the right elbow.

Stick release—4. Once the stick has been released it normally will be in a raised position, high above the left shoulder. From this position a butt smash can immediately be delivered to the throat or jaw area. Practice in this type of release will develop great confidence and make it a very rare occasion when any rioter is able to wrest the stick from its owner.

Another very effective means of releasing the baton if grasped by the rioter. The counter must be immediate so that the policeman is not pulled off balance. The kick to the knee joint, plus the extra support given by the thong, will usually effect the release rapidly. Note that the body of the policeman is leaning in the direction of his pull.

Using the baton to strike a blow or a lifting effect against the testicle area. Many times it is necessary to clear a crowd from around a speaker or agitator and approach is made from the rear. The force of this blow can be as the situation dictates. A jab to the kidney is also an alternative.

The riot stick can be used as a defensive weapon against over or underhand attacks with cutting or bladed weapons, clubs, bottles, or other weapons.

In the upper illustration a block is being made of the rioter's overhead blow. This must be followed up either by withdrawing to an on-guard position or by immediate offensive action against the enemy. From this position a follow-through butt stroke to the rioter's head and jaw area is indicated.

In the lower illustration a blow is being delivered to the inside of the wrist. Note that the blade is still out of range of possible contact. A blow to the inside of the wrist will force the fingers of the hand holding the blade to open and drop the weapon. One to the outside of the wrist, if forceful enough, will have the same effect. Generally, blows with the baton delivered to the same areas that are vulnerable to edge-of-the-hand blows will be most effective

PRACTICE with use of the long baton is vital. Training must be of the type that will give the policeman the "feel" and have confidence in the stick as a weapon of offense. It is not enough to simulate thrusts and blows. A durable canvas bag filled with a substance such as sawdust that will give slightly with each blow is best for use in training. Kicks are also delivered against such a training aid.

RIOT UNIT. A diagonal view of a squad equipped with riot sticks and, in this case, short 37mm gas guns. Note that the squad leader is in the rear with a submachine gun. A formation of this type, with each member of the group giving flank support to the other, whether it is a squad, platoon, or company, can present very formidable offensive action. If the formation is not broken and the men are disciplined, there can be no real opposition to it from the unarmed mob. If pressure of numbers is too great, the riot unit should not be committed until gas munitions are used. Always in the reserve should be the necessary firepower to back up violent opposition.

THE BLACKJACK

In addition to the baton, many police officers carry, as an article of issue or personal choice, the blackjack (slapjack, sap, persuader, pacifier, billy). This striking instrument consists of a somewhat cylindrical leather case with a lead shot filling in its striking end. It may or may not have a spring handle.

The blackjack ranges, in design and size, from the so-called vest-pocket model—which is round and about 5 inches long and three-quarters of an inch in diameter at the striking end—to a larger variety, which is about 10 inches long and is either round or flat on the striking end. Although such a weapon is most useful in handling unruly prisoners, it can be dangerous. Lack of appreciation of its efficacy has caused many officers to use it too freely and too forcefully.

The Blow. In subduing dangerous criminals with the blackjack, blows are usually directed against the head. Blows against the face will cause bad bruises and may break bones in the facial structure, but are not always sufficiently stunning. The blackjack is best used against the top portion of the back of the head. Blows should be struck no further forward than a point opposite the ears and no lower on the back of the head than ear level. Because of the structure of the skull,

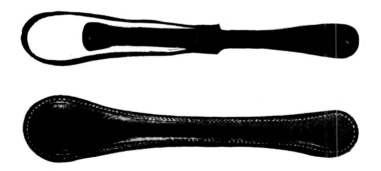

COMMON TYPES OF BLACKJACKS

At the top is shown a common type blackjack, carried by police officers. It is made of cow-hide, is lead-filled on the striking end, and has a spring handle. The thong is so made that it can slide back and forth, making different grips possible.

The blackjack shown at the bottom is an effective type and is safer for general law enforcement. It stuns, but does not have as much cutting or abrasive effect. Because of the wide striking surface, concussion is less likely.

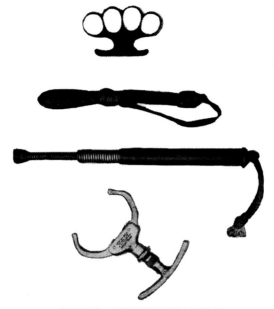

MISCELLANEOUS WEAPONS

At the top are brass knuckles, a well-known implement for use in hand-to-hand fighting.

Next is shown a heavy-type, round, blackjack with spring handle and thong.

Third from the top is the most vicious type of blackjack known. The brass knob on the end of the telescoping spring shaft will easily penetrate the skull bones. This weapon was developed during World War II and was used in underground warfare.

At the bottom is the iron claw, the most effective of all mechanical come-along devices. This is particularly suitable for handling unruly prisoners. Its use should be advocated where departmental regulations permit.

a stunning or knockout blow can be effected with less danger in this area. Very hard blows against the temple or against the top of the head, or the forehead, can easily cause skull fracture and concussion.

Those blackjacks which are entirely round or are only slightly elliptical on the striking end, tend to localize the force of the blow in a small area because of their shape. This type is more likely to cause a fracture, a cut, or a bad contusion, depending on the weight of the weapon and the force of the blow.

Of all the types of blackjacks, those with a flat striking end about 3 inches wide are the best. They have as much stunning effect as is needed and, because of the width of the striking surface, the full force of the blow is not pin-pointed on a small area. There is therefore less probability of a cut or fracture. Blackjacks which contain either a flat or coil spring in their handles will deliver harder blows with less manual force, because of the whipping effect of a snappy wrist action.

It should be remembered that the blackjack is a dangerous instrument when used improperly or too forcefully. The officer who carries it should experiment on various objects before attempting to use it in subduing a criminal. By lightly tapping on the back of his own head with his blackjack, or by using it against the back of his hand, he will more readily appreciate its effectiveness and be better able to judge the amount of force he should use in its application.

METAL TELESCOPING BLACKJACK

At the top is shown the metal telescoping blackjack in the carrying position. It is usually carried with the thong around the wrist and the weapon lying in the palm of the hand.

Below is shown the extended striking position. Note the metal ball on the end of the spring. The tremendous "whip" given the striking end by the spring will cause skull fracture with very little effort. This type weapon definitely is not for police use, since it is intended to maim or kill, not stun.

EMPTY GAS GUN AS WEAPON

Left: Thrust blow with muzzle to stomach area. The man armed with the empty gas gun still has a potent weapon to strike blows. Although the shorter gas gun is not designed for use as a weapon for close-in fighting, it can be used as such when necessary and the man armed with it is in close contact with the mob. All men armed with the gas gun should have practice and confidence in its use as a striking or thrusting weapon, even though they normally are protected from actual physical contact by their comrades armed with batons.

Right: Butt stroke from the port position, striking with the toe of the gunstock. A butt smash can be delivered to the head on the follow-through when the gun is being returned to the port arms or ready position.

Left: Two-handed blow to the jaw area from the parade rest position. This is usually a surprise blow and can be accompanied by a knee to the groin. The gas gun can also be used to shove a mob member to the rear in a situation where no actual violence is taking place.

Right: Thrust to small of back or kidney area.

STRANGULATIONS

In addition to the strangles which use the bare hands or the victim's garments (see chapter 2, *Offensive Unarmed Combat*), there are three other types which have long been used in military and criminal circles. Some or all of them have been taught in military training centers where close combat instruction is given.

These strangles, from the attacker's viewpoint, are much more efficient and deadly than those employing the bare hands. The necessary mechanical aids are always available or can be easily improvised.

The Garrotte. Thugs in India have long been known for their method of strangling, called garrotting. It can be executed with a rope, strong cord, or piece of twisted cloth —about three feet long with a noose in one end. This is a garrotte. Properly applied, it produces a deadly, silent strangle.

Slip the noose over the forefinger of the right hand so that the loop lies down across the palm toward the little finger. Close the right hand and pick up the free end of the cord with the left hand, so that the thumb and fingers are on the inner side of the cord and the end is even with the little finger. Approach the victim from the rear and, opening the right hand, throw the loop over his head with the left. Use the left hand to draw the noose through the right hand until it is nearly taut about the neck. Then close the right hand about the noose at the back of the victim's neck and twist as you would in applying a tourniquet. With your hand against the back of his neck and your right arm stiff, the victim is held at arm's length and is unable to free himself from the strangling cord or to reach his attacker. A hard pull to the rear at this point will make the victim fall backward and cause his chin to fold down over the cord, thus adding his body weight to the pressure of the strangle.

Other cord strangles can be effected with the noose, in the manner in which the cowboy uses his lariat. They are not nearly as reliable, however, because the user does not have the extra hand to twist and tighten the noose, as in the case of the garrotte.

The Stick Strangle. This very efficient strangle can be done with a stick, cane, or similar object, 18 inches or more in length and roughly one inch in diameter. The stick should be gripped in the right hand 6 inches from the end, with long end of the stick parallel to the forearm. Approaching the victim from the rear, with the stick gripped correctly in the right hand, place your right foot against the inside of his right knee, to knock him off balance. Placing your right hand over his left shoulder, slip the long end of the stick underneath his chin from the left side. With the left hand reach across, grasp the loose end and exert pressure to the rear.

This strangle has been used in combat areas with definite effectiveness. With the stick across the throat against the windpipe, but little pressure is necessary for complete strangulation. By throwing the victim off balance and applying this strangle quickly, you leave no hope of escape. It is probably the fastest of all known strangles, because the windpipe is crushed instantly.

The Cord Strangle.   Another type of strangulation, as old as history in the Far East, is accomplished with any light cord or wire of good tensile strength, about 18 inches long. The thinner the cord or wire, the quicker will be the effectiveness. Tie a loop at each end of the cord, or tie small wooden blocks on the ends, so that a secure grip can be taken. Approaching the man from the rear, throw him off balance, as with the stick, with your right foot against the inside of his right knee. With a hand on each end of the cord (the cord held taut), bring the cord over the victim's head and back against his throat. Cross the hands at the rear of the neck and apply pressure both ways. Strangulation is quick and silent. The advantage of having one end of the cord in each hand and the cord held taut when putting it over the victim's head, is apparent when you consider that he may wear a hat or helmet, or the light conditions may be poor, thus preventing a noose or loop from being thrown over accurately.

Chapter 13

CHEMICAL MUNITIONS FOR CONTROL OF MOBS AND INDIVIDUALS

THE use of tear gas and other chemical agents should be considered as an effective weapon to be used, with discretion, against the individual and collective enemies of law and order. Preservation of the peace with less bodily harm and violence to all concerned is the end result.

The past decade has seen increasing use of tear gas (CN) and nauseating gas (KO or DM) by military and police units throughout the world. This method of maintaining "law and order" and protecting life and property has many advantages over the use of guns, bayonets, or brute force in general.

Tear gas when properly used is the most effective means known to swiftly and temporarily incapacitate and break up a mob or capture and subdue dangerous criminals or insane persons. When employed in the correct manner, it is the most humane way possible to handle a dangerous situation with the least risk to law enforcement officers and minimizes the possibilities of loss of life and property, and of bloodshed.

Unfortunately, the proper use and value of tear gas and other chemical agents have never been fully explained or understood by many police and military agencies. There has always been, and remains, a certain amount of mystery and lack of full confidence in the use of this relatively modern humane weapon.

Military personel and members of law enforcement agencies will find the following manuals to be informative and helpful in using irritant gases: Field Manual 19-15, Field Manual 21-11, and Technical Manual 8-285. These may be purchased from the Government Printing Office, Washington 25, D. C.

Types of tear gas, means of projecting it, and techniques

in its use, have improved much since the World War II period. Increasing world tension, nationalism, and racial unrest, combined and motivated by doctrines and creeds such as world Communism, have now reached a dangerous stage. Directed mob violence is now one of the means most commonly used to gain or destroy political power. Tear gas and other chemical agents, when properly used, in the right concentration at the right time, are often the only means to control an ugly situation without resorting to actual bloodshed. Many times the use of extreme force and deadly weapons only increases the violence potential.

Tear gas has equal value when used to subdue, capture, or restrain criminals and insane persons. Discipline in penal institutions and control of prison riots are usually largely dependent on the use of chemical agents. Tear gas, released by special "trip" devices, is now commonly used to protect banks and vital industrial plants. Plant police in many large factories are now equipped with tear gas munitions.

To properly use tear gas, the individuals or agencies employing it must understand its nature, limitations, and effects and after effects on the individual, as well as the correct tactics of employment. Once there is confidence and there has been success in its use, police will seek increasing opportunities to use it.

Tear gas and other chemical agents manufactured and used today are generally projected and liberated by three methods: Grenades, projectiles, and cartridges.

In nearly every case where the use of gas has failed to produce the desired results, it has been caused by using too little gas or because of a lack of training or proper equipment.

SOURCES

Tear gas, other chemical agents, and equipment for their use are manufactured in the United States by two companies: LAKE ERIE CHEMICAL COMPANY, 30120 Lakeland Blvd., Wickliffe, Ohio and by FEDERAL LABORATORIES INC., Saltsburg, Pennsylvania.

The products of both companies are well known and are used throughout the world. Both companies also manufacture their products under special contracts for the United States and foreign governments.

TYPES OF GASES

Tear gas (CN-Chloracetophenone) is manufactured in two forms, liquid and crystalline. Both are used in grenades and projectiles. At the time of exposure of either type to air, the gas is released.

The liquid, invisible type of tear gas is generally considered to be the most modern and effective. It is contained within the grenade, or projectile, in a hermetically sealed glass vial. At the time of the explosion of the grenade, or projectile, it vaporizes instantly and totally.

The crystalline type tear gas (powder form) is released at the time of the explosion of the grenade, or projectile, by a burning process; the CN powder mixed with an inert material is activated by a special powder, as a fuel. The gas, during the burning process is more slowly liberated and is accompanied by a distinctive white smoke created by the burning process. Tear gas is also released by the dust dispersion method. Fine tear gas particles in the form of dust deposited as a thin coating on some inert carrier material are blown into the air by the force of an explosion or by a blast of air or nitrogen from a pressure cylinder.

VISIBLE TEAR GAS

Visible tear gas takes up to 60 seconds after the explosion of the grenade, or projectile, to be entirely dispersed from its carrier by the burning process. The white smoke, created by the burning process which liberates it, indicates the area of the gas cloud and coverage.

Visible tear gas in combination with smoke sometimes has a beneficial initial psychological effect on rioters, by tending to discourage them. It also enables the police or users of the gas to locate by means of the smoke cloud the concentration of gas released, so they can increase coverage and concentration in a given area when necessary. If all of the police are not equipped with masks it also indicates areas to be avoided, etc.

By its very nature of operation and liberation, visible gas has three definite disadvantages when the combustion or burning-type of gas release is used:

(1) The smoke cloud containing the gas can be seen, so it is easy for individuals or mobs to avoid the gas concentration as they as well as the users can see it. The burning type grenade or projectile usually needs 20 to 40 seconds to dispel its gas contents. This permits plenty of time to avoid or bypass it, even when it is thrown into the midst of the crowd. The projectile dispelling the gas, being on the ground with the smoke pouring out of it, is usually easily visible, day or night.

(2) One of the worst disadvantages of this type of tear gas projection is that individuals in the mob *have time* to pick up the grenade and hurl it back at the police, or kick it aside, if it is too hot to handle. This has happened countless times in the past, in action against aggressive mobs.

(3) The burning type grenade also provides a fire hazard. Because a burning process is necessary to liberate and dispel the gas, this must always be considered when these grenades or projectiles are used in areas, rooms, and buildings where there is flammable material such as grass, gasoline, paint, waste paper, etc. Injudicious use of this type of grenade and projectile in the past has resulted in severe fires and personal injuries brought about by the fire hazard always present.

During World War II, the fuse time on the standard U. S. Army fragmentation hand grenade had to be shortened. Even though the grenade had a 5- to 8-second explosion time after it left the thrower's hand, enemy troops often picked up the grenade and threw it back. The fuse time was shortened to 3 seconds to eliminate this possibility.

The burning type hand grenades heat up during the discharge period. Anyone trying to throw them back can be burned on the hands. This is only a partial deterrent. Many times during the hysteria of a mob action this does not discourage the rioters. In recent planned Communist inspired riots, the participants have even come prepared in advance, wearing heavy gloves, to enable them to grasp and throw back the burning type gas grenade.

INVISIBLE TEAR GAS

Invisible tear gas, being in liquid form, is volatile and instantly dispersed at the time of the explosion and release from the grenade or projectile. Being liberated in *one blast* at the time the grenade explodes, the entire concentration covers the target area immediately, so that there is no time to run away from it or avoid it.

Being invisible, this also has a much greater psychological effect especially if a heavy concentration is created. Something that is unseen but felt always causes more hysteria and panic, as it is intangible.

Because of the rapidity of the release of the gas, grenades and projectiles carrying the liquid type tear gas cannot be effectively thrown back. The time element is such that any grenade, thrown back by the rioters, is only an empty shell, having already ejected its contents.

As there is no slow burning action necessary to liberate the gas, the fire hazard, when used around flammable material, is also eliminated.

Early objections to the use of liquid type gas being placed in the grenade or projectile in a sealed glass container are now not valid. The manufacturers now use special cushioning devices and specially tempered tough glass ampules to eliminate premature breakage in handling, transit, or in action.

In commercial advertising it is claimed that the burning or combustion-type gas grenades liberate more gas in relation to size and weight than do those of the blast type. This may be true but it is of little importance in a major mob action, especially when the necessary wind conditions are not present to aid in the dispersion of the gas. The important factor is that the mob members or other recipients of the gas attack must get a heavy *concentration of gas instantaneously, in such a manner that they cannot avoid it.* By actual scientific test the burning type grenade may give off more gas by volume than the liquid type gas delivered by blast dispersion. However, the burning type grenade needs up to thirty-five seconds to liberate its contents. Meanwhile, the rioters can see the area covered by the gas cloud and can avoid it. They may even throw the grenade back or kick it aside. It would therefore appear that the greater gas content claimed for the combustion-type grenade has little practical effect on the situation.

THE EFFECT OF TEAR GAS ON THE INDIVIDUAL

CN is easily generated and is promptly effective. It produces severe irritation to the eyes. The nasal passages and throat are also affected. Tears flow profusely. When a dense cloud of tear gas strikes a victim, the latter involuntarily closes his eyes and endeavors to keep them closed in an effort to escape the irritation and discomfort. A feeling of helplessness and personal panic is created.

All tear gases are toxic to varying degrees. However, tear gas has no lasting damaging effect on the lungs or eyes in any concentration that will be met with in the field. Following exposure to the tear gas, there will be some discomfort, but this is of relatively short duration, except in those cases of exposure to very high concentrations for a prolonged period. The discomfort to the eyes will last from several minutes to several hours. In rare cases of extreme exposure by a high concentration for a prolonged period, the discomfort to the eyes has lasted as long as 24 hours.

Eyes should not be rubbed. Fresh air is the best cure. Treatment for persons exposed to tear gas usually consists of merely washing the eyes with a solution of boric acid or sodium bicarbonate. If the clothing is wet, the tear gas has a tendency to be absorbed by the cloth, therefore it has a more lasting effect. Such clothing should be removed.

The main principle to practice and remember in using this humane means of controlling, subduing, or capturing mobs and individuals is that *it should be used in heavy enough concentrations at the beginning so that the initial impact is severe.* If this is done, the individuals or mobs will be more easily controlled or dispersed at the outset.

Although tear gas causes *no permanent* damage to the eyes or lungs, lack of knowledge of this fact coupled with malicious propaganda (sponsored by subversive groups) as to the "deadly" and "permanent" ill effects of tear gas have in the past, unfortunately been successful in discouraging its use by forces of law and order. Trained agitators are usually persons who have previously been exposed to tear gas. They will minimize its effectiveness to their adherents, but even they will not be able to withstand the gas or control and direct mob action if the initial concentration of the gas is heavy enough.

Pure tear gas (CN) can be and has been combined with other chemical agents to increase its effectiveness.

Experience has shown that, unless a very heavy concentration of pure CN gas is used, a determined or dedicated individual can still do a lot of damage. He may be crying profusely but he still has vision. He will always try to avoid visible areas of gas concentration. In those instances when he is subjected to an intense concentration, such as when trapped in a room or building, the concentration of pure tear gas will eventually subdue him.

On the other hand, in the control of mobs and individuals operating in the open air, the actual effect of producing a lot of tears does not necessarily stop the action. This is especially true when the mob is made of, or led by, experienced agitators who continually whip up the emotions of the participants. A crying person can still do a lot of damage.

During recent years CN gas has been successfully combined in liquid form with another tear-producing chemical, EBA (ethyl bromacetate). EBA is a powerful eye, nose, throat, and skin irritant. Rather than producing tears profusely and immediately, it prevents the tears from coming during the initial exposure. The eyelids stay tightly closed until the CN can produce some tears and relieve the effects of the EBA so that the eyes can open. With the eyelids tightly closed, a person or mob cannot do damage, and more individual panic is created.

This combination of chemicals with its temporary blinding effect better serves the purpose. It results in incapacitating the mob or individual at the outset, providing the gas concentration is great enough. It has no more harmful after effects than the pure CN.

Tear gas has little effect on horses. Mounted police can be very effective in mob control and fortunately can operate without special masks for their mounts.

NAUSEATING OR SICKENING GAS

The effects of this type gas are much more spectacular and severe than those of tear gas.

Sickening gas has a continuing disabling effect that can last as long as 24 hours when the victim has been exposed to a severe, prolonged concentration. It should be used judiciously and only in extreme cases of emergency. Adverse publicity, political repercussions, and the effect of the gas on innocent bystanders must always be considered. This chemical agent should never be used in an unrestricted manner. In most cases, normal tear gas will perform the job. The decision to use nauseating type gas should be made well in advance, when possible, and after due consideration has been given to the factors mentioned above.

This gas was originally designated by the military and manufacturers as DM (diphenylaminechlorasine). It can be used in its pure state or combined with tear gas (CN-DM). It is released by both the burning process and in liquid form. Although called a gas when actually released by the burning process, it is an irritant smoke. The effects are produced by the action of the smoke particles on the respiratory system. DM irritates the nose and throat more violently than it does the eyes.

This agent produces: first, sneezing and coughing; second, choking and gasping; then sickness in the stomach and uncontrollable retching and vomiting, followed by violent headaches. Severe cases will frequently collapse and faint. The prolonged nausea leaves the rioters weak and helpless with no desire for further participation. The reaction is so violent that the effects can last up to 24 hours.

The delay time of the burning process of DM gas release along with the smoke generated, may enable some of the rioters to avoid the concentration. Previous comments regarding the merits of visible and invisible tear gas apply equally in this case.

The combination of the sickening gas with a tear gas is to be recommended because it is always necessary for a certain time element to pass before the sickening gas takes effect. Consequently, tear gas with its initial impact slows up the initial individual or mob action until the more severe nauseating type gas takes effect. Generally, all current DM (sickening) gas is mixed with CN (tear) gas by the manufacturer.

Nauseating gas is also currently available and projected in liquid form. Its manufacturer designates it as KO gas. This is a combination of tear and nauseating gas which is especially effective.

After one minute of exposure to KO gas, the following effects begin to set in 2 or 3 minutes later. Great irritation is caused to the upper respiratory tract, the sensitive peripheral nerves, and the eyes. The irritation begins in the nose, as a tickling sensation, followed by sneezing, with a flow of viscous mucous, similar to that which accompanies a bad cold. The irritation then spreads down into the throat and coughing and choking set in until finally the air passages and the lungs are also affected. Headache, especially in the forehead, increases in intensity until it becomes almost unbearable. These symptoms are accompanied by an oppressive pain in the chest, shortness of breath, and nausea which soon causes retching and vomiting. The victim has an unsteady gait, a feeling of vertigo, weakness in the legs, and a trembling all over the body. These effects usually reach culmination in about 15 minutes after exposure to the KO gas and continue until exposure ceases. After 15 minutes in uncontaminated air, the symptoms begin to disappear and in from one to two hours recovery is nearly complete in the average case.

Treatment for persons exposed to KO gas consists of: rest, fresh air, and removal of contaminated clothing. Wash the nose and throat with saturated solution of boric acid. Relief for the burning of the nose and throat is afforded by inhaling the following mixture:

Alcohol	40%
Chloroform	40%
Ether	20%
Ammonia	5 to 10 drops

The ammonia will also give some relief from the nausea. Glycerine and menthol lozenges also help to allay the burning of the throat. Aspirin may be used to relieve the headache and other pains, and single dose of morphine will usually relieve the worst of the symptoms. No treatment other than symptomatic is required, since almost all victims will make complete recovery in the course of a day or two.

It would be possible, under extremely high concentration conditions, to develop a near fatal effect on a victim of DM or KO gas. This situation is very unlikely to happen in normal field use. Sickening gases are best used against mobs and rioters in open-air conditions. The effectiveness of this gas, which is very volatile under these circumstances, automatically prevents the concentration from developing dangerously.

Generally, the necessity should seldom arise for using the nauseating type gases against persons or groups confined in rooms, buildings, etc. If it is used, provision should be made in advance so that the victims can be taken out into the open air as rapidly as possible. Again a heavy concentration of tear gas will produce the same desired effect with less complications.

Another factor that must always be considered when using DM or KO gas, is the protective quality of the masks used by the police. Unfortunately, many masks in the hands of law enforcement officers today are out-moded and of types that will not give protection against nauseating gases. The nature and after effect of this gas is such that if there is any doubt or lack of confidence in the protective equipment issued to the users, there will be a very natural reluctance to use the gas.

It is a simple matter to train units or individuals in the use of tear gas, where the after effects are mild after exposure to limited quantities such as used in training. It is not the same when nauseating type chemical agents are covered in training sessions. It is not generally advisable to expose trainees to effects of this gas. Its effects need only be described. At the same time the effectiveness and confidence in the protection provided by the masks to be used when it is employed against mobs and rioters must be emphasized.

SCREENING SMOKE

Smoke (HC) is very useful in riot control. It is generally projected by grenades or by slow burning candles. It is also loaded in projectiles in place of tear gas for use during visual training.

HC smoke is non-lethal and when released forms a dense white cloud of great obscuring value.

Smoke also is very useful in determining wind direction prior to release of CN or DM-KO concentrations. Naturally, smoke is best used for screening purposes when the prevailing wind is favorable. Once released, the air currents prevalent will dictate its value during a given mob action.

The use of a smoke screen permits police or troops to conceal their final movements before making actual contact with the mob. Used properly, smoke enables police or troops to approach mobs and individuals in barricaded buildings so that gas munitions can be more safely and effectively employed.

Photo Courtesy of Lake Erie Chemical Co.

Lake Erie gas mask, Lecco No. 45, is of modern type affording protection against tear gas and nauseating gas. It is packed in its own box for storage and carrying. This mask is light, compact and gives full protection when properly fitted and the wearer is trained in its use. It does not fog up, and enables good side vision.

A heavy smoke concentration used against a mob also tends to separate the various individuals so they cannot maintain visual or physical contact with one another. When individual contact is lost the capacity for collective mob action, around which riots are born, is also destroyed.

A large mob can often be split into sections by using smoke screens in the form of distinctive boundary lines. Once this is achieved and the mob is split into various sections without contact with one another, it can be more easily dispersed.

Smoke screening grenades or candles used in combination with tear gas are most effective. The psychological effect is quite great. Lack of visibility and profuse tears plus separation from his companions normally will panic the individual rioter, especially if he has no physical way of avoiding such a gas-smoke concentration

Gas-smoke concentrations are of particular value when there is no necessity for the police to enter the smoke and gas covered area. In this type of situation, police units can cover the *edges* of the smoke and gas area, and can pick up individual mob members as they finally emerge.

Screening smoke and its use in combination with tear gas should not be confused with the type of smoke emitted by the burning type tear gas grenade. This smoke is generally not heavy enough to cut off visibility entirely as does HC, developed especially for this purpose.

Many times rioters can be "suckered" into positions that will disorganize them even more rapidly than normally by use of a combination of smoke and invisible tear gas grenades. A concentration of smoke and tear gas is laid down directly on the rioters. As they begin to leave the smoke gas concentration by an escape route purposely left open for them, they can be met with a concentration of the invisible type tear gas. This strategy is very effective, particularly when it is desired to apprehend the individual rioters, their leaders, etc.

Available on special order from Lake Erie and other firms are large "smoke pots." These contain their own igniters and are capable of giving off large quantities of screening smoke. They are relatively inexpensive and the smoke is available in various colors such as orange, red, yellow, and blue. The use of these quantity-producing special smoke pots against rioters has a definite psychological effect, apart from the screening function. Instinctively, mob members are affected by the colored smoke. It is a new experience for many but more important it leaves the uninitiated with the impression that they will become indelibly stained by contact. More panic results. Civil police would be well advised to take advantage of this harmless but very useful tactical weapon.

TRAINING IN USE OF GRENADES

Chemical agent grenades are commercially available in several distinct types. They can be loaded with either pure tear gas or nauseating gas or combinations of both, and smoke.

Generally they are used by police when in close contact with rioters or individuals.

Commercial grenades containing tear and nauseating gas will vary in size, shape, and diameter. They will weigh from one to two pounds. None of them are of such type that they are inconvenient to throw or carry. All are designed for practical use and are the result of many years of manufacturing experience in meeting a need.

These grenades contain a delay fuse that is activated when the striker of the ignition mechanism hits the shotshell type primer in the fuse body. The delay fuse burns for approximately two seconds and then either initiates gas dispersion by the combustion process or by means of an explosion that gives instant release of the gas contents. It is important that police and military understand that their tactical use of the grenade must be based on the distance the grenade will travel in the two-second interval during which the delay fuse is functioning. It is not the maximum distance that the grenade can be thrown that is important; claims of superiority of one grenade over another due to its lighter weight which enables it to be thrown further may therefore be discounted. By practice and training, men must be taught to throw the grenades so that they do not burst in the air above the heads of the rioters. This is especially true of the blast dispersion types, that are designed to be thrown directly amongst the rioters. (Combustion type grenades are NOT recommended for this purpose).

The best manner to throw the grenade will depend on the individual. Any type of throw can be effectively used. Baseball type throw, stiff arm, or underhand are all acceptable. The individual grenade thrower should be permitted to use the method easiest and the most accurate for him. For reasons mentioned above, the distance factor is not important and any normal individual can launch any of the various com-

Left: The STRAIGHT ARM THROW is one advocated with the heavier type grenades to avoid possible injury to the thrower's arm or elbow joint in action and practice. As shown in the illustration, the throwing arm is kept straight and a sweeping motion over the head is used. The free arm is used to maintain balance and points in the direction of the target area. The grenade thrower is just ready to launch the grenade. In this and the other illustrations it is assumed that he has just pulled the safety pin with his free hand.

Center: The BASEBALL THROW is good for those men who can use it with accuracy. The man who has had baseball experience usually uses this one best. The lighter gas grenades are more suited for this type of throw.

Right: The UNDERHAND THROW is often the best for close range where it is desired to hit a specific target, such as a window. Persons who have never participated in baseball will usually find the underhand throw more accurate.

In the case of gas grenades the maximum range of throw is not always the desirable one. Gas grenades are usually equipped with a two-second fuse. The range of the throw is therefore that which enables the grenade to explode at the time of impact. This causes the gas to rise up past the faces of the mob members and provides maximum exposure. Longer throws are not advisable, as they cause the gas to disperse in the air above the mob and are more subject to air currents. A 30-yard throw is generally indicated with the arc or trajectory high enough to go over the heads of anyone standing close to the thrower.

mercial grenades the distance necessary to take advantage of its full capabilities of gas dispersion.

Advertising claims that one type grenade can be carried in more quantity than another, due to less weight, are also meaningless. To the writer's knowledge, there has never been any action yet where this was an important and limiting factor. Normally, grenades are carried into action either in improvised sacks or bags or in special belt holsters. Whether the grenade weighs one pound or two should not prevent the normal individual from carrying sufficient numbers to meet any known situation.

While the blast dispersion type grenade cannot be thrown back by the rioters, it should be thrown in such a manner that it bursts on impact with the ground among or at the feet of the mob elements. In this manner, the gas will rise up past the faces of the rioters and full advantage is taken of all the contents of the grenade. A distance of 25 to 30 yards is normally the recommended distance for a throw into the mob. This will take about two seconds of travel through the air, and will result in the burst being timed properly with relation to the delay fuse element. There may be some slight variations due to make and model of grenade and this should be learned and compensated for in training.

GETTING READY TO THROW. Grenades should be so placed in their pouches that they can be taken out with the throwing hand, with the safety lever in the correct position between the thumb and forefinger. This enables faster launching and eliminates the "juggling" around in the hand to get the grenade in the proper throwing position. In the midst of action, anything that can be done to eliminate the human error factor is indicated. If the grenade is grasped in a faulty manner, many times it will be dropped by a nervous individual within his own unit, or allowed to explode in his hand. Grenades are normally thrown on order and are taken from their pouches and thrown in a "by the numbers" fashion. Grenades are best not carried in the hand when in close contact with the mob. The safety pin is drawn only just prior to throwing. The possible exception to the rule of not carrying the grenade in the hand would be in those cases where the scene of action and throwing is not known or uncertain, such as in a dark alley or inside a building.

GRENADE CARRYING POUCHES. Note that each grenade is carried in a separate pouch. In this manner the individual can be equipped for action with any variation of grenades and types, as the situation demands. Normally, single blast gas grenades are carried in front. The heavier Jumper Repeater types are best carried in the rear. Special grenades such as those loaded with nauseating gas and smoke can also be best carried in the rear, to avoid errors during action when such special type loadings are used on command.

It is essential to conduct intensive practice sessions in grenade throwing to improve accuracy and range of throwing. Dummies of grenades made in approximately the same size and weight as the live grenades actually stocked are very useful in training. Empty beer cans filled with sand or cement to the proper weight make good practice grenades.

Circles can be outlined on the ground as simulated mob targets. Skeleton door and window frames can also be constructed for the same purpose. Practice throwing of grenades at a simulated window frame placed above the ground level is recommended. Not only are grenades expensive, but misses when trying to throw them into a building can cause them to bounce back at the feet of the thrower. If used against armed, barricaded individuals, there is often a lack of opportunity for a second try. Accuracy in grenade throwing is also important when gas guns and the more accurate longer range gas projectiles are not available. Underhand throws can also be used where the range is short and the target is a small one such as a small window.

During the training period men should be made to practice the proper method of handling the grenade with the safety lever being held down against the body of the grenade between the "V" of the thumb and the forefinger of the throwing hand.

The motion of pulling the safety pin should always be simulated in practice at the time of throw. Untrained persons using grenades for the first time *under tension*, have been known to throw grenades without pulling the safety pin first. On other occasions live grenades have been dropped amongst the throwers due to lack of training and excitement brought about by the action itself.

The practice of pulling the safety pin in advance and carrying the grenade in the hand for a prolonged period, prior to actual throwing, is not recommended. In this situation it is too easy for the grenade to be dropped or accidentally knocked from the hand during or prior to the action.

United States manufactured grenades available today can, with few exceptions, be thrown directly into the mobs and crowds with little danger of causing serious injury. About the only hazard involved would be if an individual is struck by the grenade while it is in flight. At the time of the explosion of the modern gas grenade, the body of the grenade stays intact. The gas pours out through numerous vent holes in the sides, top, and bottom, depending on the type.

During training periods all trainees should be exposed to tear gas concentrations with and *without* masks. Small, special training tear gas ampules are commercially available for this purpose. A closed wall tent, placed in an open field, in which a quantity of gas has been released, is a simple but effective way of training. Trainees can be exposed to tear gas, in the tent, using this system with and without masks for any desired period.

In the above manner, the effect of tear gas is actually ex-

Left: Applying gas mask—Step 1. Note that the rubber face piece is turned back fully and evenly on both sides so as to permit the mask to be placed on the face quickly with a minimum of risk of damage to the mask.

Right: Applying mask—Step 2. Notice the chin being thrust well into the mask, preparatory to adjusting the bands on the head.

Left: Applying mask—Step 3. After the chin has been thrust into the mask, the elastic head bands must be adjusted evenly so that a tight, uniform pressure on each band causes the face of the mask to fit tightly without too much pressure, making a perfect seal around all edges of the face piece.

Right: Applying mask—Step 4. When the mask is correctly fitted all elastic bands will have even tension. Each man should have his own mask that has been adjusted to his own face and *tested* by him in gas training chambers, in which he can have full confidence. There should be no interchange of masks. All adjustments to insure perfect operation should be made during the training period. After this phase the mask should be kept in the wearer's possession or marked for his personal use in action.

perienced and any mystery as to its action and nature will be revealed. This in turn leads to greater confidence by the user in its use and effectiveness.

The fire hazard presented by the burning type gas grenade (used by many police agencies) should be covered in training, particularly if this is the type grenade which has been purchased by the department.

Individual confidence must also be developed, during the training program, in protective masks against tear gas, nauseating gas, etc. Normally, police using grenades will, or should be, wearing masks. The proper care of the mask, drill in putting it on rapidly, and practice in wearing it over prolonged periods, should all be covered in the training program.

The modern commercial type gas mask is generally light in weight, gives good visibility and, when properly fitted to the individual wearer who is trained in its use, will give complete protection.

For obvious reasons, training in the use of grenades and

masks should be simultaneous. Grenades can and have been used, out of necessity, by police without protective masks. However, the situation can usually be foreseen in advance to eliminate this possibility.

COMMERCIAL TYPE GAS GRENADES

Lake Erie Model #34. This grenade discharges its gas instantaneously in a single blast in less than two seconds after throwing. The gas is invisible and is liberated so rapidly that there is no time for kicking the grenade aside or a throwback. There is no fire hazard. It is available loaded with pure tear gas, nauseating gas, or combinations. It does not rupture or explode and can be thrown directly into the mob. The invisible gas cloud liberated is about twenty feet in diameter. There is no fragmentation.

Lake Erie Jumper Repeater. This instantaneous grenade, with-

Photo Courtesy of Lake Erie Chemical Co.

TWO TYPICAL GAS GRENADES

Left: the Lake Erie Jumper-Repeater grenade containing invisible tear gas which is discharged in three heavy blasts during a four-second period as the device bounces amongst the rioters. Right: the smaller Lake Erie Model 34 grenade which discharges its contents of invisible gas in a single blast two seconds after throwing.

Photo Courtesy of Federal Laboratories, Inc.

Federal Triple Chaser hand grenade. This grenade breaks into three sections (as illustrated) two seconds after being thrown. Each section travels in a different direction, functioning as an individual grenade and covering a wide area quickly with visible gas.

out rupturing the grenade body, discharges in rapid succession three heavy blasts of gas. As each blast occurs, the device jumps ten or twelve feet in a different and unpredictable direction. The first blast or gas discharge occurs two seconds after the grenade leaves the hand (this represents between 40 and 50 feet of travel). The two succeeding blasts occur at one second intervals. The total discharge of all gas in the grenade is completed in four seconds. There is no opportunity or time for a throwback. The invisible gas released is in a very heavy concentration. The manufacturer states that the total gas discharged is approximately 35 percent more than the Army Fast Candle or the standard size burning type grenade. No fire hazard is present. It is available in smoke. It can be thrown directly into a mob. Each blast of invisible gas is about ten feet in diameter.

Federal Spedeheat. This is a burning type grenade that begins its action at the time thrown. The entire content of gas is discharged in about 35 seconds. This grenade is nonexplosive and becomes extremely hot during the burning period. This makes a throwback difficult. The grenade discharges a heavy visible gas smoke concentration through the openings in the top, bottom and sides. A fire hazard is present. It is available in tear gas or nauseating gas. The grenade body does not rupture. Due to the throwback hazard, the manufacturer recommends that it be used some distance from the mob with a favorable prevailing wind. It is not recommended to be thrown directly into the mob. The diameter of the tear gas burst can easily be observed by the smoke cloud that accompanies its release.

Federal Triple Chaser. This non-explosive grenade separates into three gas producing sections in about two seconds after being thrown. Each section travels in a different direction, functioning as an individual grenade. A good volume of visible gas is thus discharged in three places practically simultaneously. The sections travel with a sizzling, hissing sound brought about by the burning and moving action. This has a definite psychological effect. In this particular grenade the hazard of throwback is minimized and a heavy visible concentration of gas is delivered over a larger than normal area. This grenade is available with pure tear gas or with sickening gas. The individual sections do not rupture and it can be thrown directly amongst the rioters.

The Federal Triple Chaser and the Lake Erie Jumper Repeater type grenades are best employed among rioters, and in situations where the mob members are rather widely dispersed. Densely packed masses of rioters are best attacked by using blast type grenades such as the Lake Erie Model 34 that can be thrown directly into their mob or by using the Federal Spedeheat grenade in conjunction with a favorable wind.

A blast dispersion type grenade that throws off a cloud of tear gas dust is now produced by Federal Laboratories. Their Model 121 has an aluminum case that rips open but does not throw any dangerous loose fragments. This grenade, according to the manufacturer, does not create any fire hazard. Users are warned, however, not to permit the grenade to go off accidentally in the hand as serious injury can result. An earlier blast type grenade listed by Federal was their Model 120 which had a fiber body that disintegrated at the time it released its charge of tear gas dust. This grenade is not now manufactured as apparently there was danger to the user from fragmentation.

In years past Lake Erie also produced a bursting type grenade called the Green Band. It was very effective but due to fragmentation of the metal case at the time of gas release, it also has been discontinued. At the present time all Lake Erie grenades are of the instant blast dispersion type but their steel grenade bodies remain intact and there is no fragmentation. Gas is dispersed instantly through holes in the grenade body but there is no danger due to flying metal fragments.

Smoke Grenades (Candles). Both Federal and Lake Erie produce a large grenade for use in smoke screens and air current testing. The smoke (HC) is oily white and very thick. This type smoke is generally considered to be non-irritant and non-toxic but a long exposure to a heavy concentration can result in irritation and discomfort.

For a heavy, prolonged smoke screen, it is recommended that burning candles be used. They burn continuously for several minutes. By placing the candles to take advantage of the wind, streets and other critical areas can be more completely blocked and obscured for longer periods.

Shoulder Gas Guns and Projectiles. The development of the 37mm gas gun (1½" caliber) along with accurate short and long range projectiles has given law enforcement another very potent weapon to use against barricaded criminals, insane persons, and mobs.

These guns, and ammunition for them, are manufactured by both Lake Erie and Federal. They are shoulder fired and equipped with sights that, after practice, enable their accurate use at ranges well out of physical contact with dangerous mobs or individuals.

Photo Courtesy of Federal Laboratories, Inc.

FEDERAL 37mm gas gun for use with long and short range gas projectiles against persons and mobs with barricade type shells.

Photo Courtesy of Lake Erie Chemical Co.

LAKE ERIE TRU FLITE 37mm GAS GUN

Training is necessary in their use and firing to develop accuracy, as it is with any other type of firearm. Special individuals or units skilled in the use of this equipment will "pay off" in saving lives and property and counteract all other negative effects of individual and mob violence. Practice projectiles are available from the manufacturers for training.

Tear gas and nauseating gas projectiles and combinations can now be launched against targets up to 350 yards distant. Accurate shooting with tail-fin projectiles enable consistent hits up to 75 yards on ordinary window-sized targets after training.

Lake Erie 37mm shells are usable in the gun manufactured by Federal and vice versa. Sight adjustments are necessary when using the barricade shells in guns of the opposite make.

Short-Range Gas Shells. These 37mm shells are quite effective against rioters at close quarters. They are excellent for protection of gates, entrances, or narrow approaches to buildings. The gas is blasted directly from the muzzle of the gun with effective ranges up to 35 feet (in still air). A cloud of about 15 feet in diameter is released containing a heavy concentration of gas.

It is recommended that masks be used in this type of gas projection. If masks are not available care should be taken not to fire against an adverse wind. Due to eye danger from flying particles of wadding from the shells, the gun should be aimed at the feet of the persons toward whom the gas is directed. Tear and sickening gas are loaded.

Long-Range Gas Shells. This type has proven most effective in controlling or dispersing mobs beyond the effective range of hand-thrown missiles. They are best used against large mobs and are not intended to be fired directly at individuals as is the short-range type.

With the long-range shell it is possible to lay down gas barrages on the windward side of a mob or in the rear if wind conditions make use of hand grenades impracticable. If the gas concentration is heavy enough, all physical contact with the rioters can many times be avoided. Both tear and sickening gas can be loaded in these projectiles. The gun is usually elevated from 30 to 60 degrees for this type projection. Some guns have adjustable sights that have been developed to determine definite ranges, but again training must be done to achieve efficient use of the long-range gas projectile. The various manufacturers supply practice projectiles and others containing smoke for training purposes.

COLT AR-15 GAS GRENADE LAUNCHER MISSILES

The versatility of this new arm and its application to police use has been increased greatly due to the fact that Lake Erie has produced special grenades and missiles enabling its use in riot control with tear gas, KO, and smoke.

Above: With the special gas grenade now manufactured, it is possible to hurl a charge of tear gas approximately 400 feet when the gun is held at a 30 degree angle.

Below: A finned barricade projectile can be fired with accuracy at a window at ranges up to 75 yards. It will penetrate a one-inch thick pine board.

Left: Types of leather carrying cases for 37mm gas gun projectiles. The policeman can carry a number of projectiles comfortably in this manner. On one side in front long-range projectiles can be carried and short-range on the other. In back, barricade shells, smoke, and nauseating gas can be carried.

Right: Firing position used for shooting short-range gas shells at close range directly into the front of the mob. This is also the position for firing special finned projectiles into windows against barricaded criminals or rioters.

The Federal long-range gas shell has a three-second time fuse. It burns expelling visible gas for between 20 and 30 seconds after the fuse has activated. The kick and throwback hazard during the burning period is present. The fire hazard must also be considered. Range claimed by the manufacturer is 325 yards.

The Lake Erie Company manufactures a projectile of the liquid gas type. The claimed range is 450 feet. All the gas is expelled in a single blast. The casing of the projectile tears open rather than shatters. Invisible gas is liberated over a 20-foot circle. This projectile has a six-second time fuse. When fired at a 30-degree angle the time fuse will explode the gas charge at about the time the projectile hits the ground. Lake Erie claims that, due to the type of gas used and the container in which it is carried, their shell liberates three times more gas than the standard long-range burning type projectile.

COMMERCIAL LONG RANGE PROJECTILES AND BARRICADE GAS SHELLS

This type of projectile is designed for projecting tear or sickening gas into barricades, defended rooms or buildings,

Left: Firing position when firing a long-range gas projectile in front of, back of, or into the mob. The angle of the piece will dictate the range. Practice with specially designed practice ammunition will enable the shooter to hit his objective with sufficient accuracy for tactical use. Note that the weight of the shooter is on the forward leg.

Right: Loading the gas gun is normally done from the port arms positions and all loading is done by the numbers, by command. Normally, the gas guns are not carried loaded, but are charged with the appropriate type of projectiles on command. In some cases, where the action has been pre-determined and the time element will be short, prior loading instructions can be given, but for obvious safety factors loading is best done just prior to discharge of the piece. Cocking of the gun is done just prior to firing.

industrial plants, prisons held by rioters, or against barricaded criminals or insane persons.

These projectiles are equipped with tail fins that spring into position when the projectile leaves the gun muzzle. These tail fins (like an arrow) keep the projectile from tumbling and keep it pointed toward the target. Good accuracy at window-sized targets from the smooth bore 37mm guns at ranges up to 100 yards is possible, after practice.

This type projectile is *not designed or intended for direct* use against crowds and persons, since its velocity and penetration potential is such that death or serious injury can result.

The barricade type projectile that releases its charge of gas on impact, can be used against mobs and rioters by firing it so as to hit a wall or building above or near the rioters, to release the gas charge.

This type of projectile is available in a number of loadings. Tear gas and nauseating gas are the most common charges.

On special order WP (Incendiary) practice smoke, practice inert, fragmentation, and high explosive loadings can be obtained.

Because of the varied loadings available, law enforcement units now have, through use of their 37mm gas guns, a type of firepower for extreme situations that is similar to the military.

The Lake Erie Company manufactures its TRU-FLITE barricade shell for this specific type of law enforcement. This shell has a stated maximum range of 350 yards and an accurate

Photo Courtesy of Lake Erie Chemical Co.

Left: Lake Erie long range Tru-Flite tear gas shell with projectile. This projectile is designed for use against criminals or insane persons barricaded in rooms or buildings. On leaving the muzzle, tail fins spring into position, permitting accurate shooting at window-sized targets up to 100 yards. Right: Lake Erie long range riot shell for use in laying down gas barrages, from a distance, against mobs.

Because of criticism of its Model 230 and numerous throwbacks, Federal has recently introduced a new blast type barricade shell that explodes on impact and disperses a cloud of tear gas dust. The new shell Model 232, should better serve the purpose and it is claimed that the fire hazard is also eliminated.

range of 100 yards. It delivers its gas charge, on impact, at the end of the flight, in one blast. An impact fuse that is activated after the projectile is in flight, sets off the gas-detonating charge. The body of the projectile rips open and allows the gas to be instantly dispersed. The impact fuse is not overly sensitive, so that the projectile can penetrate window glass and light board partitions before the gas is released. There is no fire hazard, or fragmentation..

Federal manufactures its #230 FLITE-RITE projectile for the same purpose. Claimed range is up to 325 yards. Good accuracy is claimed up to 100 yards. The Federal projectile carries a time fuse that automatically ignites the grenade to start the burning process, liberating the gas, at a flight point about 50 yards from the gun muzzle.

This projectile continues to burn and expel its gas for about 30 seconds after it is activated. The projectile body stays intact and will penetrate window glass and light board partitions due to its velocity. The burning process of gas release makes the projectile very hot to handle and minimizes the possibility of a throw back. The fire hazard is present.

Many police officers annually are wounded or even lose their lives when attempting to dislodge desperate armed criminals or insane persons from barricaded rooms and buildings. This is one of the most hazardous aspects of law enforcement. The 37mm gas gun and special barricade shells provide a solution.

Newspaper files and police department records are replete with reports, good and bad, concerning this particular phase of law enforcement. The two newspaper articles below are very indicative of the possibilities.

MURDER SUSPECT CORNERED, KILLS SIX

Springfield, Mo., Jan. 2—Sheriff Marcel Hendrix and five other officers were slain late today when they attempted to capture Harry Young, 25, and several companions in a farm house five miles west of here, and late tonight the killers were believed to have made their escape into the Ozark Mountains.

After a siege of several hours a new force of officers and citizens stormed the house, only to find Young, who was wanted for the slaying of a city marshal at Republic, Mo., and his companions had gone.

Young and his pals escaped from the house after greeting the officers with a hail of machine gun lead that killed five outright and fatally wounded a sixth.

Then started a vengeance-maddened search through the hill country. To the officials and guardsmen were added farmers, armed with shot-

guns, who traveled in groups and talked quietly of a "lynching party."
The dead are: *Deputy Sheriff Wiley, Mashburn, Green County;*

> *Sheriff Marcel Hendrix, Green County;*
> *Detective Chief Tony Olver, Springfield;*
> *City Detective Ollie Crosswhite, Springfield;*
> *City Detective Disney Meadows, Springfield;*
> *Patrolman Charles Houser, Springfield.*

—Cleveland Plain Dealer

KILLS OWN FATHER
Drink-Crazed Soldier Captured
After Augusta Squad Used Tear Gas Gun

MILLEN, GA. April 26—(Special). After killing his own father and wounding a night policeman, David Humphreys, 28, a drink-crazed ex-soldier, barricaded himself in a room at Hotel Autery early today and for four hours defied officers to "come and get me."

Millen officers sought unsuccessfully to rout him from his fortress, in which he had two shotguns, a case of ammunition and a half gallon of corn whiskey.

Officers Employ Tear Gas Gun

The slayer refused to budge and threatened with death any one who approached. Then, for the first time in the history of dealing with criminals in this section, a new weapon was brought into play on behalf of the law. A short gun, of wide bore, gave a blast which alarmed the neighborhood; a large projectile hurtled through the window pane into the room where the slayer was holding out; a gas arose from the floor; in a few seconds, the cries of defiance had changed to one of "Come and help me out." Humphreys, the fight taken from him, staggered out of the room, hands over head, into the arms of Lieutenant Walter H. Holly, of Augusta, who had fired the gas projectile into the room. An incident which without the new weapon would have been a bloody battle was settled without further bloodshed.

—Augusta Georgia Herald

Compiled statistics show that over 90% of barricade cases occur in the second story of a house or building. Trajectory and ballistics for barricade gas missiles are developed with this in mind. Training targets should be constructed at varying heights up to 20 feet above the ground so as to develop better accuracy and realism.

Parachute Flares. Illuminating parachute flares are also manufactured in 37mm to be used in the gas rifle. These cartridges shoot a brilliant flare into the air to an altitude of about 225 feet. The period of illumination is about 40 seconds and lights up an area such as would be covered by a circle 600 feet in diameter.

The brightness of the illuminating flare is such that, during

night action, individuals, mob elements, and police disposi-
tions, are easily located in the lighted area. It is advisable
to plan to be at some high point above smoke, gas, etc., such
as the top of a building, at the time the flare is released, so
that all advantage can be taken of the brief observation period
furnished by the flare.

Chemical Projectors and Billies. There are now available on
the market a number of hand tear-gas projecting devices.
The better types are especially manufactured by Federal and
Lake Erie for use by police, plant and prison guards, and
night watchmen. These devices are effective in direct proportion to the size of the shell and the amount of gas projected in relation to the range used.

In addition, the general public can buy small imported .22
caliber automatic pistols shooting very small amounts of tear
gas plus a wide variety of tear gas fountain pens in calibers
from .38 to 410-gauge. The actual effectiveness of the concentration of tear gas released from these devices is variable
and questionable.

Gas projecting billies and prison riot sticks such as manufactured by Lake Erie and Federal have a definite value as
they are multi-purpose weapons. They carry enough gas to
be effective against one or several individuals who are closely
grouped together. Discharge of the gas cartridge can be followed up with use of the billy or riot stick for striking purposes. The user has the advantage of utilizing offensive tactics
while the element of surprise and immediate effects of the
explosion, plus the gas, temporarily disconcert the recipient.
The officer can utilize the short period after the release of the
gas to use his billy as a weapon, draw a firearm, retreat, or
close a door or gate.

In those cases where an officer is alone and in doubt about
the intent of an individual or group who approaches him, he
can utilize the gas in the billy either as a threat or by firing
to improve his position and thereby assume the initiative before coming into bodily contact. As the gas is basically harmless no permanent damaging after effects result, therefore,
when in doubt, he should not hesitate in its use. Should it
develop that the parties on whom it has been used had no
actual hostile intent, still no real harm has been done.

It must always be remembered that gas billies, pens, etc., are
"one-shot" devices. A positive immediate follow-up action
must be taken as soon as the gas is fired.

Where possible this strategy should have been decided on in advance. The officer should not just stand immobile and expect the victims of the gas to be and remain completely

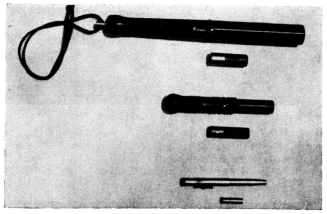

HAND TEAR GAS PROJECTORS

Top: Lake Erie 12 gauge police billy that carries a spare gas shell in handle. Middle: Detective gas billy manufactured by Lake Erie in 20 gauge. Bottom: Caliber .38 tear gas fountain pen of a type commonly sold commercially for individual protection.

Generally speaking the 20 gauge tear gas shell such as used in the Lake Erie Detective Gas billy is the smallest caliber gas projectile that can be expected to give positive results from this type of hand-carried weapon. The billy itself is approximately six inches in length and can be comfortably carried almost as easily as the smaller .38 caliber fountain pen type. It discharges five times more gas than the .38 caliber shell. In addition the round knob on the end of the billy provides a potent striking weapon for a follow-up against the adversary after the gas discharge has been made.

The .38 caliber and smaller sized cartridges are so limited in their gas carrying capacity that too much reliance must not be placed on their effectiveness against dangerous persons.

helpless. In some cases determined individuals can and will still attack, use firearms, etc., in spite of having received a gas discharge. The officer must take advantage of the surprise and the immediate effect of the gas to assume the offensive, retreat, or whatever else is indicated under the circumstances.

Gas billies and riot sticks as projectors have little use in mob control. In this case, officers equipped with standard riot sticks reinforced by grenade throwing units or individuals in their rear, can best handle large groups of rioters.

Gas guns and billies which must be used at close range to be effective should always be pointed at the middle or chest of the victim at time of discharge. Otherwise, particles of sealing compound from the end of the shell and wads may injure the eyes.

At the time of the discharge the element of surprise along with the noise of the explosion usually causes the recipient involuntarily to open his eyes and gasp, thereby automatically absorbing a good dose of gas.

On the other hand, if the blast is expected, an experienced individual will immediately start moving, with his eyes closed to avoid the gas cloud.

If the officer is confronted with a small group of individuals who are close together, he should fire the gas without any provocation, if he sees the group beginning to spread apart or to reach for what may be concealed weapons. After firing the gas discharge the officer should move rapidly from his firing point so as to disguise his physical position and to confuse his enemies while they are still under or avoiding the effects of the gas cloud.

Lake Erie manufactures billies and riot sticks for use with a 12-guage shell that blasts a five-foot cloud of gas approximately 15 feet. Provision is made in their products to carry a spare shell in the handle and a special safety device presents accidental discharge.

Federal gas billies utilize a ten-gauge shell. One model projects a gas cloud of larger size at about the same range as the Lake Erie. This company also manufactures a special billy that fires through a choked opening a three-second continuous gas discharge. This permits moving the billy from side to side to achieve a spraying effect. A special safety device prevents accidental discharge.

Twelve-gauge shells available in tear and sickening gas are also manufactured by Lake Erie for use in *standard commercial type* shotguns. This provides the private citizen with a means of gas projection at no more than the cost of the cartridge. Police units equipped with riot guns also can utilize this type shell to advantage. Unfortunately, few police units or individuals realize that this type of munition is available for use in the standard sporting type arm.

Lake Erie has also introduced in recent years a very effective double action twelve-gauge, tear gas revolver. This hand weapon fires five cartridges as rapidly as the trigger can be pulled. It is possible for an individual officer to lay down a respectable barrage of gas with this weapon. The concentration of gas developed coupled with the psychological effect of the explosion of the individual shells on the victims, make it a very useful weapon. It is best used against small groups

Photo Courtesy of Lake Erie Chemical Co.

The Lake Erie five-shot 12-gauge, double-action, tear-gas revolver, model 512. This is a very effective weapon for use by the individual officer in laying down a maximum gas concentration. The five separate charges can be fired in a three-second period. This weapon is especially useful against small groups of rioters and in capturing criminals or insane persons in confined areas. Due to the recoil factor it can many times be more advantageously fired by using a two-handed grip. A five-foot diameter cloud of gas is projected by each shell at ranges from ten to fifteen feet.

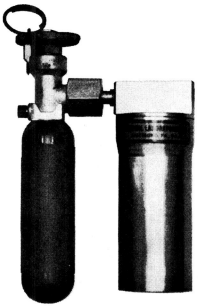

Photo Courtesy of Federal Laboratories, Inc.

FEDERAL TEAR-GAS DUST PROJECTOR

This is a very useful device which will shoot tear-gas dust into rooms through small openings where there is no possibility of projecting tear gas to subdue the occupants in any other manner. Keyholes, cracks under doors, etc. can be utilized as ports of entry.

in street and prison riots or in capturing criminals or insane persons when they are cornered in rooms.

Federal and other manufacturers also market a complete line of tear gas projecting devices designed to protect safes and vaults. These devices are usually placed inside the safe, etc., and are activated when the safe is *forcibly opened.*

Other gas devices are available for use in protecting banks from armed robbery, industrial installations, etc. They are activated automatically or by convenient and strategically located hand and foot controls which can be set off without danger to the individual.

Cost of Gas Munitions and Equipment. The seemingly high initial cost of gas equipment many times discourages its purchase or inclusion in the police budget. This is particularly true in departments where it has never been used with success, previously, and the members and officials are untrained in its use and potential.

Most modern police departments now maintain inventories of gas equipment and train in its use. Many times gas munitions on hand and in reserve are not enough to handle any large and long-sustained mob action. Reliance is generally placed on being able to get additional munitions from the manufacturers quickly, or on a loan basis from other police agencies.

Gas munitions, like raw camera film, have a stated shelf life which is usually three years from date of loading. This is usually stamped on the grenade or projectile at the time of manufacture. This is only an approximate figure but should be used as a basis for purchase and consumption. Much depends on the storage conditions. Humidity, extremes in temperature, and other factors affect the actual "shelf life" of gas munitions. The manufacturers do not know under what climatic conditions their products will be used and therefore give a dating for approximate guidance of the purchaser that is within all known safety limits. The procedure in modern police departments that have purchased their initial inventory, is to replace on a yearly basis those gas munitions that have been expended. If any materiel is "outdated" or soon to be, it is used in training. In case of any action the munitions with the oldest "dating" are used first.

Generally, liquid type tear gas munitions will last longer in storage due to the fact that the gas content is hermetically sealed in glass containers. In extreme humid or hot conditions, munitions loaded with powdered or crystalline type tear gas, are more vulnerable to deterioration. Moisture enters into the grenade body and starts deterioration of the CN crystals. This in turn starts an oxidation or rust action on the inside of the grenade case, which is usually of steel. This process cannot be avoided over a period of time because the body of the grenade itself is perforated and the holes for emission of the gas are covered with adhesive tape that seals off the grenade contents for a limited time only.

Commercial type shotshell primers are used in the fuse as the detonator. These primers are copper jacketed and are well sealed against action of the elements. However, the delay element or fuze, that is ignited by the explosion of the primer, is the most susceptible to moisture penetration. Failure of "outdated" grenades and projectiles to expel their contents is many times due to the malfunction of this element.

Taking into consideration the above comments, serious thought should be given by responsible officials to the *actual economy* of gas munitions and equipment.

The savings in life, property, and casualties must be placed on the opposite end of the scale from the initial cost. The increased efficiency and high morale of department members equipped and trained in the use of gas munitions must also be considered. To dismiss, or to fail to buy, gas equipment for reasons of economy is a very shortsighted and ill-advised action.

Dollar value of the life of an individual officer cannot be determined. On the other hand, the expenditure of a few

Photo Courtesy of Lake Erie Chemical Co.

LAKE ERIE SPECIAL GAS GUN OUTFIT

Weight of complete outfit, 51 pounds. Carrying case dimensions: length, 32 inches; height, 15 inches; width, 5¾ inches.

The outfit includes: 1 Tru-Flite 37mm Super Long Range Gas gun; 4 Tru-Flite Super Long Range Tear Gas Barricade shells; 4 Standard Long Range Tear Gas Projectile Riot shells; 4 Short Range Tear Gas shells; Illuminating Parachute flares; 4 Model 34 Tear Gas grenades; and 1 leatherette carrying case.

A kit such as the above costs approximately $275.00. Its contents are especially selected to enable a flexible all-around use of tear gas in small actions and emergency conditions.

Every police and sheriff's department, no matter how small, as well as plant guards and other organized protective units, can afford and should have this type of equipment. They are designed for rapid easy transport and many departments have these kits permanently assigned to each roving vehicle.

hundred dollars worth of Jumper Repeater or Triple Chaser hand grenades to break up a large and dangerous mob, that if unchecked would have caused possible loss of life and property and damages running into thousands of dollars, would seem to be a definite practice of economy.

The principal thing to remember is, that gas equipment must be on hand along with personnel trained in its use. It cannot always be anticipated in advance when emergencies will appear.

U.S. ARMY GAS MUNITIONS EQUIPMENT

It is important that civilian police and others have knowledge of gas equipment in current use by the U. S. Armed Forces. Under emergency conditions this equipment may be made available to civilian police units or it may be used in support of civil law enforcement agencies by National Guard or Army units in certain situations.

Generally, commercial equipment such as 37mm gas guns and the variety of gas grenades and projectiles offered give more flexibility to civil police units in mob actions of moderate size. In very large operations where thousands of demonstrators are involved, the Army equipment such as mass gas dispensers is many times more applicable.

In 1960 the Army announced a new irritant gas agent for riot control, designated as CS this gas is crystalline in nature but is soluble in certain liquids. It is stable under ordinary conditions of storage.

CS causes copious tears, a burning sensation in the eyes, coughing and difficult breathing, a stinging action on moist skin areas, sinus and nasal drip, involuntary closing of the eyes and nausea in high concentrations. It has a pungent pepper-like odor and is accompanied by a white cloud during release. Its lasting effects are not harmful and most disappear after 5 to 15 minutes in fresh air. CS is also used by the Army for training purposes to simulate more toxic types of gases. Its nature and psychological effects are stronger and more varied than those of ordinary tear gas (CN). Projection, handling, and decontamination procedure of CS demands thorough training under the supervision of skilled officers.

CS is also used in bulk form for mass projections from planes, helicopters, special portable tank units like those of a flame thrower, and special mounted blowers such as are used in crop dusting. Grenades of the combustion and instantaneous bursting type are also loaded with it.

The U. S. Army also still issues CN hand and rifle grenades and smoke candles for riot control operations.

From examination of all available data it would seem that

the CS gas, due to its special characteristics, is not ideally adapted to use by civil police, even if it were made commercially available.

The U. S. Army CN tear gas grenades in current use are of combustion and baseball fragmentation types. Special rifle grenade launchers and adapters are issued. The U. S. Army does not issue the commercial type 37mm gas gun and projectiles.

It is interesting to note what the most recent U. S. Army manual (FM 19-15, Sept 1958) recommends regarding tactical use and limitations of its CN grenades. The hand grenade M7A1 uses the combustion or burning system of release of tear gas. It takes from 20 to 60 seconds to dispel its contents, with the characteristic white smoke, which indicates the area covered by the gas. The following statements are quoted: "Riot control gases of the combustion type are not thrown into the mob because they may be thrown back. . . . The burning type grenade should not be used where combustibles are present because of the intense heat generated by the grenade and the danger of starting a fire."

The baseball type hand grenade M25A1, containing tear gas is constructed with a frangible plastic case that shatters into small fragments when the grenade bursts. Finely pulverized powdered tear gas is dispensed over the impact area in from 1½ to 3 seconds after leaving the hand of the thrower. Dispersion is caused by an internal explosive element like a blasting cap. The manual says "The average distance that the baseball grenade may be thrown before bursting is 35 to 50 yards. Grenades should be lobbed into the air so that the burst will occur several feet over the heads of the members of the mob on the up-wind side and *should never be thrown directly into the faces of the individuals in the mob, as permanent blindness may result from ruptured eyeballs torn by plastic fragments of the cases.*"

There are several other points pertinent to use of this baseball type of grenade that should also be noted. (1) To use the grenade as directed, by throwing so it bursts over the heads of the rioters, is a very difficult thing to do under stress of combat action. Usually in combat, the tendency is to throw the grenade directly into the mob elements. To be able to judge correctly the bursting time so that it will occur as recommended, is extremely difficult and not practical in mob action. Even the listed fuse time is too variable. Much training is necessary. (2) If the grenade is used as recommended, and it bursts over the heads of the mob, a great deal of gas will be wasted in a windy condition. The gas cloud will be global in shape and the wind will carry away the gas that is not blasted directly downward over the rioters. (3) There is definitely also another dangerous safety factor when using the blast type, frangible case grenade. At times in the excitement of mob action, the thrower will pull the safety pin and release the safety lever accidentally or unconsciously. When this happens and the grenade explodes in the thrower's hand the serious results can well be imagined. (4) Misuse of this type of grenade so that a mob member will be blinded is almost as bad as causing a fatality. Publicity and public reaction can be very adverse.

GENERAL COMMENTS

An unruly mob or riot can be caused by anything; labor, religion, politics, or the price of beans. Gas munitions are used to dispel riots, not to settle disputes. Practical experience now proves that chemical agents control these situations much better than bullets. The policy of all law enforcement should be to control riots by first, the presence of police or troops; secondly, the use of chemical munitions; and lastly, by resorting to gun fire. The objective to be achieved through the use of the gas is to create panic, confusion, and dispersion of the mob.

In the employment of gas munitions it is basic that they be projected in quantity so that there is a sufficient concentration to discourage and destroy concerted action of the mob. In the long run it is much more economical to use more munitions at the outset than to have to repeat launching lesser quantities several times to achieve the same result. The majority of the rioters must individually feel the pain or discomfort of the gas fumes if they are to be effective. A few grenades thrown into the fringes of a violent mob will have little real or lasting effect. The center, rear, and flanks must feel the effects also.

Advantage of favorable prevailing wind is always taken when possible but the fact that the wind is unfavorable must not limit the projection of gas munitions. Long-range gas guns and instantaneous dispersion blast type grenades are available. Therefore strategy and tactics in employment of gas munitions must not be entirely developed around the prevailing wind concept. Most mob actions take place in cities where there are buildings which can block off air currents or diminish them to a point where effective tactical use of gas in combination with a favorable wind cannot always be made.

The combustion type grenade is particularly dependent on favorable wind conditions. Tactics recommended for use by the manufacturer are always based around this key factor. In a condition of light or no wind, the combustion type grenade will liberate its contents so slowly that a great deal of effectiveness is lost. Blast type grenades give instant dispersion without depending on the wind factor, and get a rapid concentration into the faces of the rioters.

Hand grenades and gas guns with short and long-range projectiles can all be employed. The principle most advocated is to keep up the pressure and flow of gas against the mob. It should be remembered that in the case of large mobs an avenue of escape must always be left open through which the rioters can flee.

Don't fire a few gas grenades and visibly retreat to await results. Avoid if possible, hand-to-hand contact by concentrated use of chemical agents. The less actual physical force used in restraining the mob the more lasting will be the resultant peace.

Tear gas and other chemical agents are humane weapons to be used to preserve law and order. Communist and other type agitators who use riots as a means to power will always directly and indirectly try to destroy the effectiveness of chemical munitions by minimizing their usefulness and by malicious propaganda as to the "deadly qualities" when employed. In Communist dominated countries, such as East Germany, tear gas is also used, but the overwhelming tendency is to use the less expensive bullets from rifles and machine guns to achieve their purpose.

Another very important factor in favor of the use of chemical munitions in mob control, is that it will not injure the so called "interested bystander," as bullets can. Every scene of violence, real or potential, always draws its share of curious spectators. Physical damage to this type of person usually results in bad publicity, law suits, etc. Here again, in an indirect way, chemical munitions aid law enforcement in carrying out its mission.

Police elements used in mob control should wear masks, especially those in close contact. Protective masks are as an important a part of the equipment as the gas itself. The use of gas grenades involves close contact where variable wind conditions can always expose the thrower as well as the target. Another interesting side effect is the psychological impact

World Wide photo

TEAR GAS SCATTERS DEMONSTRATORS

The above illustration was taken from a press release covering a demonstration of teachers in Lima, Peru in October 1961. According to the Associated Press news story, the demonstration was broken up by the police, utilizing tear gas and night sticks.

The photo clearly shows that tear gas grenades of the combustion type were used. A burning grenade with its distinct accompanying cloud of smoke generated during the burning process can be seen in the center. Individuals on the left have received a dose of the gas. Those on the right can be seen running away from the grenade and its cloud of gas, thereby avoiding the fumes. This is one of the disadvantages of using the combustion type grenade. It is also interesting to note that the cloud of gas being released in the smoke is not being dispersed but is moving straight up, indicating a lack of wind. This is visual proof of the recommendation that combustion type grenades are best used with a favorable wind, so as to disperse the gas among the demonstrators. If, instead, an instant dispersion-blast type grenade had been used with invisible gas, a much more effective concentration that the demonstrators could not see or avoid, would have been the result.

caused by the weird appearance of the gas-mask wearing, grenade-throwing police elements.

Determined rioters will many times try to improvise protection against gas. This may take the form of goggles such as worn by skin divers, handkerchiefs across the nose, or impregnated cotton stuffed up the nostrils. These expedients will only delay the action and will not stand up under a heavy concentration of gas.

For further information on mob control, see chapters 14, 15, and 16.

Chapter 14

CIVIL AND DOMESTIC DISTURBANCES AND THEIR CONTROL

A WIDESPREAD public disturbance which is not immediately suppressed but instead is permitted to grow, becomes a threat to the effective functioning of legally organized government. Violent and uncontrolled mob action destroys public morale and confidence in police and military forces. Loss of life, property, and other deleterious side effects always accompany mob violence.

Causes of Disturbances. The causes of such disturbances are varied. Social, economic, and political conditions have a marked bearing, as does the failure of existing authority.

Social. Racial and religious clashes and differences have always been a major cause of disturbances. Community activities which draw together large numbers of people to celebrate a specific act, or a sporting event, have some times degenerated into serious civil disturbances when tension exists.

Economic. Extreme poverty, poor housing conditions, lack of food, differences between labor and management, devaluation of currencies, high cost of living, and allied economic factors will cause civil unrest.

Political. Efforts to gain or to destroy political power outside of lawful means is now a common motivating factor of mob violence.

Absence or Failure of Constituted Authority. The failure of civil police or military authority to cope with a mob crisis due to indecision, inability, or absence from the scene, can ignite further action. In the absence of legal restraint, the mob members begin to feel that they can act with impunity and can impose their will, however capricious may be their desires.

HOW MOBS FORM

A crowd is not a mob. It is a gathering of people for either a casual or intentional purpose that is legal under traditional rights of assembly. Members of such a crowd think and act as individuals and are without any definite organization or united purpose. However, under stimulation of an act of violence, or under the manipulation of professional skilled agitators, this same crowd can turn into a violent mob. When the crowd changes into a mob its purpose or objective becomes a unified thing. Its members lose their identity as individuals and merge into a cruel, primitive body, which has lost civilized restraints and suddenly has no respect for law and order nor for those law enforcement forces that resist it.

Influences Affecting Mobs. *Hate and revenge,* brought by such incidents as racial tension, lynching, or inflammatory political issues at local or national levels, provide strong motivation.

Numbers and anonymity. The individual loses his self-consciousness. His normal moral restraints break down. At the same time he gains a sense of strength and security due to the presence of other people acting in concert with him. Almost instinctively present within him is the feeling that he has lost his identity as an individual and therefore will not be personally blamed for his actions.

Suggestion and agitation. Under the influence of the professional agitator, a dominant personality, or a "crackpot" who assumes the mantle of leadership, the mob member reacts to exhortation and suggestions without giving any rational thought to consequences. There is no follow-through in the thinking processes.

Imitation and contagion. There is a primitive urge to do what others are doing and "to get into the act." A mob tends to increase in numbers automatically. The communication of ideas and influence from one member of the mob to another is quick and contagious.

Newness and novelty. Subconsciously an individual welcomes anything new which breaks his normal routine. Any novel and strange circumstance, such as joining a demonstration, will many times be welcomed enthusiastically. If the individual has had no previous experience and is lacking in restraint, he will easily pass from the crowd to the mob phase, wholly neglecting his usual pattern of reasoning.

Repressed desires. Those desires that have been repressed or unsatisfied are many times released in a mob action. The individual loses himself among the other mob members and now may have an opportunity to do things he has always wanted to do but did not dare do alone.

Mob Types. There are at least three types of mobs: aggressive, escape, and acquisitive. The *aggressive* type mob attacks and terrorizes. Mobs activated by agitation, racial conflicts, lynching, desire to overthrow existing governments, and prison riots fall in this category.

The *escape* type mob is motivated by panic. Its members are trying to escape from some feared or existing situation by physical flight. Terror and lack of reasoning are present. Escape is sought from the presence of some man-made or natural disaster such as an explosion, flood, or earthquake. Characteristic activating factors are the breakdown of communications, transportation, utilities and blockade of normal means of exit.

The *acquisitive* mob has as its principal incentive the purpose of acquiring some specific thing. A mob action bent on securing arms, equipment, or food would fall in this category.

The Heavily Armed and Organized Mob. The types of mobs just indicated can most of the time be dealt with by normal or reinforced civil police units. However, when mob members appear armed with firearms, in quantity, of the high power or military type, police tactics must be changed or revised. The use of extreme force is indicated and this must be done using heavily armed combat troops or military police units. A mob armed with submachine guns, light machine rifles, bazookas, demolition equipment etc., must be dominated with similar and superior weapons. This type of an action is normally countered by use of Regular Army or National Guard combat or military police units.

Civil police are not normally equipped or trained to counteract this type of mob, which degenerates into armed insurrection.

U. S. Army Field Manual FM 19-15 adequately covers this type of action. No clear definition can be made as to exactly when to apply military force to reinforce or replace a conventional civil police force. Each situation will differ and local and national conditions will dictate at what point military force must be used to replace, supplement, or reinforce the civil police.

THE ELEMENTS AND PRINCIPLES OF MOB CONTROL

There is a distinct divergence of ideas as to the type, tactics, and general concept of mob control as it is employed throughout the world. Values placed on human life, types of equipment available, historic precedents, and general police concepts as to the dangers of the mob, vary.

This does not mean that the correct and best mob control measures are always employed by the police. It does mean that each force has to face up to its own situation and deal with the mob as best it can, based on its own experience and the judgment of its officials.

Unfortunately, too little has been written about this increasingly important phase of maintaining law and order. An ominous note is the growing use of mob agitators and subversives in various countries as a covert phase of cold war.

It cannot be said that the tactics employed in Caracas, Venezuela are the same as those which should be used in a somewhat similar situation in Cleveland, Ohio.

The purpose of this chapter is to outline a number of general principles and basic precepts and to project some new ideas which can be adapted by a military or police force to its own situation to enable it successfully to cope with mob violence.

As previously indicated, the point where control of a given mob situation should pass from civil to military authority depends on the individual situation. In the U. S. the civil police of city, county, or state are first in direct control and have the prime responsibility for civil disturbances. When the civil police force fails to control a serious riot situation, the procedure has been, and still is, to call for military units either from the National Guard or the Regular armed forces. Recent disturbances in Little Rock, Arkansas are a case in point.

In many countries in the world the professional army and the police force are identical. In some countries (such as the Republic of Panama) no army exists as such, and there is only a national police force. In Latin countries, the army generally acts as the national police force even though the various municipalities may have local police elements which are civilian in nature and organization. Generally, municipal police forces in Latin countries do not have either the numbers, training, inclination, or equipment to cope with large, violent mobs. Exceptions to this are not many, but do exist. Mexico City, for example, maintains a large permanent special riot group, which is part of the city police force. This group has enough incidence of action to justify its permanent existence, and cost.

It is therefore suggested that the tactics and techniques to be outlined hereafter, be not considered as definite, rigid, fixed patterns in the control of civil disturbances, but as guide lines to aid in shaping the best solution to meet the local situation.

Riot Control in the U.S. by the Civil Police. In the United States riots of any size and scope are, or at least have been, relatively infrequent during recent years. There are reasons for this, which do not necessarily apply in other countries. The police force and the individual policeman are regarded by the general public with respect, not fear. The great majority of the American public, like the British, considers its civil police forces as guardians of law and order and a professional body of men whose sworn duty is to keep the peace and protect the individual citizen and his rights under the law.

Consequently, when riots occur in the U. S. they are usually short lived and spontaneous in nature which can be quelled without resort to extreme force. Apart from the racial issue there are no real issues of basic conflict. The public maintains a respect for forces of law and order and does not regard its police as an oppressive force.

For this reason our police forces, with their high-type personnel, good equipment, and training are able to handle most civil disturbances with a minimum of bloodshed and violence. Tear gas as a means of mob control is well-known and has been employed successfully to break up most domestic mob actions in the U. S.

There have been very few large, violent, mob actions that have been professionally organized and directed. On those rare occasions where the National Guard or Regular Army units have been called out in support of civil police, the mere display of force by the troops has generally been sufficient to prevent mob action.

In addition to this, the average police department which is faced with the possibility of a mob forming in its area normally maintains a good intelligence operation, and can usually break up any pending action by taking into prior custody the leaders and agitators; or by a prompt show of force disperse the mob in its early formative stage.

Larger state and city police forces usually have previously prepared civil disturbance and disaster plans ready for emergencies. These are covered in training programs and are relied upon to meet a riot situation on those rare occasions when one threatens to occur. These plans are usually part of the civil defense effort and are coordinated with all interested government agencies.

It is not economically possible, nor is it presently tactically necessary, for U. S. civil police to maintain on permanent assignment special riot police units. In some departments selected officers are given special training in riot control, use of tear gas munitions, and riot formations. These officers lead the riot squads or groups when the need arises. The bulk of the members of the civil police making up the actual riot force are drawn from "off duty" elements, from men on other routine assignments, and from other areas where they are on duty but calm prevails.

Larger departments that have had to control disturbances in the past and have a mob potential will maintain what is called a permanent "gas squad," which may vary in size from five to fifty men. This squad trains together at given times, and receives special instruction in all phases of mob control. This type of operational planning is very good because, when the emergency arises, its members can be assembled together from their respective regular duty assignments, thus providing the department with a more competent trained unit available for this special duty.

At times, especially in the southern part of the U. S., local civil disturbances of varying sizes have taken place due to racial problems. It is interesting to note, that, even though emotional feelings have been high, these disturbances have been handled by local police with a minimum number of casualties. In most cases there has been no bloodshed, due to the physical presence of the law enforcement units in strength, the occasional use of tear gas munitions, and the good judgment of both the police and even the leaders of the demonstrations. This is further proof of the statement that the U. S. public, when not subjected to professional agitation with international motivation, is an orderly and law-respecting one.

There has been one recent mob experience in the United States where the hand of the professional agitator was strikingly evident. In May 1960 the Congressional Committee on Un-American activities held hearings in San Francisco, California. These hearings and the police guarding them were the target of planned Communist-inspired demonstrations in which many college students took part. This was a relatively new experience in the U. S. law enforcement field but it followed closely the classic mob pattern that is now occurring in Latin America. The entire incident was well covered by news cameramen and reporters. The House Committee later published its conclusion and findings on the incident and Federal police agencies such as the FBI also took notice of the nature and origin of the manifestation. A film has since been made ("Operation Abolition") that is being exhibited throughout the country. The film has been the subject of controversy but it is of value for training purposes to law enforcement agencies due to the coverage made, regardless of political overtones.

While the public attitude toward police in the U. S. is one of respect, the same cannot be said of some other parts of the world. Especially in those areas where much illiteracy and poverty exist, police and even the military are frequently regarded as the instrument of oppressive forces.

It is also a fact that we are living in an era of great social change and upheaval brought about by extreme nationalism and a desire of the poorer segments of the population for better living conditions and opportunity for advancement. The greater the unrest, the greater has been the Communist effort to foment agitation and disturbance.

Although we hope that, in the domestic U. S., calm will continue to prevail, the world situation is such that we are no longer isolated from our neighbors and are therefore not immune to alien influences. The threat (and certainly the aftermath) of nuclear war could greatly disrupt civilian calm and order. During times of tension the professional agitator will seek to foment unrest and disorder. For this reason the police of this country had better look ahead to the possibility of more troubled times and prepare for use of mob control techniques which previously have not seemed necessary to our internal security and situation.

The Role of the U.S. Army and National Guard in Mob Control. Rarely, during the past decade, has the U. S. Army been called upon to control a civil disturbance. Usually the National Guard, under orders of the state governor, is called out in the rare case when troops have been needed to support or replace civil police unable to control a serious civil disturbance.

Regular Army units are generally called into action only as a result of a national emergency or a situation where a civil disturbance in a given area presents a serious threat to the security of the nation or vital installations and operations which the federal government must protect in the common interest. It will be remembered that Regular U. S. Army paratroop units were ordered to duty in Little Rock, Arkansas for a time, to insure the maintenance of law and order.

U. S. Army Field Manual 19-15 covers legal considerations, and policies and procedures regarding the control of domestic disturbances. When national interest is at stake, the national Government may employ Army units to maintain or restore order. When this occurs the decision as to the degree of force to be used must be made by the Army commander. The manual covers this aspect completely and it is recommended that every civil police organization of any size, with a riot potential, be familiar with it. The tactics outlined are basic and sound for military units but they are not necessarily those which are best adapted to use by the civil police because, once troops are committed, the desire to avoid casualties among rioting elements may be impossible to realize. The Army by its nature, training, doctrine, and equipment differs in its basic concept of riot control. Any and all necessary force will be used when it is finally committed to action.

Because of the numerous and sometimes complicated legal restrictions on the use of military personnel in riot control, it is recommended that all officers in command of Regular or Reserve units of platoon size or larger acquaint themselves with the contents of the following Army Regulations: 500-50, 500-60, and 500-70. These, and FM 19-15, should be kept available at all times in the unit files.

Chapter 15

COMMUNIST TACTICS AND STRATEGY IN DIRECTING MOB VIOLENCE

THIS might well be called the era of the Communist *professional* mob. We are at present in a period of "directed" mob violence. The manipulation and exploitation of this mob violence, and physical mass pressure, is a non-secret weapon which the Communists are employing on a world-wide basis with far reaching results. They are using this instrument of cold warfare for purposes of Red diplomacy. The Kremlin, using trained Soviet agents and agitators, by this means is trying to force the hand of governments and to achieve victory preferably without the necessity of firing a single shot or loss of a single soldier.

There is no lack of evidence of this serious phase of the cold war. The disturbances in Bogota, Colombia in April 1948 were Communist-inspired and were directed against the American delegation headed by General George Marshall. The purpose was the torpedoing of the Inter-American conference, which had been called to plan resistance to the threat of international communism. This riot, which cost hundreds of lives and millions of dollars in property damage and almost upset the Colombian government, was the first of many in this hemisphere in the last decade that have been Communist-organized and directed. In May 1958, Vice President Richard Nixon was the center of Communist-inspired riots in Caracas, Venezuela. These organized manifestations caused the Vice President and his party humiliation and could have cost his life. Another riot of serious proportions was organized and directed against the American Embassy, in March 1959, in La Paz, Bolivia. During May and June of 1960, riots were staged and organized in Tokyo, Japan that forced President

Eisenhower to cancel his proposed visit. The riots were so violent and of such nature that the Japanese Government did not feel it could guarantee his personal safety. At the time this is being written (February 1962) Caracas, Venezuela has just undergone another series of riots organized and led by Communists. It was 72 hours before the manifestations and terrorism could be brought under control by the government and at least 40 lives were lost. A Communist student, when interviewed by a newspaper man, stated that the Communists had expected and hoped that the government would have reacted *more forcefully*, in its suppression of the manifestations, so that more "martyrs" could have been created.

Public incidents are used or fabricated to spark riots. In the case of the above-mentioned riots in Caracas, a transport strike was the basis for the beginning of the mob action, which could have set off a full-fledged revolt against the government. It has become standard Communist practice, in the course of mob incitation, to develop a situation that will produce a "martyr" in whose memory mob emotions can be centered and raised to fever pitch. This was especially the case in Bogota in 1948 and in Japan in 1960.

Elsewhere in the world, similar tactics have recently been, or are being, employed. It is to be expected that mob manipulation will be a continuing form of Communist strategy due to its frequent success in the past. The overall strategy is one of armed revolution and subversion, supported and fostered from outside the target nation. Guerrilla warfare is coordinated with sabotage, espionage, terrorism, and mob violence. In actual fact, violence in a planned mob action can be characterized as just another form of guerrilla warfare, although waged in urban areas.

Communist minorities with party members strategically located in places of power and influence in the press, communication networks, labor movements, universities, and in positions of trust in local and federal government have been known to instigate mob violence to overthrow the existing government.

The discrediting and destruction of regular police and military forces whose responsibility is the maintenance of law and order, is a prime objective. When police and military forces are divided, destroyed, or rendered incapable of action against the directed mob, the Communists can move rapidly into power. After power has been seized, the new government acts rapidly to disband and destroy the professional military and police forces. Records, files, and all other collected evidence of Communist activity are destroyed. Cuba under Castro is a classic example of this tactic.

Recent U. S. Congressional hearings have further pointed up this new threat which must be met and dominated by the legitimate forces of law and order. On June 13, 1961 the U. S. Senate Internal Security Subcommittee held a secret hearing. Mr. Lyman B. Kirkpatrick, a high official of the Central Intelligence Agency, gave testimony. The secrecy classification has since been lifted and Mr. Kirkpatrick's testimony is now a matter of public record. It is entitled "A Communist Plot Against the Free World Police." This valuable and interesting testimony can now be secured by sending fifteen cents to the Superintendent of Documents, Government printing Office, Washington 25, D. C.

The police and military organizations of the free world are foremost guardians of our democratic institutions and freedom. Therefore, they are prime targets of the Communists. The better the police force, the more the Communists desire to destroy it. All types of tactics are used to discredit the police, who may suddenly find themselves the target of vicious and organized opposition. A natural antipathy exists between police and Communists. The police are always among the first to become aware that the Communist party (regardless of its local name and affiliations) is not a "home-grown" political movement, but that it is an instrument and part of an international conspiracy bent on destruction of democratic institutions.

Not only must police be properly trained and equipped, but they also must have knowledge of the techniques and tactics that may be used against them. Communists will do everything possible to slander, discredit, or prevent the development of a strong police force. This will vary from attacks in the press and outright subversion in the force itself to a publicity campaign aimed at the reduction of appropriations of funds for police payrolls and equipment.

Police and military officials must have a basic knowledge of Communist tactics with relation to mob disorders so as to be able to foresee potential danger spots, better direct their own intelligence operations, and to train their own units adequately in mob control and riot duty.

GENERAL COMMUNIST TACTICS IN FORMATION OF MOBS AND CREATION OF DISORDERS

These tactics and strategy are based on teachings given to Soviet agents and selected Communist party members in various countries. Schools for this purpose have been and are now being conducted in the USSR, Czechoslovakia, Cuba, and other "iron curtain" countries. Some of these centers for training the professional revolutionist in the science of creating civil disturbances and civil war have been in operation for many years. This training activity has recently been stepped up to meet the demands of the current world situation. Those forces in the democracies responsible for law and order should understand what they are up against. The tactics may be summarized as shown below:

(1) Generally, there will be no overt action by known Communists. All agitation will be done behind the scenes, using uninformed and excitable teenagers, students, illiterates, and others to form the body of the mob.

(2) Unfavorable local economic situations will be exploited. As a rule the Communists wait for some situation or suitable local issue to arise so they can provoke mob excitement. If no issue exists they create one, preferably one including a martyr.

(3) In order to minimize police and other suppressive action, the Communists will often ally themselves openly with other groups with political power and thus seek to form a united front. At the same time they will continue mob agitation and incitation in a clandestine manner. It should be remembered that in most cases the Communist party will not be flying its true name and colors. Its local party or organizational name will not be any indication of its true nature and affiliation. In fact, the organization will probably be under some name with a claimed purpose which would indicate to the more gullible the exact opposite of its true nature.

(4) As a matter of policy, the Communists do not deplore bloodshed and violence. The concept is that martyrs and violence will excite the mob to even greater violence.

(5) A planned mob action will usually be thoroughly worked out in advance. There will be preliminary mass meetings, printed leaflets distributed, radio broadcasts, provocative cartoons and newspaper articles, and even assassinations. Local

police counter-riot tactics will be studied and plans made to circumvent them.

(6) The immediate targets of mob action will be police stations with their vital records, radio stations, newspapers, utilities, and communications. In foreign countries, Communist-dominated labor unions connected with these prime targets will usually be focal points for great preliminary agitation and activity. Later these same union members will be called to join the mob, even though the action may have been initiated by a separate movement such as a student group.

(7) If the Communist party is operating openly, it may officially disclaim all responsibility for mob violence. At the same time the party members will normally be the channel through which agitators are furnished, and funds and propaganda material provided, along with whatever else may be needed to incite a mob. In some cases, if the situation so indicates, the local Communist party will be kept entirely apart from any direct activity and association with the mob activity. In this fashion the party serves as a decoy while the principal operations will be centered around or through some other local or national political movement. The Castro take-over in Cuba is a case in point.

(8) It is standard practice for Communist-trained and led mobs to be armed with non-military weapons such as stones, clubs, and homemade bombs of gasoline or other flammable liquids. The armament may be supplemented by sporting firearms and crude explosive devices. Looting of local commercial outlets to secure arms and explosives may be part of the preliminary action phase. If any arms are actually supplied to the rioters prior to the action, they will probably be of commercial sporting types. They will probably not be makes and types that can definitely be traced to Communist sources. On some occasions arms supplied will be those of the army or police who must confront the mob. Planned raids on military and police arsenals are made in advance for this purpose. Arms may even be obtained by subversion within police ranks through ample use of funds or other means. Effort is made to obtain arms without prior police or public knowledge.

Communists Using Mob Violence as an Instrument of Cold War Consider Themselves To Have the Following Advantages:

(1) Police or army units of any given country are likely

to become demoralized when called upon to attack their own people, especially young students, women, and veterans.

(2) Rioters can be armed with homemade weapons that can be secured without outside aid.

(3) Communists will use people and elements of the country under attack for destruction of the government. There is no need to use Soviet soldiers.

(4) Mob violence has a tendency to grow and gather momentum due to its very nature. If the mob is allowed to grow and is not checked at the outset, its strength will increase automatically and it will draw many types of non-affiliated elements to itself.

(5) If the government is weak and hesitates to restrain the demonstrators, the Communists will make increasing demands. When violence does occur, either provoked by the initiative of the mob or by government forces, the government will be blamed. The issue can then be used for national and international propaganda.

(6) Communists are trained to select and use the most provocative and incendiary types of propaganda slogans. Simple ones are easy to understand by the masses of the people and they need not reveal any Communist connection.

(7) Democracies operate at a disadvantage, especially when under attack, as they are dedicated to the principle of safeguarding human life and liberty. This makes the democracy vulnerable under mob attack, as it will use every means to avoid bloodshed. In contrast, a Communist country does not hesitate to use unlimited ruthlessness and mass killings, as was done in Hungary.

Communist Mob Management Techniques. An example in Iraq of effective mob management by a very small number of Communists, and a description of the control techniques they used, in the words of Mr. Gene Methvin, of Washington, D. C., follows.*

"The Communist Party of Iraq in the militant period of 1948-50 used well-designed mob management techniques. Although a tiny minority, the Communists, by carefully disguising the Communist direction of their demonstrations, were

---

*An extract, used by permission of the author, Mr. Gene Methvin, from an article in ORBIS, No. 2 Summer 1961, Foreign Policy Research Institute, University of Pennsylvania (copyright © 1961 by the Trustees of the University of Pennsylvania), a condensation of which appeared in the March 1962 issue of *The Military Review*, U.S. Army Command and General Staff College, Fort Leavenworth, Kansas.

able to give an impression of great size and support. The techniques used were fairly representative. They consisted of the following:

"*External command.* This was composed of demonstration commanders well-removed from the activity, stationed whence the entire 'battlefield' could be observed; if a moving demonstration, it would stay apart from the crowd.

"*Internal command.* This was the Communist cadre within the crowd. They were responsible for directing the demonstration, under the external command's orders. Great importance was attached to protecting the leader of this unit.

"*Bravadoes.* This group acted as a loose bodyguard surrounding the internal command, protecting the leader from police, and screening his escape if necessary. A line of these guards would flank processions and protect banner carriers as well.

"*Messengers.* They stayed close to leaders, carrying orders between internal and external commands. Generally, they would wheel their bicycles along the sidewalks, keeping abreast of, but removed from, the demonstration.

"*Shock guards.* These men were armed with stout staves and accompanied the Communist faction, but marched along the sidewalk where they were screened by spectators. They would dash into the mainstream of mob action only as reinforcements if the Communists were attacked by police. Their sudden and violent descent on the battle was designed to provide sufficient diversion to enable an orderly retreat of the main body of Communist demonstrators who, upon signal from the external command, would melt quickly into the ranks of spectators, leaving the milling bystanders, unwitting excitement seekers, and fellow travelers to the police.

"*Banner carriers.* The slogans used by this group and the 'cheering section' were adapted to suit the prevailing mood. At first they displayed banners with slogans expressing general grievances, but as the demonstration gained momentum and frenzy drove out reason so that real issues lost meaning, the slogans were exchanged for direct Communist propaganda.

"In any Communist demonstration anywhere, key agitators can often be found keeping close to certain conspicuous banners. The carrier may be a sincere non-Communist protestor, entirely innocent of his true role as an important part of the internal command's communications network. By assigning key men to stay near specified banners, the command knows their location at all times and can dispatch messengers to them with instructions for stepping up the tempo, shifting slogans, or inciting violence.

" '*Cheering sections.*' Specially briefed demonstrators were carefully rehearsed on the slogans they were to chant and the order in which the cries were to be raised.

"Using these tactics, a group of 200 to 300 party members could create a demonstration in which as many as 10,000 would take part.

"Still another efficient mass action was organized in Buenos Aires on 3 April 1959 to turn a demonstration against electricity rates into a bloody riot. To inhibit countermeasures by the police, or at least to embarrass them, women and children were recruited to help set fire to automobiles. Supervising the vandalism were the party's top leaders. Sixteen cars were overturned and burned, and 30 persons were wounded and 144 arrested—some of whom admitted they participated under party orders."

Communist Mob Training Manual. The Communist training manual on creation of mob violence and destruction of police opposition sets forth four specific objectives, as listed below:

(1) Make investigations and report on the activities of all police and security services.

(2) Make every effort to penetrate police and security services, so that they can be better repressed and counteracted.

(3) Infiltrate police organizations to find out how much they know of Communist activities, to steal documents, and to destroy records and files that may be of value to the organizations concerned.

(4) Undermine police authority and prestige, weaken police efficiency, create the impression that the police are basically a repressive force, that the officers are incompetent and in pay of a foreign power, and that the police are not true representatives of the people.

The Communist handbook contains some very simple sketches and elementary drawings illustrating how the mob, under leadership of its trained agitators, can be maneuvered to crush police opposition and otherwise bypass the police in order to carry out its purpose. A few selected illustrations of Communist mob operations from this handbook are shown.

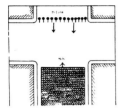

Fig. 1. Shows the mob advancing toward its objective. It is faced with only a few policemen, who will attempt to block off the path.

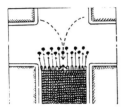

Fig. 2. Shows how the police have deployed into two lines to oppose the mob, and have advanced to meet it before it enters the intersection. At contact, selected mob members in front engage police units in combat, permitting the rest of the mob to surge out around the flanks into the intersection and continue toward the objective.

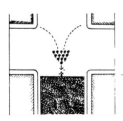

Fig. 3. Shows that the police meeting the mob have formed into the classic phalanx or wedge formation for mutual protection. Again the formation has advanced to meet the mob before it breaks into the intersection.

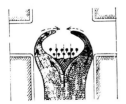

Fig. 4. Shows the police phalanx being engaged by selected hard core mob members and the beginning of an envelopment action. This action will result in the police unit being surrounded while the mob moves on to its target.

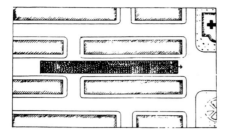

Fig. 5. Shows a mob moving forward which has not yet met any police resistance. During this period scouts are sent out and intelligence organized so the mob leaders will know where and what kind of police resistance can be expected. Here the mob has not made any provision for protection or counter police action, so is vulnerable to police action. See fig. 6.

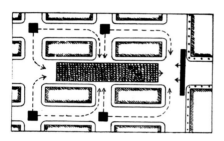

Fig. 6. Demonstrates how the police would take counter action against a poorly planned and unprepared mob action. This shows police units blocking the advance and having reserve units in adjoining streets that can move in any direction to penetrate the mob and force its dispersal.

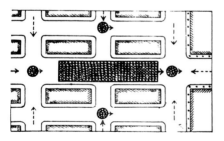

Fig. 7. Demonstrates how the mob should advance into action against planned police resistance. "Action units," specially armed and trained, protect front, flanks, and rear of the mob against the police.

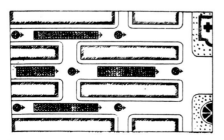

Fig. 8. Another tactical formation of mob approach, advancing along parallel lines in segments, each being preceded by an "action unit." This formation gives great flexibility for envelopment tactics and forces the police to extend over a wide area.

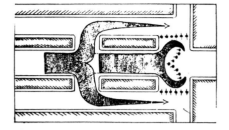

Fig. 9. This is the military type envelopment technique. The central mob column meets and surrounds the police units from the front and at the same time the two columns on the parallel streets flank the police lines guarding the center.

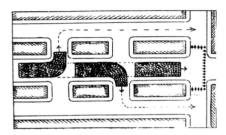

Fig. 10. This is another technique to meet the same police formation as in fig. 9. In this case the single mob column breaks into three segments, one moving to the right, the other to the left, in order to flank the police lines.

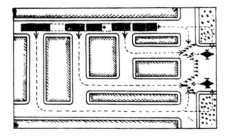

Fig. 11. In case of police roadblock, the mob column splits into four groups that enables a coordinated attack on the police elements from all sides.

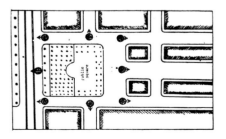

Fig. 12. A plan to protect a public square where a meeting or demonstration is being organized. "Action units" are stationed at all points of entrance to the action area. These action units will divert the police, delay police entrance into the square, and protect and permit the crowd to build up to where it can be incited to mob action.

WHAT TO EXPECT FROM THE MOB

This is a very flexible subject, as the scope of mob action is limited only by its motivating factors; the arms, supplies and other materials available; the number and type of the individual mob elements; and whether or not trained agitators are present to direct the action.

The location of the action also plays an important part, as the activities of the mob itself and its capabilities for violence will be limited by the space available for movement and maneuver. The size of the city square, direction and width of the streets entering into it, and the location and type of buildings will also affect the course of action, in the same manner as does terrain on the battlefield. Temperature and other climatic factors have influence. For instance, cold, rainy weather has a slowing down effect on mob activities, movement, and organization.

The tactics employed against the police will also indicate, to the trained observer, the nature of the mob leadership and degree of professional organization present. Evidence of advance preparation would be previously prepared handbills and posters, possession of weapons of types and quantities not normally available to mob members, and simultaneous yet coordinated incitation by agitators strategically located throughout the mob.

Abuse. Police elements can be subjected to both verbal and written abuse. Taunts, ridicule, jeers, and obscene remarks and shouts are to be expected. Derogatory pamphlets or handbills may be distributed to the crowd and to bystanders before and during the action. Propaganda may be sent to the police units themselves or distributed in a clandestine manner before and during the disturbance. Posters may be carried depicting police brutality, or demanding vengeance for past acts. Sound trucks or agitators using hand-powered transistor-type megaphones may be used to direct the mob and to heap abuse on the police units in an attempt to demoralize them. Slogans and derogatory material may be painted on the sidewalks, buildings, vehicles, and other likely places.

Noise. A large mob action is always noisy. The shouts, cries, and chants of the mob members are usually supplemented by the use of fireworks, noise makers, sirens, and whistles. Very effective use has been made of chants or the shouting of slogans in a definite rhythm pattern, sometimes aided by whistles and drums. This type of crowd incitement is very effective when well organized and directed. Rioters sing songs of an inflammatory nature, and chant slogans. They readily respond to man's instinctive attraction to jungle drums and primitive rhythm as exemplified in a war dance. These tactics have the effect of increasing the aggressiveness of the mob, especially when there are large numbers involved. Police may become demoralized if they have not been trained in what to expect.

Thrown Objects. Every conceivable object has been thrown at police units in mob actions. Listed are a few of the more common: Garbage, animal and human droppings, rotten fruits and vegetables, eggs, bricks, rocks, paving stones, bottles, cans filled with dirt, plastic bags and balloons filled with liquid ammonia or chlorox, bags of pepper, containers full of stain (also dye and acids), birdshot, tacks, firecrackers, jagged pieces of scrap metal, improvised fire and explosive bombs, powdered glass, chunks of window glass, chimney soot, coal and coal dust, plates, triple-pronged fish hooks, tin-can lids, links of chain, short lengths of barbed wire, or any other similar object.

Primitive type catapult devices, slings, sling shots, and similar devices using old inner tubes have been used to hurl objects from within the mob at police who are out of range of hand-thrown objects. Thrown objects can not only be expected from the mob in immediate contact but also from members on roofs, inside windows, and on buildings adjacent to the action.

Hand Weapons. Mob members may be armed with hand weapons secured from local sources such as looted hardware stores. The following have been encountered in action: wooden clubs, pieces of pipe, pointed sticks or improvised spears, short lengths of concrete reinforcing steel, wooden clubs with lengths of chain or barbed wire tied to the end, baseball bats, golf clubs, hockey sticks, hoe handles, hammers, machetes, hand sickles, shovels with edges sharpened, pitchforks, axes, all types of knives, handguns, mattocks, ice picks, bows and arrows, and air pistols and rifles.

If the mob is a spontaneous one, hand weapons will normally be fewer in number and less dangerous in nature. The longer the mob has to organize and prepare, the more armament must be expected. Police officials, by using their intelligence services and observation facilities, must always consider the degree of mob armament when planning a suppressing action.

Shoulder Weapons. A mixture of sporting-type firearms may be encountered, if the opportunity has been present to secure them by looting or to assemble them in the prior planning phase. Normally, a well-disciplined mob led by trained agitators will not desire to employ too many firearms. Sniping tactics will be employed rather than mass use of these weapons. Heavy use of firearms will result in counter firepower from the police, who may be replaced by heavier-armed military units if the situation deteriorates. The mob, of course, would prefer to combat the lighter armed and less deadly civil police units.

Isolated sniping can normally be expected in a large action. For this purpose .22 caliber arms are very effective, as the report is not loud and the location of the sniper is more difficult to determine. Expert riflemen with scope-sighted rifles can also be expected in a mob in a well-organized and serious operation. These men usually have instructions to "pick off" the key police officials directing the counter mob action. This is one reason that a police unit, trained for riot action, must have its own counter snipers available.

Use of Fire and Explosives. Mobs under professional direction often blow up or set fire to buildings and vehicles in order to create more confusion, increase the excitement of their own mob elements, and to try to create a diversion by drawing the attention of the police from the main scene of action.

If the mob is moving forward, it may contain within itself special groups or individuals who are equipped to start fires as the action progresses. Other special groups may be designated to go in advance of the fire-setters and rip open doors, windows, and gates with heavy crow bars, so that access can be secured to the interior of buildings. These same tactics of breaking open doors also make it easier for the inevitable looters to operate that follow in the wake of the mob.

Normally fire hydrants will be destroyed in conjunction with a deliberate torch action. Areas between the police and the mob may be flooded with gasoline and set off to prevent police contact. Flaming torches may be utilized at night for mob illumination purposes and also to further arouse primitive emotions. Gasoline-soaked waste is often used along with other gasoline-saturated, flammable objects such as cushions and pillows hurled at police elements from roof tops and windows. Fronts of buildings can be drenched with gasoline and set fire.

The "molotov" cocktail is a favorite mob weapon. This is usually a glass bottle filled with gasoline and corked. Around the neck of the bottle will be tied a piece of gasoline-soaked rag. The rag is set on fire and the bottle thrown at some object against which it will shatter on impact. By using a shotgun with a blank shell, a crude but effective long-range launcher for the "molotov" cocktail can be devised. In place of a cork, a long, round stick is used as the bottle stopper. The butt of the gun is placed on the ground and the stick placed in the muzzle of the gun against the blank shell. The bomb is ignited and the trigger of the gun pulled. The gas charge of the blank shell against the end of the stick will drive the fire bomb a considerable distance. A little experimentation as to the proper angle of the piece will develop a fairly efficient, long-range launcher.

Gasoline stations and gas and gasoline-storage tanks are all prime targets for mob action and sabotage, prior to or in conjunction with mob action. Fire not only has a tactical use by the mob but it also is very effective in inciting primitive emotions among the mob members thereby increasing the violence potential.

Utilizing commercial sources for explosives, secured either in advance or during looting, a trained mob will use the destruction of key buildings as a diversion action to draw the police. Booby traps and bombs placed in heavily-populated buildings will be part of the action. Explosives can be more easily concealed, and timing devices readily improvised. Consequently, this tactic must always be expected against planned targets such as utilities and communications prior to the actual disturbance. Planned explosions blamed on other parties are always a good way to fabricate martyrs.

Attacks On Small Groups and Vehicles. Many times a mob is incited to violence by a directed action against some small, specific group of individuals or their property. In this manner hatred can be aroused that may result in beatings, and killing or burning. Racial minorities are often the object of such an attack. This type of tactic can be used as a diversion or as a target to set off explosive violence that can later be directed at the principal target.

Vehicles such as trolleys, buses, and privately-owned cars or trucks that are unfortunate enough to be parked in the action area are always potential targets. Trolleys and buses are derailed or turned over and set on fire. Flaming newspapers are forced into gas tanks, or cars can be drenched with gasoline first and then set on fire.

Buses and other vehicles can be commandeered by the rioters. They can be set on fire, or driven under their own power, in the direction of the police lines, the driver jumping out before contact. The same tactics with or without drivers can be used to break blockades or damage buildings. At times these vehicles are loaded with explosives.

Tires of parked cars may be slashed and upholstery ripped open and windows broken. Many times large tacks to damage tires are scattered in the streets along routes police vehicles will use to approach the mob.

On occasion trucks, buses, and similar vehicles have been stalled, or accidents created that will block off streets and prevent police elements from entering areas or leaving their headquarters.

Looting. It is a standard tactic to organize or to encourage looting. In this manner, the uneducated, non-dedicated mob elements will be attracted. Promises of easily acquired wealth, either in the form of material goods or money, is always a sure way to attract mob members.

Liquor stores, hardware stores, banks, gun stores, jewelry stores, and food stores are all prime targets. In conjunction with the general looting by the uninitiated, the professionals will concentrate on police stations, newspaper offices, telephone, radio and television and telegraph stations, government buildings, and banks.

Communications and Utilities. These are prime targets of any large, well-organized mob action. This does not mean that the mob itself will first attack them. Many times planned sabotage will take place in conjunction with or prior to a mob action.

Cutting off electric power and telephone facilities is one of the first moves to be expected in support of any organized mob action.

Demonstrations. A demonstration is described as an assemblage of persons exhibiting sympathy against authority or with some political, economic, or social condition or movement.

Public demonstrations frequently are the planned forerunners to mob violence. Due to skillful leadership and knowledge of mob psychology, a seemingly harmless or peaceful demonstration can in minutes be turned into a howling destructive mob. Police are often taken by surprise in such instances and find themselves unprepared to meet the sudden change in the situation.

Sometimes a series of demonstrations will be called by the organizers before the scene is set for actual concerted mob action, or enough strength of numbers and confidence is developed to touch things off.

The parading of the bodies of so-called martyrs in their coffins in the streets as victims of claimed government or police brutality and the parades of groups of women dressed in black as pretended widows of the dead, and of so-called martyrs, are examples of this type of demonstration activity.

A crowd of persons may gather as a result of some event that arouses interest and curiosity. The crowd can be turned into a mob if it can be held together long enough and the thinking of the individuals ignited by agitators into mob action. On the other hand, the planned demonstration is already far advanced along the path to mob violence as the participants are already drawn to the scene by the united thinking and interest.

Much attention must be given by police elements to the planned demonstration. Continuous surveillance must be maintained and good intelligence accumulated before, during, and after demonstrations.

The Planned or Fabricated Incident. When elements bent on civil disturbances lack an excuse for one, they will manufacture an incident around which to develop and prepare the mob action. This will vary from planned assassinations to the blowing up of monuments and buildings. The means is not important if the results are obtained.

The planned assassination of the popular figure, Dr. Jorge Gaitean, in Bogota, Colombia in April 1948, was used to set off destructive mob violence; it cost millions of dollars in damage. The popular Latin slang expression, "bogotazo" is now commonly used to describe a destructive, planned, mob action.

Miscellaneous Mob Tactics. It is now common practice to make full use of unarmed women and children in mob actions. They are usually placed in front of the mob in direct contact with the police elements. Wounded and incapacitated war veterans are similarly used. Agitation continues behind the protective screen of women and children and at the indicated time, they are pushed against the police lines by those in the center and rear.

Many times the rioters in front of the police will also be waving the national flag and singing national anthems.

Such tactics make it very difficult for police to break up the mob by use of physical force; tear gas munitions are usually the best solution.

In June 1960 when President Eisenhower was visiting Okinawa, Communist-inspired riots and demonstrations took place. U.S. Marines were ordered to fix bayonets and clear away the crowd. Young Okinawan college girls are reported to have unbuttoned their blouses, bared their breasts, and dared the Marines to advance against their naked bosoms.

Rioters often take advantage of a hillside or an incline by rolling vehicles, old auto tires and wheels, or barrels at the police line.

Domestic animals can be driven in front of the mob against police. On some occasions delayed-action explosive charges have even been tied to animals which were driven toward the police lines.

When mounted police are used against a trained mob, its members may try to hamstring the horses by cutting their leg tendons.

Combustion or burning-type gas grenades and 37mm projectiles are, due to their use over many years, well known to the experienced agitator. Specific persons will be designated to pick them up and throw them back. Instructions are also given to the mob members to kick these munitions aside and to avoid the white smoke cloud created during the burning process that liberates the gas, and discloses the area covered. Thus being forewarned, they can avoid any visible gas concentration that does not completely saturate the entire scene and to continue aggressive action against the police. In many recent actions, selected mob members have entered action wearing cotton work gloves that enable them to pick up and throw back combustion-type tear gas grenades and projectiles without burning their hands on the hot body of the grenade. The fact that this type of grenade heats up is only a partial deterrent to throwback.

Chapter 16

THE PROFESSIONAL RIOT CONTROL UNIT

ALTHOUGH this text continues to be of great value to the combat soldier and the law-enforcement officer in any type of individual hand-to-hand combat, armed or unarmed, it has recently been greatly enlarged so as to be of specific assistance also in the training of police and military units in riot duty. The incidence of riots is increasing throughout the world in this epoch of social unrest and upheaval. American law enforcement agencies have not yet had to face the type of major, directed, mob violence that is now frequently occurring in some other nations. Let us hope that our own domestic tranquility continues, and as a measure of insuring that this hope may become reality, let us train and equip our defense forces, both military and police, so that they will not be caught unprepared if suddenly called upon to quell mob violence.

Some of the material in this chapter will not seem to apply directly to our current domestic situation, but rather to be "slanted" toward problems of mob control arising more frequently outside our borders. The material is included as useful background information to help each individual law enforcement agency develop its own training and techniques in mob control to meet any eventuality in its local situation.

THE PROFESSIONAL UNIT

In many countries throughout the world the army is actually the national police force and is maintained principally to keep domestic order. This is especially true in Latin-American nations, in the Middle East, and the Orient.

In such a situation a combination of the best techniques of the military and of civil police can best be employed by the army-police force to dominate a riot situation. The cost of maintenance of a permanent standby riot control unit to keep conditions stable need not be prohibitive. Due to the potential or actual incidence of disturbances, such a force may even be considered necessary to keep the government in power. Whether civilian or military as to uniform and nomenclature, the basic purpose of such a unit is to control and dominate any mass manifestations that would menace local and national authority.

The maintenance of such a professional unit to handle mob violence would seem to be an urgent need in countries which may have to face planned, professionally-led, Communist-inspired mobs. In the past, the failure of the civil police, where they existed, resulted in calling on the regular troops. Usually the mere presence of regular troops was sufficient to control the situation. But the professional leadership of some of today's mobs is less impressed by a show of force. When the presence of troops fails to halt an aggressive mob, and gas attack proves inadequate, the final alternative is to order the troops to fire. Commanding officers cannot expect their men to stand up in a passive manner to the tactics, abuse, and threats of a professional mob, even when orders have been given *not* to fire. This is particularly true in countries where the troops themselves are illiterate or poorly educated and lacking in discipline. The troops may believe that they must fire to dominate the situation. They are quite likely to use their firepower to protect themselves and the dignity of their unit and uniform. No final alternative remains but the use of force. Yet, especially when regular troops are used against civilians of their own nation and locality, the situation plays into the hands of the Communists, who will be quick to criticize as more martyrs are created.

Another aspect of mob control in countries that are not highly developed, and where there is little public discipline, is that most local and civil police forces and their members do not want any part of a violent counter-mob action. When faced with a "home-grown" mob, they have numerous personal, political, and other reasons for being reluctant to aggressively suppress it. They all realize that they have to live there after the incident is over. The fact that students, women, children, and war veterans are used in the formation of the mob also makes the position of law enforcement personnel all the more untenable, as the individual policeman may be forced to use strong measures or extreme force against neighbors, friends, and even relatives.

These handicaps may be largely avoided by organizing and training an adequately-equipped special riot police force to control threatened mob action. The purpose of this group is to avoid, when possible, the heavy casualties that may occur when military infantry tactics and armament are used, but at the same time to be able to use whatever force is necessary to control the situation.

What is needed is a para-military police organization that contains within itself all the armament, training, and discipline necessary to dominate the mob by application of only the "necessary force." This idea is not entirely new but it has been little used to date. The unit must include only specially selected officers and men, and its training must be thorough. All members must understand that the mission is to dominate

LEFT: The formidable appearance of an entire unit of riot police wearing masks is very effective in discouraging mob elements. The "Man from Mars" aspect with its psychological impact on the mob may discourage the uneducated, less aggressive type rioter without need of force.

CENTER: Policeman equipped with gas mask of the latest type, which protects him against the effects of tear and nauseating gases and at the same time gives him maximum visibility and carrying comfort. The mask is carried in a locally-made special pouch. All masks should be clearly labeled so that each man wears his own, which he has previously tested and adjusted to his own head and face.

RIGHT: A riot policeman equipped with baton and carrying tear gas grenades in special holsters. With the baton he has a potent and offensive weapon. Knowledge in its use also creates great self-confidence. He can be equipped with gas and smoke grenades. If desired he may carry a pistol. The baton-grenade members of the squad (grenadiers) are also responsible for the protection of the members who carry the gas-launching guns.

a mob with a minimum of casualties yet at the same time be ready and able to change quickly and efficiently to more (or less) drastic tactics depending on the temper and action of the mob. It is really an "in-between" force that because of its flexibility, can adapt to any given mob action.

BASIC PRINCIPLES OF ORGANIZATION

The organization of the unit is based on the squad as the smallest operating tactical element. Individual soldiers or police are not trained or encouraged to operate individually in mob control.

All tactics are such that the same formations, movements, and actions against the mob can be used by a squad, a platoon, a company, or a battalion.

The squad and larger units carry the weapons and firepower designated, which are to be used only on order of the leader. Thus the commander may prescribe that some soldiers be armed with a caliber .45 automatic pistol, some with gas grenades or gas guns, others with a caliber .30 carbine. If riot sticks are also to be used, the carbine may be slung across the back. The squad leader may be armed with a submachine gun, riot gun, or sniper's rifle.

Members of the squad are divided into two groups, a front rank and a rear rank. The front rank is to be ready for contact with mob elements and will usually carry tear gas grenades and the baton, or riot stick. These men are used to attack the mob with the sticks, to launch or throw gas grenades, and also to protect the rear rank, consisting of three squad members carrying special gas guns.

In the platoon formation there are usually two squads in line armed with riot sticks and grenades. The gas guns are in the rear. The reserve squad is armed with carbines and other special weapons, according to the situation.

All action in which launching of gases is ordered, either by grenade or gun, is done on command. There is no indiscriminate use of the gas munitions. Use of the baton and changes in tactical formations are only on command of the commander of the unit, who stays behind the line of contact with the mob in order better to observe and control the action. The commander maintains his reserve under his immediate control. He is the only one that can authorize the use of firearms. In this manner the responsibility can be placed directly on the officer, in case firearms are used with consequent casualties.

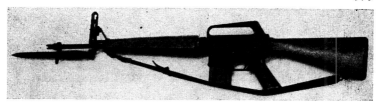

COLT ARMALITE AR-15 Cal. .223 Rifle

This is a new combat rifle that is recommended by the factory for both police and military use. It weighs less than seven pounds with a loaded 20-round magazine. It is recommended for use at ranges up to 500 yards. The high velocity of the small diameter bullet gives it extraordinary penetration. Firing can be either semi- or full automatic. Grenades can be launched from the rifle and a scope can be mounted on the carrying handle for sniping. The rifle has penetrating power against metal objects such as car bodies and engine blocks, that is superior to any other arm in its class. Those departments that have use for its special characteristics will find it a welcome addition to the arsenal.

FORMATIONS

Formations in mob control are generally based on standard infantry formations. Police and troops with knowledge and training in normal drill formations will have no difficulty in adapting to the small variations needed for more efficient mob and riot control.

There are four basic formations that are used for riot control. These are the column, the skirmish line, the wedge, and the diagonal formations.

The *column* formation generally is used for approach to the riot area. When coming into the view of the rioters for the first time and in approaching them, this formation should always be moving in *double time*. This fast tempo of march is very impressive, psychologically, to the mob members. In fact, all changes of formation in front of the mob are best performed in the faster tempo. This is not only for the visual effect but also for tactical reasons when formations must be changed rapidly in close contact. All practice should be conducted likewise at double time.

The *line of skirmishers* is for use when confronting the mob, to advance against it, for a display of force, or to block off an area. This is the usual formation when the unit is in line confronting the mob but not in action or contact. From this formation gas can be launched and the wedge or other formation can be assumed rapidly.

SQUAD LINE OF SKIRMISHERS

This formation is used when confronting the mob, or advancing against it. It is also used in a display of force. In this illustration, grenadiers with batons are in the front rank. Three squad members with 37mm gas guns are in the second file. The squad leader is in the rear and is armed with a submachine gun. The men with the 37mm gas guns can be placed in the front rank during a display of force, or can advance and fire short-range shells into the mob from positions between the grenadiers. They also can fire long-range shells into the mob from the position shown. Men in the front rank, when not in mob contact, can on command kneel while long-range shells are being fired. In this formation, the 37mm guns are protected by the grenadiers. They can also be considered as a reserve to fill in the line, if necessary.

The *wedge formation* is used in clearing streets and splitting the mob. It is an offensive formation. In case of change of direction or of withdrawal, the formation can be converted into a triangle or diamond by using the reserve to fill in the base.

The *diagonal* ("right echelon" or "left echelon") formation is assumed from the line of skirmishers or from the wedge. Its principal use is in movement against the mob when it is desired for the entire unit or elements of it to drive the mob members in a given direction, such as down a particular street.

All of these formations can be used by squad, platoon, company, or battalion. They are basic. Descriptions in detail with the commands on how they can be formed are available in any standard U.S. infantry manual on formations, including FM 19-15 previously recommended as a reference text.

Rules for Use of Formations. (1) The formation must be such that it can be maintained and the line held in the face of direct mob action and physical contact. The guiding principle is that movement in the action, whether it be offensive,

SQUAD IN WEDGE FORMATION

Grenadiers form the "V," with a squad leader armed with an automatic weapon in rear of the point man. Three men with 37mm gas guns are in column in rear of the squad leader, acting under his orders as a reserve.

SQUAD IN DIAGONAL FORMATION

The diagonal can be formed from either left or right. It is useful when it is desired to move the mob members in any given direction, such as into a side street. The diagonal formation must be practiced so that it can be assumed rapidly in the midst of any action and from any other basic formation. In this case the man on either end can act as a pivot in case a wheeling action is ordered.

PLATOON IN WEDGE FORMATION

This is an offensive formation used for splitting up mob elements, and advancing and clearing streets. In the illustration two squads carrying batons, grenades, and 37mm gas guns make up the front or "V" of the formation. Squad leaders are behind armed with submachine guns. Directly to the rear of the point is the officer in command, with a radio man on his left. The third squad is in reserve in the rear of the officer. It is armed with automatic weapons, extra 37mm gas guns, and special rifles for sniping, etc. It also can carry extra munitions and special equipment. The third squad is used to reinforce the line, protect the rear and flanks, for counter sniping, and any other special use brought about by the circumstances. It operates under the direct command of the officer. It can be in column or dispersed as shown. This basic formation can be used in units of company and battalion size with equal effectiveness. The line of skirmishers, diagonal, or any type wheeling movement can be assumed from this formation, on command.

defensive, or static, is always to be *undertaken as a unit*. This is true whether the unit is a squad, platoon, company, or battalion. Individual members of the police units must never be permitted to operate separately, both for reasons of safety and efficiency. The strength of the police unit is the strength of its combat formations, much more than the individual prowess of the men.

(2) Each formation should have a reserve, which will serve under the officer in command as he dictates, to meet the demands of the situation. Members of this reserve can be used as messengers, to reinforce the line, replace wounded, perform special firing missions, handle prisoners, or perform other essential tasks. It is never advisable to commit all the unit reserve to the action, if this can possibly be avoided.

(3) The officer commanding the unit during action must always be in the *rear* of the line of contact. This is necessary so that the leader can be in a position to observe the action, send messages, give orders, and otherwise control the action. The leader's exact position behind his unit during the action is not fixed; it is the position from which he can best perform his mission of control.

(4) The choice of formation and tactics used must always be such that no members of the mob can get in its *rear*. If a situation develops that makes this a strong probability, the formation should withdraw.

(5) It is never advisable to commit a small formation too deeply into a mob or crowd; otherwise the unit may lose maneuverability and control and its avenue of retreat cut off.

(6) If the unit formation is small and the crowd or mob very large, contact should be avoided and the mob handled from a distance, taking advantage of the use of smoke, long-range gas guns, and other tactical means.

(7) If a retreat becomes necessary because of an unforeseen change in the situation, this retreat should always be made *in formation*, slowly so as not to give any indication of panic, and with the *face* of the men *toward the mob*. Any situation that will indicate panic on the part of the police units will only encourage the mob and make it more aggressive. Even the members of the mob will initially respect the uniform worn by the unit, and the unit formation and discipline must be maintained to keep this respect.

(8) Changes in formations and movements are always made quickly. Surprise is to be achieved wherever possible. The offensive is always to be maintained once an action has begun.

(9) Should any mob member lay hands on a member of the unit and try to capture him or withdraw him from the formation, other members must instantly converge on the adversary and overwhelm him with blows from the baton or other weapon.

(10) In addition to disciplined formations, the uniforms of men and officers must be neat in appearance. This helps develop the impression that the mob is not dealing with individuals but with a unit. Any offense against an individual policemen must be considered as an offense against the entire unit.

Basic Principles in Dealing with a Mob. In initiating operations against a civil disturbance where the potential of mob violence exists, the police commander should employ the following measures and, if possible, in the following sequence:

(1) Make a show of strength to demonstrate to the mob by means of military appearance of his unit, changes in formation, and display of armament, that the unit is there for a serious purpose and is able to use all necessary force to disperse the mob. (This is done without any threats and is in fact by implication.)

A DISPLAY OF FORCE

In this simulated mob scene the riot unit is shown facing the mob but not in contact with it. This is the period when display of armament, fixing of bayonets, mounting of gas masks, changes in formations, and drill movements are employed. This will many times be very effective in dispersing the crowd or mob in its early formative stage. This phase is followed up by a warning to the crowd to disperse peacefully.

(2) Make a proclamation to the crowd to disperse, giving a time limit. Sound trucks, hand megaphones, or other available means to deliver the demand to disperse in a peaceful manner, are to be employed. In some cases leaders of the agitation can be called to the presence of the commanding officer for this purpose. This will depend on the motivation and the attitude of the crowd and how close it is to the mob stage.

(3) If, after waiting a reasonable time, the mob does not voluntarily disperse, resort to an offensive riot-control formation and move against the crowd or mob using batons to disperse it. This procedure will depend on the attitude of the mob members and many times is best employed at the stage before the crowd members have arrived at unified purpose or objective.

WARNING THE MOB TO DISPERSE

This is the second phase after a display of force and if possible, is made prior to any contact. In the illustration, the riot unit leader is warning the crowd to disperse and is giving it a time limit before proceeding with "necessary force" against it. The hand-carried, transistor-type megaphone is indispensable for this purpose. The officer advances until he is near the mob in order to give it the order to disperse. Note that he is accompanied by members of the unit who act as flank guards. When he and his men return to the unit they normally walk backward, always facing the mob. Psychologically as well as practically it is never advisable to turn the back to a mob, especially when there is a potential for violence.

(4) Lay down a concentration of tear gas. This to be followed by nauseating gas, if indicated. Smoke also can be used at any time in combination with the gases. The gas barrage is normally followed up by an aggressive attack on the mob elements, or the attack can be made at the same time the heavy concentration of gas is delivered. Normally the attack is made after a short interval has passed, to see if the gas alone was sufficient to disperse the gathering. Usually gas should be followed up by use of batons with the unit wearing gas masks.

(5) As a last resort, order firearms to be used. This is best done by first ordering a limited number of expert marksmen to fire. These marksmen should be from the reserve unit. If they are not sufficient to break up the mob, full firepower of the entire unit must be used. Full firepower would mean the continued use of all chemical agents as well as firearms.

The above sequence of action may not be practicable if

the mob action is already under way when the unit arrives; in such case steps 1, 2, and 3 may have to be omitted.

The decision as to use of sickening gas in place of or with tear gas is entirely up to the judgment of the officer in command, based on his analysis of the temper of the mob. Logically it would be the last step before use of firearms. It is assumed in this discussion that the riot control unit has strength and armament to dominate the situation. If it does not but attempts and fails to do so, a more chaotic situation results. Mobs must be dealt with from strength and any possible situation that might give the rioters the upper-hand, even temporarily, should be avoided.

If strength is not available the mob cannot be dominated; it can only be attacked from a distance with the hope that long-range use of gas munitions will disperse or delay it until sufficient forces are accumulated.

All operations in mob control and dispersion should invariably be preceded by study or prior intelligence from all sources, including consultations with local law enforcement officers or units already on the scene. All standard military procedures to arrive at an intelligent estimate of the situation before contact should be employed. Arrangements for liaison with other units, communications, medical service, reinforcements, etc., should be completed before physical contact with the mob is made or the unit is committed to the attack.

MOB CONTROL TACTICS AND SUGGESTIONS

The following precepts and ideas must be adapted by the individual riot force to meet its own situation. All will not apply. Type, size, and motivation of the mob; location; quantity of gas munitions available; number of men in the riot control unit; reserves and weapons available; and other pertinent factors will all affect planning and tactics. Each situation will be different. The following ideas and comments are offered, accordingly.

(1) Never try to bluff a mob. Don't threaten to do things that you cannot do or enforce. Should your bluff be "called," the mob thereafter becomes more lawless and dangerous. A threat is always antagonizing and may be accepted as a dare. Be able to back up what you say or don't say it.

(2) Do not attempt to do more than you can *reasonably*

expect to accomplish with the forces you have available. If the mob is too large, split it up, use gas munitions in quantity, and create delay while awaiting reinforcements.

(3) In extreme emergency situations make an *advance* decision to use firearms as a last resort. Let the mob know it and put no restrictions on your men and their use of firearms at the proper time and signal, once the action has begun. Do not resort to firearms under panic conditions just because you happen to run out of gas munitions or don't have gas in sufficient quantity for the job. It is much better to plan to use live ammunition from the outset and tell the mob so, rather than commit yourself to a policy of gradual attrition of your men and gas equipment ending up using bullets as a desperation measure.

(4) If your forces are badly outnumbered and faced with a potentially dangerous, but still inactive, mob, stall for time until reinforcements can be secured. Don't put too much reliance on the old axiom "one riot, one ranger" when dealing with a large potentially violent crowd which badly outnumbers your forces, fire power, and chemical agent capabilities. If violence breaks out you should have planned in advance your position, and stand in an area where you can make the best use of your limited forces, taking advantage of terrain, narrow streets, and buildings.

(5) Keep your men under tight discipline and control when facing a mob. Do not let members of the mob aggravate your men into premature action by "name calling." Begin any offensive action on your own orders. Do not let mob members set things off by "baiting" individual members of your forces. The reasons and need for this should be clearly covered during the training program and reiterated, if possible, just before any mob contact or action.

(6) Training in the use of riot sticks is always desirable. Many times a *crowd* can be kept from becoming an unruly *mob* by their use or threat. Back up your stick men by gas and grenade throwing units in the event the use of the riot clubs alone can not handle the situation. Develop, during training, a signal for orderly withdrawal of your stick men at the time grenades and other munitions are projected over their heads into the crowd. Do not have your stick men withdraw by turning and running. This gives the mob the idea that the forces of law and order are in a state of panic, which in-

TWO FORMATIONS USING THE BATON

Above: Using the baton to extend the line to block off given areas. Each man extends his baton and it is grasped by the tip by the adjacent squad member with his free hand. This is a good formation to use when there is no physical contact taking place with the mob and the situation is passive.

Below: An interlocked arm formation that presents an unbreakable front to the mob. This formation can be used to block off a narrow street or doorway. It can be maintained against a passive mob that is merely pushing against the line.

In both of these formations note that the squad leader is in the rear with his automatic weapon. The 37mm gas guns are also in reserve to be used in any sudden change of the situation. Short or long-range shells can be fired into the mob either from the line or from the rear.

creases mob aggressiveness. The stick men in their withdrawal, after gas munitions have been launched, should do it *in formation*, walking backwards, always facing the hostile elements. If your stick men in the front rank are without masks, have a reserve group of stick men (if possible) with masks, to step into the line when the gas munitions are launched.

(7) When in close contact with apparently unarmed mobs, you must anticipate that bricks, stones, clubs, or other missiles will be thrown or used against your men. Protective helmets are a must. The light, tough, fiber glass protective helmets

used by miners and structural steel workers are ideal. They can usually be secured at low cost and many times can be the difference between aggressive action and retreat. The fear of injury to the head, eyes, and face from thrown missiles or blows is always present. When these helmets are worn this danger is greatly minimized with a resulting increased self-confidence. Protective helmets can also be painted in distinctive colors to enable better identification and control of your own forces during periods of poor visibility, such as use of smoke, gas and night action.

(8) Make provision for first aid and medical treatment for your own men prior to any mob contact or action. It is very important that your men *know* that they will be taken care of if and when they become casualties. Arrangements should be made for special ambulances, to be held in reserve. Do not permit those persons or medical units assigned to this task to be diverted by attending injured rioters. Have separate units for this purpose, if desired.

(9) You should always, where prior planning and manpower permit, keep a reserve of men, gas, and equipment to commit to the action in an emergency. This reserve should be used to replace injured men and reinforce weak areas. When the mob is breaking up, it can then be committed to special tasks, such as to pick up mob leaders.

(10) Commanding officials should always be at a vantage point where they can see the *entire* action. Binoculars used from buildings or roof tops, etc. are very useful. Two-way radio contact with subordinates on the scene is always essential in a large action. This contact must also be maintained with the reserve unit, medical aid groups, etc. Do not make the mistake, if you are the leader, of "plunging into the fray," with your men. You then lose control of the action as you cannot see what is going on. Cover this point and the reasons for it thoroughly in training.

(11) Tactical squad or company formations for use in riot control such as the flying wedge or other offensive and protective formations should be practiced in training. Signals for offensive action, retreat, and formation changes, should be developed. Hand signals, whistle blasts, commands from megaphones, and flares are all available for this purpose. Colored flares are particularly useful at night and in a daytime action when the noise and smoke of a large action make other means impractical. The commanding officer should also always arrange to have assigned and accompany him, indi-

viduals for use as messengers. He can utilize members of the
reserve if the manpower situation is critical. Remember, that
in a serious situation, headquarters office personnel can be used
in noncombatant jobs such as first aid and as messengers so
as to release the regular forces.

(12) Special tactics and formations should be developed in
training to enable physical penetration of the mob body by
the reserve unit or other groups in order to seize leaders or
agitators or rescue injured or outnumbered personnel. A riot-
stick wielding wedge formation is usually advocated with the
reserve and leader inside.

THE WEDGE OFFENSIVE FORMATION

In this simulated mob action, the upper illustration shows the unit
beginning to advance after it has just assumed the wedge formation
from the previous line of skirmishers. At this point gas would normally
have been launched into the mob from the long-range gas guns, or gas
grenades thrown taking advantage of favorable winds. Masks would
be donned and the batons would be used to further disperse the mob.

In the lower illustration it will be noted how the wedge formation
has closed or tightened up as it gets closer to the mob. Note how the
reserve has bunched up so that it is close to the unit leader and immediately available in support of the line.

(13) Grenades can be used very effectively to break up a loosely dispersed *crowd* before it becomes a *mob* by penetrating it with a siren-blowing vehicle from which the grenades can be thrown by hand and dispersed over a wide area.

(14) Hand-thrown grenades can be and have been used effectively through skylights, down chimneys, through door transoms and from roofs or rooms in buildings overlooking the rioters, especially when police are without masks.

(15) If the area in which the mob is going to concentrate is known in advance, grenades can many times be placed in concealed places in advance, to be activated from a distance by trip wires when the time is ripe.

(16) When necessary to enter and disperse rioters in large rooms, halls, etc., police should enter the door and their formation should then move along the walls, ejecting a small part of the crowd at a time.

(17) The use of fire department members and their high pressure water hoses should always be considered in handling a large mob action. Especially if the forces available are limited and gas munitions are short. In some cases self-contained hose, tank-truck units are very useful when placed at strategic spots. Rioters can also be sprayed with a specially colored or tinted water to enable identification and capture later after the mob is dispersed.

(18) During the past few years the helicopter, with its obvious advantages, has become a very valuable piece of military and police equipment. If available, helicopters should be utilized to hover above the center of large mobs both to drop tear gas grenades, to more effectively make use of the powerful hand electric type megaphones for mob control, and for observation purposes.

(19) Generally, troops or police on riot duty should never have specific instructions as to the limit of force that they may use. The commander of the military-police unit should be instructed to use the *necessary amount* of force to subdue the mob and control the situation.

(20) The mob control unit should contain within itself the entire range of arms necessary to control the situation. This will vary from batons, to gas munitions, to automatic-type firearms. When he must, the commander should use them all if the situation requires such action.

(21) It is useless to carry firearms without ammunition or under instructions *not* to use them. If the mob ever finds this out, there will be immediate disruption of the morale of the

riot unit and loss of control of the situation.

(22) In a police action against the mob, it is best for the commander to have the firepower of the unit (small arms such as rifles, carbines, sub-machine guns, etc.) in the reserve part of the formation. This gives him better control and enables him to make more efficient use of these arms when necessary. When the men in the front against the mob, who may be armed only with batons and grenades, know they are backed up by firearms, they will perform with more aggressiveness and confidence.

(23) The least violent and courageous members of the mob will be found in the rear, where there will also be spectators. It is often a good tactic to launch a surprise attack by gas against these rear elements. Normally, such attacks will cause panic and these rear elements will disperse more easily. Fear is highly contagious. If a part of the mob takes flight, the remainder will tend to be thrown into panic and confusion. The sight of members fleeing can also demoralize the more determined mob members.

(24) Escape routes must always be available when using gas to disperse crowds or mobs. It is obvious that the mob members, in order to get away, must have free avenues of escape against gas concentrations.

(25) When it is apparent that mob members in front in contact with the police cannot retreat, because of pressure from the rear mob elements, the pressure on the front is retained while the rear and center of the mob is attacked with gas.

(26) Chemical smoke projected by use of grenades or candles has great tactical value. Smoke can be used to block off or deny mob assembly areas, to disperse crowds by splitting them up into sections, to provide cover for closer approach to the mob or persons barricaded in buildings, and to conceal tactical movements. It can be used inside buildings to force their evacuation. In combination with tear gas, smoke is even more effective in creating a panic condition.

(27) Extreme discipline must be maintained before and during the action to gain and keep respect of the mob members and spectators. A well-disciplined, silent, well-armed unit with every member intent on the mission of controlling the mob, creates the impression of a powerful, competent machine.

(28) Blank cartridges should never be used against a mob and should never be issued for riot duty. Their only possible

use is in training. Volleys of "live" ammunition normally should not be fired over heads of rioters.

(29) When confronting a mob for the first time, steps should be taken so that the mob members can *see* and *know* that firearms are available for use. A show of strength by formation and exhibition of weapons before an action is always advisable. If there is nothing to use to give the impression of complete dominance of the situation by numbers, weapons, or formation, all close contact with the mob must be avoided.

(30) When firearms are used against the mob, they are best aimed low so as to hold down the mortality rate and also avoid hitting innocent persons who may be in the rear of the mob as spectators.

(31) It is the responsibility of the leader to see that the unit has protection from snipers, or persons firing from windows, roofs, or trees. He should protect his men from this kind of attack. If the situation is such that he cannot, by his own means or with help from other units, cover the dangerous areas through which he may be moving, he must change plans and routes of approach.

(32) First-aid training and equipment must be made available to the members of the mob-control unit. In an action, cuts and bruises and lacerations are to be expected. Mob members will hurl rocks, bottles, and other types of missiles at police. The unit should contain, within itself, first-aid kits for prompt treatment of wounds. It will also be advisable to carry, in addition to the normal medical first-aid supplies, some sort of eye-wash preparation. If the police operate without eye protection, they must expect to suffer this sort of injury.

(33) Gas is used in conjunction with the prevailing wind. If the wind is against the mob, a cloud can be ejected that will carry the gas into it from the front. If the wind is against the police elements, the gas must be projected by gas guns or other means to the rear of the mob so that it will be carried into the mob. Generally, gas grenades and projectiles that are not dependent on wind and of the type that can not be thrown back, are best.

(34) The burning type of gas grenade (that releases gas by the combustion principle) should not be used where combustibles are stored or where there is any other type of fire hazard. The intense heat created by the burning process that liberates the gas, can start serious fires. When vehicles

are turned over by mobs, spilled gasoline from tanks can be ignited by burning-type grenades or projectiles.

(35) Gas grenades of the combustion type should not be thrown directly into the mob. Due to the fact that they need to burn for from twenty-five to thirty-five seconds in order to expel their gas, there is plenty of time for the mob members to throw them back at the police, kick them aside, or avoid the gas concentration by skirting the edges of the light cloud of smoke that is expelled with the tear gas during the burning process of gas liberation.

(36) When only grenades are available and it is necessary to cover the entire mob with a gas concentration, have persons in civilian clothes enter the mob and assume previously determined locations in it. At a given time have these individuals drop tear-gas grenades among the crowd and begin to run towards previously selected exits. These men can shout and incite panic by yelling "Gas, let's get out of here," etc. When mob members see people running and in panic, the panic spreads. This maneuver is very effective, especially when the gas grenades are of the invisible type so that the

PLASTIC GOGGLES

Provision must be made for protecting the eyes of police members in close contact with the mob members. On riot duty, police may have almost anything thrown at them by the mob such as stones, sand, dust, offal, pepper in paper bags, plastic bags with liquid ammonia, rotten vegetables, pieces of iron, and every other imaginable object. The plastic goggles shown are the commercially available type that are normally used in factories and machine shops to protect the worker's eyes. They are inexpensive and non-breakable. Each riot policeman should carry in his pocket an eye-protective device for use when necessary.

mob cannot discover or avoid the source of gas emission.

(37) Many times a crowd or potential mob will disperse on first contact with gas. If the unit is in sufficient strength, patrols should be sent out to prevent the crowd from forming again. These same patrols can pick up agitators and hard-core mob members.

(38) A mob directed by professional agitators may seem to disperse at first and then try to reform. The more aggressive members of the professional agitators may try to create a diversion by setting fire to buildings or vehicles in the vicinity of the combat area. It is important that the commander of the police unit does not allow his men or unit to be "suckered" into breaking up his formation by such mob action.

(39) An effort should always be made to previously identify the leaders of the mob or the professional agitators. If they can be taken from the mob by use of formations and tactics at the very early beginning, this is the best procedure, provided the unit is not endangered or does not have to penetrate too deeply into the mob. An organized mob will

The IRON CLAW is a very useful device for mob control. It is especially valuable when it is necessary to extract a leader or agitator from the mob and take him into custody rapidly and without a struggle.

probably have a number of agitators simultaneously operating at different locations in the mob body. Apprehension of agitators and leaders before the mob has even formed is a basic tactic.

(40) Pictures of a given mob action, either still or motion pictures, are often very useful. The pictures can be used later to identify agitators, to study tactics, and sometimes can be useful in public relations. The fact that mob members know pictures are being taken will also dampen the enthusiasm of those who want to retain their anonymity.

(41) Every disorderly assemblage should first be dealt with as a crowd until the point is reached when orders to disperse are disobeyed and actual physical resistance, such as throwing missiles, is encountered. At this time offensive action should be taken. Do not react passively to any attack and subject your troops to physical injury while deciding what tactic to employ. Have your plans made out in advance and if possible explain them to all the men so they can anticipate the time, manner, and circumstances when offensive action will take place.

(42) Always use the element of surprise when possible. If sufficient elements are available and the location of action is favorable, hit the mob simultaneously from the rear and flanks. If the mob has been confronted in its front by police elements for some time during a static period, send units to hit it from unexpected quarters in conjunction with a frontal assault. This applies to the launching of gas munitions as well as offensive movement of baton-wielding formations.

(43) In a situation where riot troops arrive when the mob is already in action against an objective that cannot be reached in order to give it protection, use gas and smoke in quantity from flanks and rear. Utilize roof tops as a means of approach and to launch gas. Try by physical means to split the mob from the rear and create panic in rear mob elements. Normally, the least violent mob members will be on the flanks and rear. Peel them away in order to get at the hard core of the mob.

(44) If it can be anticipated where a mob action will take place, close all possible businesses in the area and order people to stay inside the buildings. Be sure that liquor stores, bars, gun stores, and hardware stores are closed.

(45) Do not split your unit into a number of small detachments and try to quell minor diversionary disorders at

scattered points. Concentrate on the main body of the mob, maintaining sufficient strength to handle it.

(46) Don't send small bodies of troops into areas where they can be surrounded. You will then be forced to rescue them and thus fail to concentrate on the main mob element. Protect your flanks and rear. Do not permit the mob to envelop your unit. Maneuverability must be maintained.

(47) If you can hit the crowd before the agitators have changed it into a mob, do so. It is basic for any well-trained riot unit to pick up leaders and agitators if known, in advance of any action. This cannot always be done but good intelligence as to identification of leaders and agitators and of the purpose of the mob always "pays off."

(48) Men instinctively protect their groin, stomach, and eyes. The baton or shoulder weapon in the hands of a trained man will enable him to enter physical contact without much fear of endangering vulnerable body areas. With respect to the eyes, plastic, adjustable-type safety goggles are recommended for issue.

(49) Gas masks of the modern type do not fog up and permit good side vision. Be sure your men have confidence in them and are not reluctant to wear them. Your men should be subjected to tear gas in training with and without masks. Train the unit to don masks while in formation, and work out a system where units in reserve can don masks and replace those in the line. Men should be accustomed to wearing masks over prolonged periods of time while performing all combat functions such as use of riot sticks and firing weapons.

(50) The psychological effect of the police advancing against the mob while wearing masks is very great, particularly if rioting groups are made up of illiterate elements. Many times a surprise initial appearance of the unit wearing masks is enough to discourage the rioters. Normally masks are not available to rioters and this is a great police advantage. Rioters may try to improvise masks but they really cannot secure much protection. Tear gas enters the nostrils, mouth, and eyes, and affects the nasal passages; all cannot be protected at the same time by an improvised means.

(51) It is advisable that each squad or similar unit of the riot group have its own motor vehicle so that it is independent of other transportation. This gets the unit into action faster, is better for discipline, and increases maneuverability.

(52) Provision should always be made for a specific vehicle

for carrying additional special equipment for use under the commanding officer's orders. Such items include flares, axes, cables, rope, reserve gas supplies, fire extinguishers, chains, searchlights, crowbars, wire cutters, tow cables, hacksaws, extra tires, and extra gas supplies and arms. It is many times advisable to keep one vehicle always loaded with special equipment and ready for action.

(53) Gloves are a must on riot control where physical contact is always possible. They give protection against flying missiles and clubs. In addition they can add to smartness in the appearance of the unit. The combination of white gloves, white helmet, white riot sticks, white shoe laces, etc., is very effective from the standpoint of unit discipline, morale, and in impressing the mob.

(54) The problem of the sniper who is operating in conjunction with the mob against police elements can be a very serious one. A skilled rifleman operating from a concealed position of advantage can "pin down" police elements and kill or wound officials and troops. This can be expected in any large, serious, well-organized riot operation. It is absolutely imperative that special riot groups have expert riflemen, preferably scope-equipped, assigned to counter this action. Usually these riflemen would be members of the reserve unit and operate directly under orders of the officer in command.

(55) Riot type 12-gauge shotguns, if available, are very useful weapons in riot control. Their wide pattern at close ranges and the psychological effect of the large bore pointed toward the mob make them ideal close contact weapons. The standard OO buckshot load will create casualties and is ideal for night work. Shells loaded with tear gas can also be used in these weapons. On some occasions very fine shot (#8, 9) has been used at long ranges to effectually stop violent mob members. The fine bird shot at a distance does little harm, except in case of the eyes, but will penetrate the skin and cause a wound that will need medical attention. On one occasion, to the author's knowledge, rock salt has been used against rioters in specially loaded shells with good results.

(56) Shields made of bullet-proof steel or fiber glass have a definite place in the "special equipment" of any professional riot group. They are very necessary to counter sniper action. See chapter 9, "Raids and Room Combat."

(57) When rioters are barricaded in a building, it is best to clear it from the top down. Escape routes such as ground floor and basement exits and roofs of adjacent buildings must

be watched. Heavy concentrations of tear gas and smoke are very useful in this situation.

(58) Vehicles used to carry riot squad members and equipment to the scene of action must be parked in places away from the action. Normally, a driver and assistant should stay with the vehicle to protect it; they should be armed accordingly. These same vehicles can also be equipped with radios to maintain communication.

(59) The use of mines, booby-trap devices, and explosive charges to prevent police from performing their function in mob control, can be expected, especially in a large, well-planned and directed action. A general knowledge of such tactics is advisable. If possible, designated elements in the riot control unit should receive some training in this field. These same men can also be trained in using explosives to clear mob-installed blockades. The increasing use by Communists of guerrilla warfare, and their training in the use and improvisation of such explosive devices, make this an important consideration. Good prior intelligence will generally determine if use of explosives will be a mob tactic.

(60) The use of a tear gas concentration, chemical smoke, or a combination of both, is highly recommended to block a street or deny an area that is the target of a moving mob or on the route to the target.

(61) The use of chemical munitions against the mob near hospitals and schools always presents a problem. Although tear gas is not harmful, bad publicity and panic conditions can result. Except in extreme cases, an attempt should be made to meet the mob in another location or else arrange for evacuation of persons in temporary danger.

(62) In training a special unit for mob control, the practice "alert" should frequently be ordered. This is especially important when elements of the riot squad are not maintained together as a unit.

(63) The transistor-type, hand-carried megaphone as well as the small walkie-talkie two-way radio, are now very important parts of mob control equipment. Those using standard flashlight batteries are recommended.

(64) Vehicles loaded with riot troops are used in controlling large mob operations. Room for maneuverability is obviously a must. Formations such as the wedge, using vehicles as its elements, are possible. Again, U. S. Army Manual 19-15 covers this type of operation.

(65) The factories manufacturing the 37mm long-range

riot projectiles recommend that these projectiles be fired from the riot gun in such a manner that the projectiles fall behind, into, or in front of the mob. They normally are fired with the gun held at a 30 to 40 degree angle and the projectile falls into the target area accordingly, there being no velocity beyond that of gravity at the time of impact. Actual combat experience against mobs has resulted in recommendations that some types of projectiles be fired directly at the mob or by bouncing the shell along the ground in the direction of the mob so as to lower the velocity. When these projectiles are fired either directly into the mob or via the bouncing method, the chances of a casualty are present even though the velocity of the projectiles themselves is only a few hundred feet per second. This technique is and can be used, if recognition is given to the fact that minor casualties may be inflicted. It can be particularly useful when: (a) the mob is beyond grenade-throwing range and there are adverse wind conditions; (b) no other means of projecting gas is available; and (c) physical contact with the mob needs to be avoided.

(66) Small pocket-size colored smoke grenades designed for signaling and spotting air drops are now in use by U. S. Army airborne troops. They can be obtained on special order from commercial sources and have a possible use in large mob actions. Police members disguised as rioters could be used to set them off in mob areas where hard core agitation is greatest, in order to bring down gas concentrations, or to indicate locations of key leaders and agitators for possible apprehension tactics. They can also be used to signal to other units the beginning of various actions or phases against the mob.

Visual signals by use of flare pistols are also very useful in coordinating action against large mobs. These flares are commercially available from police and marine equipment supply houses.

Railway-type flares in yellow and red of the type called "fusees" have a practical application also. These flares contain self-igniters and have a spike in one end that can be driven into a wooden wall. Red is best for signaling a danger area or location of a road block. Yellow flares will provide emergency night illumination of operational areas. These flares are inexpensive and will burn for approximately thirty minutes in all kinds of adverse weather including rain, wind, and snow.

(67) Simple booby traps utilizing tear gas grenades can be

rigged indoors or inside buildings where rioters may want to enter or assemble. Any type of trip device that enables the safety ring to be withdrawn by a movement such as opening a door, can be devised. Instantaneous blast-type grenades are best for this purpose.

(68) Emergency electric lighting facilities are a must for night action. In the past, car and truck spotlights have been used but again valuable vehicles lose maneuverability and are exposed to mob action and sniper fire. Portable long-range spotlights powered with dry cell or rechargeable batteries are now available. Individual mob members are more aggressive in night action under the protective cover of darkness. It is to be expected that power lines and municipal lighting facilities will be cut off by any well-planned mob action and provision must be on hand to light up the scene.

(69) Experience during the past decade has proven that a small organized cadre of trained agitators can maneuver and direct the action of a mob. numbering thousands. When the mob action meets with police or military resistance that cannot be overcome, these professional agitators leave the mob body and flee to safety or other predetermined rallying points. For this and other obvious reasons, it is vital to identify these individuals, who many times have not been operating openly prior to the action. Naturally, commanders of mob actions both within and without the mob body should be subject to apprehension orders of the highest priority before, during, and after any riot incident. Police agents dressed in appropriate clothing etc. should be placed in the mob body for this purpose or for purposes of collecting evidence and identification.

Transistor type miniature tape recorders and transceiver two-way radio sets that can be readily concealed on the person are extremely useful in this type of operation.

Powerful binoculars with built-in cameras that can take photos of subjects thousands of feet away and various other camera-telescope combinations are now being used in the surveillance field. Their application in riot control situations should not be overlooked. Likewise, miniature cameras such as the Minox have a definite use.

(70) A number of interesting new developments are now undergoing testing that should be of considerable use to law enforcement agencies and the military in the control of civil disturbances. Some may soon be commercially available, such as the following:

(a) A device used by sportsmen for throwing empty beer cans into the air for target practice. The power of a blank cartridge is used to launch the can into the air. An adaptation is now under study to enable this same inexpensive device to be utilized to throw tear gas grenades over long distances.

(b) As a result of the recent interest in combatting guerrilla warfare, an invisible spray is being developed that stains clothing and the skin. It cannot be washed off. Later examination of mob suspects through a special lens would result in infallible identification of participants.

(c) An electric riot stick that is battery-powered and imparts a strong shock of static electricity. The stick is of normal size. A spark from the tip will penetrate clothing of the recipient and does not have to contact the skin area to shock the person. The practical and psychological effects of this weapon can be imagined. The static electric shock is harmless but very effective.

INDEX

417